1.19.18
$25.95
AS-14

168

Withdrawn

D0953718

PASSING
JUDGMENT

ALSO BY TERRI APTER

Altered Loves: Mothers and Daughters during Adolescence

Working Women Don't Have Wives: Professional Success in the 1990s

Secret Paths: Women in the New Midlife

The Myth of Maturity:
What Teenagers Need from Parents to Become Adults

You Don't Really Know Me: Why Mothers and Daughters Fight and
How Both Can Win

The Confident Child: Raising Children to Believe in Themselves

The Sister Knot: Why We Fight, Why We're Jealous, and
Why We'll Love Each Other No Matter What

What Do You Want from Me?
Learning to Get Along with In-Laws

Difficult Mothers: Understanding and Overcoming Their Power

PASSING JUDGMENT

*Praise and Blame
in Everyday Life*

TERRI APTER

W. W. NORTON & COMPANY
Independent Publishers Since 1923
NEW YORK | LONDON

For information about permission to reproduce selections from
this book, write to Permissions, W. W. Norton & Company, Inc.,
500 Fifth Avenue, New York, NY 10110

For information about special discounts for bulk purchases,
please contact W. W. Norton Special Sales at
specialsales@wwnorton.com or 800-233-4830

Manufacturing by Berryville Graphics
Book design by Helene Berinsky
Production manager: Anna Oler

ISBN: 978-0-393-24785-5

W. W. Norton & Company, Inc.
500 Fifth Avenue, New York, N.Y. 10110
www.wwnorton.com

W. W. Norton & Company Ltd.
15 Carlisle Street, London W1D 3BS

1 2 3 4 5 6 7 8 9 0

For David

CONTENTS

PASSING
JUDGMENT

Introduction

HUMAN INTERACTION—between parents and children, within couples, among friends and colleagues—is permeated with praise and blame. Praise can be more restorative than food. Blame can wound and humiliate, stripping us of dignity, pride, and pleasure. Our experiences of praise and blame range far beyond specific compliments and complaints; we respond positively or negatively, with approval or disapproval, to facial expressions, eye movements, small wordless vocalizations, and physical gestures. Generally without being fully aware, we engage with praise and blame in every personal interaction.

In the first milliseconds of perceiving something we not only automatically process information about what it is, but we form an opinion, positive or negative.[1] Our more conscious thoughts may be elsewhere—on the day ahead or the task at hand—but in the background is an automatic judgment meter, a legacy from crucial survival responses that primes us to assess a person as someone to approach or to avoid. Are they friend or foe? Can I trust this person, or is the friendly appearance deceptive? So important is this response that one neuroscientist argues, "Every emotion we experience falls, at least to some extent, into one or other of the two categories . . . Whether to approach or avoid is the fundamental psychological decision an organism makes in relation to its environment." [2]

Over time, as societies became more complex, the human brain evolved more subtle, probing, and varied appraisals. We remain interested in assessing whether someone is dangerous or trustworthy, but we also have more sophisticated social concerns: whether someone would understand our problems and predicaments, whether we are on the same wavelength, whether we would enjoy eating, talking, joking, debating with someone, and whether he or she responds positively to us. Here also, two systems of judgment—approach and avoidance, approval and disapproval—shape our thoughts, emotions, and behavior. [3]

EACH morning begins with a tally of what's positive and what's negative in the people around us. My husband quietly mounts the stairs and, without speaking, hands me a mug of steaming coffee. I am thinking about my early morning meeting, the weather, and the rain gear I'll need, but these give way to a sudden rush of praise. "He is wonderful," I think and he acknowledges this unspoken judgment with a fleeting smile. The warm mug that I hug with my hands, anticipation of the first stimulating sip of coffee, my favorable bias toward my husband, the comfort I take in his understanding of my tight schedule and my caffeine craving trigger a bundle of responses that can be translated as praise. But when he turns up the volume of the radio, I feel more than irritation. There is a rush of blame: "He should know how unpleasant this is to me." For a moment I tense and the accusation—"He is so inconsiderate!"—hovers at the rim of consciousness. This must be expressed in the set of my mouth and eyes, for he raises his eyebrows. A silent query, tinged with humor and self-defense: "What have I done wrong now?" flickers across his face; then, after a minute tightening of his lips, he turns down the sound. My annoyance evaporates.

I go downstairs to the kitchen and step in as overseer of teenage daughters. There is a pulsing pleasure in the presence of these girls: "They are *wonderful*," I think, but the halo surrounding their familiar faces, bodies, movements, and smell gives way to other responses. "They are so careless, so messy," I think, as I look at the kitchen table, with its clutter of books and bags, spilled cereal, and uncovered jam, and the sticky river of juice encroaching on my papers. Before I articulate a complaint, the thirteen-year-old puts a bowl in the sink and my focus shifts. I wonder if she has really eaten anything. Our eyes meet, and I see that she is overwhelmed by some anxiety. "What's up?" I ask. I try to be neutral, knowing how easily she is offended by excessive maternal concern. Her voice is a high-pitched, childlike whine, and she launches into a narrative I cannot follow, but the gist involves conflicting demands of friends and anxiety that one will judge her as a "bad friend." I try to minimize her concern over such a negative judgment

("You can't be serious! Who could possibly accuse you of that?") but she counters with her own accusation, "You don't even try to understand." Then her forehead folds like rumpled silk; a whimper is buried in a hug, because she regrets her harsh judgment of me and worries that it may make her look "bad." The sixteen-year-old observes this with faux detachment: "Typical," she declares, hugging her sense of superiority close. As we prepare to leave the house, she is slow to locate her shoes and then asks me to sign a stained and very long document I have never set eyes on before. I tell her she is "disorganized" and wonder anxiously whether she is also being devious (Is there something untoward about the form that I have no time to read?). For a moment accusations thicken the air, until we exchange the glances of mutual love that each of us experiences as a primitive form of praise.

FOR over three decades I have been fascinated by the human obsession with praise and blame, and the central role it plays in our relationships. This fascination was awakened when, as a junior research assistant, I recorded interactions of infants with their mothers.[4] I spent hours focusing on a newborn's jerky limbs, the spidery play of hands, the searching movements of head and mouth. I would track the mother's gaze, and note the responsive tension in her arm, tightening and lifting, easing and lowering, as she held the baby. I noted the changing modulation of her voice that seemed to reference her baby even when she chatted to a visiting friend. Three

months on, in the second phase of the study, the infant's probing gaze was full of expectation. There was a need beyond
food and warmth, even a need beyond love; it was a need for
love that also conveyed, "You are delightful and admirable."
An infant's despair at failing to secure admiration was over-
whelming; the wails signaled a primitive terror, as though
of abandonment and danger, even when the infant remained
safe in a parent's arms.

The primitive stake in others' approval and disapproval is
gradually absorbed into more complex understandings about
cause and effect. By the age of three years, a child has developed a sense of his or her agency. The thrill of being able to do
things "by myself," and being praised accordingly is countered
by the terror of doing "bad things," and being blamed for the
consequences. When my research took me to a new decade
of development—from five to fifteen years [5]—I saw just how
much energy children devote to noting and trying to manage
others' judgments. As children were exposed to commonplace
discipline from parents and teachers, the possibility of being
blamed for something was a daily fear. Even as they developed
a broader context of "bad things" and learned, for example,
that breaking some*thing* is different from harming some*one*,
and that there are levels of severity in harm, being blamed
for anything at all, even just for talking too loudly or being
"a nuisance," lowered their mood and self-esteem. Being told
that they "did well" or "were very good," even if it was only
for sitting quietly or eating a meal, elicited a body-filled grin
and rush of delight.

At this time, my own children were engaged in the sideways and backward transition through late childhood to puberty. Together we dwelled within a continuous dynamic of family praise and blame. One moment, they were the best children in the world; the next moment I was admonishing them, all too often in the language of blame: "You should be more careful!" and "Can't you show some consideration?" and "How can you be so thoughtless?"

Like many other parents, in cooler moments I underlined the difference between behaving badly and being bad, but in heated moments this distinction could be lost.[6] I knew, both from the cauldron of my own family and from my research, how a scolded child is suddenly propelled away from vital engagement with her surroundings to frozen isolation. Lips press together; a large swallow signals a painful lump in the throat; arms tense against the body until the flood of emotion eases. "I'm not bad," I heard my own and other children insist, while they watched a parent to see whether this bravado would be confirmed or shot down. There were times as a parent when, riven by different demands and with limited patience, I was blamed by a child for "being unfair" or even "being horrid." There were many times when I blamed myself for lacking patience, for being meaner than necessary, for being insensitive or selfish. My own esteem would be restored only when my children assured me, with smiles and hugs and confidences, that I was an admirable mother.

Praise and blame again came to the fore in my study of adolescents.[7] As children become teens, friends shape and bolster one another's judgments while a parent's judgments are constantly, ruthlessly challenged. "I don't care what you think," is one of the most dismissive things we can say to someone, and in the hundreds of parent-teen interchanges I witnessed, I heard this cry over and over again. Whose judgment one cares about is key to who is admired and who has influence. Parents often said, "Nothing scares me as much as her rejection of my judgment," and "Nothing makes me feel more helpless than her indifference to what I think."

Yet as I decoded the frequent arguments between teenagers and their parents,[8] I realized that these apparently indifferent teens continue to care about their parents' judgments. Teenagers put "being judged" at the top of their things-I-hate list because they are trying to disengage from their obsession with a parent's praise and blame. Teens discover, and create, their own identities by distinguishing their judgments from those of a parent. Yet they long for a parent to admire their newly emerging and distinctive judgmental self. This ambivalence about parental approval and disapproval shapes the teen-parent relationship.[9]

Among friends, among coworkers, and with a partner, we glow in the presence of praise and glower in the presence of blame. The concept of unconditional love is so appealing—and so confused—because it promises a special haven from our judgmental world. But even our closest, most abiding relationships, where love itself may be unconditional, where *attachment* endures, are impacted by judgment. The toddler is adored but that does not protect her from the shame of being declared naughty, the terror she feels when voices are raised against her, or the despair when others rebuff her bids for attention. The romantic couple may pledge love until death and delight in total acceptance, yet in the course of a marriage each partner is exposed to a wide range of judgments about consideration, attentiveness, fairness, and even the quality of his or her love.

The distinctive pleasure of getting older, people often say, is release from concern about what other people think. I discovered, though, that attaining such equanimity and confidence took hard work. When I explored the so-called midlife crisis, I found that this pivot of adult development was triggered by a special urgency to reclaim control of one's own life by managing sensitivity to others' praise and blame, and putting more trust in one's own judgments.[10]

My long obsession with relational judgments was only formalized with the discovery of new, illuminating research on the evolution of our judgmental brain.[11] For 150 years, the human brain had been studied largely for its ability to process factual information, to solve problems, to recognize and use patterns, and to navigate and survive the environment. It was thought that humans' particularly large brain evolved for the special purpose of mastering these practical skills. But thirty years ago a very different hypothesis emerged as to why humans require such large brains.

A large brain is, in evolutionary terms, costly. This large organ consumes 20 percent of our total energy intake. It also increases the risk to mother and baby at birth as the baby's large head passes through the narrow birth canal. To minimize this risk, infants are born when the brain is still immature and vulnerable, though a consequence of this immature brain is a long period of dependence. As is so often the case in evolution, this cost comes with advantages: it fosters close personal bonds through that long period of dependence and it gives the brain plasticity, the capacity to adapt to different environments.

One constant as we navigate any of the variety of human environments is our need to be able to live with others. It is now understood that the large size of the human brain reflects the demands of attachment, cooperation, communication, and judgment—the bases of our sociability. In other words, our large brain results from our fundamental social bent.

This "social brain hypothesis"[12] is supported by evidence from other species in which relative brain sizes depend on whether those species are solitary or social. For example, the brains of birds that flock together are larger than the brains of solitary birds.[13] Further, the brain size of any creature—even the locust—changes as it moves from being a solitary creature to one in a coordinated swarm: as it crowds with others, it starts to pay attention to what the others are doing, and the brain areas associated with learning and memory enlarge by one-third.[14] In every species, from birds to locusts to humans, a larger brain is linked to greater sociability.

Another argument in support of the social brain hypothesis comes from a look at the development and function of the larger brain mass. At birth, our brain is only one-quarter the weight of an adult brain, yet we have (almost) a full complement of neurons, or brain cells. What we do not have at birth, but rapidly develop as we interact with others, is an extensive communication network between neurons.[15] This substantial communication network—much of it devoted to social understanding—accounts for the fourfold increase in brain weight. The communication network is essential to what Robin Dunbar, professor of evolutionary biology at Oxford, calls "the computational demands of living in large, complex societies."[16] We need to compute other people's trustworthiness and generosity and kindness. We need to compute their intentions. We need to compute their response to us: Do they find us trustworthy and generous? Do they want to befriend us? Do we get that approval necessary to be included in the group?

Some readers may initially be disturbed or doubtful that we are fundamentally judgmental creatures and that others' judgments impact so deeply on us. Some people adhere to the ideal that we should not judge others. *Judgmental* is a term normally used as a criticism and is often equated with making negative judgments. Many common sayings warn us against being judgmental: "If you don't have anything nice to say, don't say it," my teachers used to warn, and one of the New Testament's most powerful directives is, "Judge not, lest ye be judged." Such sayings underscore the vulnerabilities of human judgments to distortion and bias, and point to our own exposure to others' negative judgments. Nevertheless, we continue to make judgments, both positive and negative, because we have evolved to do so.

Another ideal is, "What someone else thinks of me doesn't matter;" what matters is "knowing who I am," regardless of what anyone else thinks. As I shall show, self-appraisal is of paramount importance, but how we see ourselves is affected by others' judgments. Self-confidence and self-belief arise within a range of relationships, some close and intimate, some more public and social. There may not be a simple relationship between thinking well of oneself and being admired by others, but the human brain has evolved to take note of others' judgments, to feel pride, pleasure, and comfort in praise, while blame saddens, enrages, and sickens us. Our experiences of praise and blame even affect how long we live.[17]

LEARNING to navigate the complexities and confusions of our judgment meter is a demanding lifetime enterprise. Praise and blame themselves are complicated judgment systems. Neither is invariably helpful nor damaging. Neither is invariably comforting nor hurtful. Both are necessary and, in my view, inevitable. I hope this book will increase understanding of how our judgments, particularly those that can be characterized broadly as praise or blame, develop within and impact the full range of our relationships, from the most intimate and enduring to the most transient and casual. Awareness that we live, day by day, in the constant company of our judgments, both subliminal and conscious, both positive and negative, and that we constantly monitor the judgments of others, particularly those directed toward us, will vastly improve our ability to manage our biases, to tolerate others' views, and to make sense of our most powerful and confusing responses to ourselves and to others.

1

The Beginnings of Human Judgment

THE HUMAN OBSESSION with praise and blame begins soon after birth. Totally dependent on others, with an impulse to form loving attachments to those who respond to us, we rapidly learn the value of others' praise. We also learn to fear the terrifying consequences of blame.

Fundamental to this learning is *mindsight*, the ability to sense the subjective world of others as like but distinct from our own.[1] Mindsight detects purpose and intention in others' behavior, and identifies others' feelings, goals, and desires.[2] It helps us judge others and understand their judgments of us. The pioneering American psychologist William James believed that such judgments were necessary to human survival: "I should not be [living] now," he reflected, "had I not become sensitive to looks of approval or disapproval on the faces among which my life is cast."[3] Indeed, a lot of what we learn about others' judgments comes from that phenomenal communicator—the human face.

Within the womb, before a baby actually sees anything, the human eye is being prepared to absorb information:[4] retinal cells send spontaneous signals to the brain and waves of activity sweep across the eye; by the time a newborn first opens her eyes, her brain has been prepared for its work in recognizing and responding to faces. With a reflex that ensures an infant turns to look toward the person who holds her, and shows special interest in a face when the eyes are directed toward her,[5] she is primed to respond to those who tend her. Parent and baby lock together in a mutual gaze, each fascinated and absorbed by the face of the other.[6]

This mutual gaze is sometimes referred to as eye-love. It is filled with adoration, it bypasses language, and it is rich with romance. Eye-love floods an infant with the same hormones that provide the high of sexual love. These chemically powerful exchanges, explains the psychiatrist Daniel Stern, introduce us to the importance of what others see and how they see us.[7]

Soon babies become skilled interpreters of the extraordinary, expressive muscle network from the forehead to the chin. They learn, in a normal or good-enough[8] environment, to expect that a face directly in front of their field of vision will show admiration; and, by two months of age, they reciprocate by smiling at someone who looks directly at them.[9] This is far more than imitation: before they can walk or talk or even crawl, babies expect that lips forming a smile will be accompanied by crinkly eyes, the chirp of a happy tone of voice, and the message of approval.[10] Soon a child will be able to process a face within 40 milliseconds and form a judgment, within 100 milliseconds, as to whether the person is friend or foe, kind or mean, desirable or disgusting, competent or inept, trustworthy or unreliable.[11]

By the age of six months, body movements, particularly of the arms and hands, add to the growing lexicon of mindsight.[12] The brain has an extensive mirroring system in which neurons, or brain cells, register others' movements just as we register our own. This mirroring system gives us an intuitive grasp on the meaning of movements. When I see another person wriggle in a chair or bite his lip or tense his shoulders and draw back, I can see he is impatient or nervous or repulsed. I do not have to make a deliberate inference from my own experiences to his. My brain does this automatically because the neural activity triggered by watching him is similar to the neural activity that occurs when I do the same sort of thing.[13] It is as though the brain performs a pantomime of the actions we are observing.[14]

We never see a person without making some kind of judgment.[15] In a face, for example, something about the shape of the mouth seems trustworthy; the eyes seem to shine with a friendly light. When drawn to someone, we may ignore danger signals. Over time, though, if a person disappoints, frustrates, or betrays us, the face looks different to us. The smile is sinister. The previously warm eyes are alarming. Similarly, a face that initially makes us uneasy may become appealing after we see the person in different contexts, discover his humor, and find him supportive and reliable. Our experiences shape our judgments, and these are constantly being reinforced or modified.

At the same time that children are developing complex judgments of other people, they are becoming aware that others judge them. If anyone has any doubt as to a child's sensitive social awareness of others' judgments, they have not seen a two- or three-year-old blush. Involuntary and uncontrollable, the face reddens suddenly, as though in response to a punch or slap. "What rule have I broken?" or "What are they laughing/glaring/staring at?" a child wonders anxiously. There is the sensation of burning and a longing to disappear or be swallowed up rather than suffer this confusing scrutiny. Charles Darwin described blushing as "the most peculiar and most human of all expressions,"[16] evolving alongside our concern about others' judgments of us. Only a child who can imagine how he or she appears to others, and who has a stake in how others see her, would blush.[17] But behind this display of abject embarrassment lies a social purpose; blushing diffuses disapproval by sending the message, "I care how you judge me; violating your standards makes me uncomfortable; I want you to accept and approve of me."[18]

Being Seen: The Importance of Joint Attention

Eyes are sometimes called windows to the soul, and indeed they reveal a wealth of subjective information. The size of the pupils registers feelings: pupils dilate with love and contract with contempt. The key to whether a smile is genuine or feigned comes not from the lips but the muscles around the eyes, which crinkle only in a genuinely felt smile.[19] Staring directly into someone's eyes is a powerful, intimate act because our gaze reveals so much.

When a small child cries, "Look at me!" she exhibits a fundamental human need—the need for positive attention.[20] An unnoticed child is a neglected child. Jealously such a child notes what draws others' attention away from her.[21] Whom are other people looking at, and are they looking with approval or disapproval?[22] This question is important to survival, and infants are quick to catch on. By ten weeks old, infants will instinctively look where someone else is looking.[23]

Infants express their fascination with seeing and being seen in their earliest game: peekaboo. An adult covers the baby's eyes, or his or her own face, and then pulls the cover away and exclaims, "Boo!" Once the baby is accustomed to the game, he or she squeals and gurgles with delight. With eyebrows slightly raised and the mouth motioning a rudimentary imitation of the adult's cry of "Boo!" the infant signals a preverbal version of "Again! Again!"

Children's play is a way of processing experiences that intrigue and disturb them. The game of peekaboo models someone "disappearing" or leaving the room, and then returning. Now-you-see-me, now-you-don't explores the anxiety surrounding a parent's absence and the delight at his or her returning attention. Disappearance and reappearance are great mysteries to an infant. Before the age of about eight months, babies have no concept that things (including people) are still there when they are out of sight. People appear, disappear, and reappear without apparent explanation. Peekaboo is an enthralling game in which a child has some control over appearances and disappearances, and in which he or she can enjoy repeated experiences of marked attention.

Later, when the child is between the ages of two and three years, peekaboo is refined into a hilarious variation of hide-and-seek whereby toddlers hide by covering their eyes, or sometimes just by closing their eyes. What is so strange about this game is that a child of this age knows full well that things are visible to others when she or he does not see them. Even in the imaginative grip of the game, a child will acknowledge that the grown-up can see his feet, his arms, even his head but persists in believing that he is hidden.[24]

This contradiction—"I know you can see my body but I am sure you cannot see *me*"—sparks tender amusement in many people but psychologist James Russell was intrigued as well as amused. Confident that this "confusion" regarding visibility is underpinned by a certain truth, Russell and colleagues in the Department of Experimental Psychology at the University of Cambridge set up a series of observations. First, Russell established that two- and three-year-olds did believe it was perfectly reasonable for them to hide by covering or closing their eyes. In fact, they believed it was perfectly reasonable for someone *else* to hide by covering or closing the eyes. In many cases children thought that even open eyes that are not making eye contact can render someone invisible. The underlying belief is,

"You cannot see me when you are not looking at my eyes and seeing me looking at you."

Meticulously assembling the evidence, Russell discovered the importance of mutual seeing. The two-year-old thinks, "I can hide from you by shutting my eyes because with my eyes closed or covered I am not engaging with your view of me. I can be hiding from you because even when you see my body, you are not *seeing me*; what matters is whether I see you seeing me.[25]

Eventually our sensitivity to others' gazes becomes so finely tuned that "in a sea of faces, we are quickest to spot the face whose eyes are directed at us."[26] The gaze may convey warm recognition or admiration, and our mood buzzes accordingly, or it conveys suspicion, accusation, or dislike. A gaze is packed with judgment, and we are quick to note shifts in its meanings. When a gaze becomes fixed and prolonged, it triggers a flare up in the emotional centers of our brain.[27] We have wildly different responses to different kinds of stares. In one case, where the eyes have a dark fixity, some primitive force beats out the question, "Are you eyeing me up as a meal?" or "Are you focusing on me as an enemy?" In another case, the stare contains a caress. In this context the message "I could eat you up" carries a very different meaning; the urge to devour suggests enclosure, safety, and approval.[28]

Beyond Vision: Judging Voices

Vision plays a key role for most people in assessing others, but the visual world is not the only route to mindsight. A parent's voice is a powerful attraction to an infant. When the mother speaks, the baby turns toward her nearly 100 percent of the time. The father's face is the second strongest attraction; the baby turns to the father's voice 85 percent of the time.[29] Children who are blind are thus quickly inducted into their interpersonal world. They also demonstrate, in time, the same sensitivity to others' judgments as sighted children.[30]

The human voice is flexible and expressive, with a distinctive range of tones and sounds, a complex creativity, and a vast expressive scale. For over 40 years Philip Lieberman has conducted research that demonstrates the remarkable interplay between the evolution of the human voice and the brain's powers of understanding and judging others. The basic apparatus we share with chimps—the lips, voice box, throat, and lungs—is able to perform a range of functions far beyond other primates' capacities. A more flexible tongue began to develop about 100,000 years ago as the human mouth became smaller and less protruding. Over the next 50,000 years, the human neck became sufficiently long, and the mouth sufficiently short, to engage in what Lieberman calls the "vocal gymnastics humans have and use every day."[31] The result is a vocal tract that extends beyond grunts of greeting and warning to "singing opera and speaking on the phone."

These abilities come, however, with a price tag. As the mouth adapted for talking, its newer structure altered the nasal equipment and the power of smell was compromised. This trade-off makes sense in evolutionary terms only if the gains are substantial, and the substantial gain is language.

Language opens up possibilities for sophisticated relationships that extend well beyond family connections; it also facilitates communication across generations, enabling information to be embedded in culture. Language generates vast nuances in our judgment meter, and ensures our ability to share our judgments with others.

Humans are so adept at processing and producing language and syntax that any child exposed to a language during special critical periods of brain development will naturally learn that language. Brain-language power is used not only for decoding the meaning of what is said. Humans have a very peculiar capacity for distinguishing and making a range of tones and sounds that trigger emotional responses. The inferences we make from vocal sounds would be (nearly) unthinkable outside language.[32] We distinguish age and sex and character in a voice. We make inferences about intentions, desires, and fears from a voice. Through the vast and subtle variations of a voice, we form judgments about people.

Even when infants are asleep, they process and respond to vocally expressed feelings. Alice Graham, Philip Fisher, and Jennifer Pfeifer at the Oregon Social Learning Center, home to many groundbreaking studies on relationships, looked at the brain scans of infants sleeping while recordings of human voices were played. The actual words were gibberish, but the emotions in the voices ranged from extreme to moderate anger, and from neutral to cheerful tones. The results, published under the intriguing title "What Sleeping Babies Hear,"[33] showed that even as they slept, infants as young as six months of age respond to the emotional valence of voices.[34] From the first months of life, we look to the voices of people around us to provide clues as to whether they are expressing approval or disapproval.

Infant Judgments

It was once thought that very young children did not really judge others; they simply liked or disliked them. It was thought that their sense of good and bad was an egoistic proxy for "giving me what I want now" or "withholding from me what I want now."[35] So, "Someone who feeds me when I am hungry" is "good," and "Someone who fails to pick me up when I need comforting" is bad."[36] New research shows, however, that even before the first birthday, a child judges others, and these judgments can be both profound and subtle.

At around eleven months of age babies prefer others who like the same things they do. Neha Mahajan and Karen Wynn identified these emerging judgments in children who had not yet acquired speech, by giving these babies a choice of puppets as toys.[37] When one puppet showed enthusiasm by saying "mmm-mm" for food the baby liked, 80 percent of the babies chose to play with that puppet rather than a puppet that "disliked" the food they liked. But babies go well beyond simple affiliations based on liking the same things. They are attracted to those who can teach them how to take the next step into their social lives.

One way we reveal what we like is by letting our gaze

linger over a face or figure. Very young children spend more time looking at other children than at adults who are not related to them, and it seems they have a special preference for children who are just a bit older than they are. A baby girl is likely to pay more attention to other girls, and a baby boy is likely to pay more attention to other boys.[38] They prefer those who will be most helpful in inducting them into their social world.[39]

But babies' preferences go beyond practical issues. Many are shaped by deep moral principles. When a child, even as young as six months of age, watches one puppet pick up and return a ball that a second puppet drops, while a third puppet picks up the dropped ball and runs away with it, the child is very likely to choose the helpful puppet as her preferred toy. When a one-year-old watches the same puppet show and then allocates treats to the puppets, the helpful puppet is the winner[40] while the unhelpful one loses out—and even has treats taken away.

The evolutionary anthropologist Michael Tomasello, who has been called "one of the world's leading experts on what makes us human,"[41] argues that a prehuman ancestor, perhaps the last one we shared with the great apes, would have already had embedded in its genes a strong admiration for those who helped and cooperated with others and strong disapproval for those who do not.[42] Qualities such as helpfulness and cooperation are so fundamental to the question, Is it safe to approach this person? that we make instant judgments about people that psychologists call a "welfare trade-off ratio."

We rapidly learn that other people have both good and bad traits. We accept that we may gain a great deal from their company, even when they pose some potential threat. To assess another person, then, we size up our ability to manage possible risks. Will I, with my particular strengths and my weaknesses, be capable of managing what may be dangerous in that person while benefitting from what is good? As we automatically and, perhaps, unconsciously calculate trade-offs, we feel approval or disapproval, and make the key decision whether it is safe to approach or include or interact with them, or whether we avoid and exclude them.[43]

So important is it to distinguish between whom we approve of and want to approach, and whom we disapprove of and want to avoid that these different responses are segregated in different hemispheres of the brain.[44] Richard Davidson, one of the leaders in the field of affective neuroscience—the study of the brain mechanisms that underlie emotions—explains: "When we must avoid a harmful or threatening stimulus, it is important that nothing get in the way of our escaping a rock slide or a cave bear. Evolution seems to do this by keeping the two contrasting responses—approach and avoidance—on different sides of the brain; this means that there is almost no chance that [the wrong judgment] will be activated by mistake."[45] Balancing the value of this neurological "certainty" against our judgment meter's susceptibility to errors of bias, simplification, and confusion, is, as we shall see, one of the most important tasks in our interpersonal life.

Common Questions About Commonplace Judgments

Some philosophers and psychologists believe that our judgments are mere preferences that we dress up with explanations and reasons.[46] Are the responses that we call judgments simple, subjective preferences? Are they preset and permanent, rather than reasoned evaluations? Does their early emergence in infants prove that they are imprinted and unchangeable?

Judgments are subjective and also evaluative, packed with meaning, both emotional and conceptual. When we praise and blame, when we admire or condemn, we are logging a response that has far more meaning to us than a personal preference for salted pretzels versus sweet doughnuts, for neutral versus bold décor, for lazy versus strenuous vacations. Our judgments express deep-seated values forged by early experiences of love and acceptance, trust and anxiety, fear and rejection. When someone disapproves of us, finds us distasteful or fearful, we may try to console ourselves with the view that it is a mere preference, but, particularly when we care about that person, we experience that judgment as a kind of blame for being less than we should be. Others' judgments, however distorted or excessive, shape our relational landscape.

One of the most colorful discussions about the emotional and intuitive nature of judgments comes from Jonathan Haidt, professor of ethical leadership at the Stern Business School based in New York University. Haidt, frequently described as one of the top global thinkers of our time,[47] says that the human mind is constructed with "moral machinery." Just as our minds are designed to "do language, sexuality, music, and many other things," they are designed to be judgmental. The judgments we make are intuitive rather than rational. They have evolved along with our social brains and through our dependence on relationships and communities.[48]

To model the intuitive and emotional nature of our judgments, Haidt uses the analogy of a person riding an elephant and believing that he or she has full control of the elephant's movements. However, the elephant is much stronger than the rider, who (unless he engages in careful and prolonged reflection) has minimal effect on this irrational, instinctive, and powerful animal force. As the rider goes through various routines, he clings to the delusion that he is in charge.[49] In the realm of ordinary judgments, Haidt argues, people believe they derive their judgments from reason, when the beliefs are actually shaped by unreflecting and often biased intuition. When we think that our judgments are grounded in reason, we are as deluded as the rider who thinks he or she is in charge of the elephant. After all, research shows that two people, looking at the same evidence, will assess it differently according to whether it supports their intuition-based judgments.[50] However strong the evidence, it is weaker than our feelings.[51]

All too often, exposing the emotional elements of our judgments is seen as a reason to silence our emotions when we pass judgment. The emotional nature of our everyday judgments, however, does not make them irrational, nor does it untether them forever from carefully reasoned argument.[52] These "affective (or emotional) responses" that detect "goodness" or "badness," positive or negative, [53] illuminate our deepest values and guide us in our relationships. The sources of our judgments stretch back in time, over our full emotional history, to the desires and fears arising in early attachments, to unmet needs and terrible losses, to our experiences of guilt or inadequacy, and to expectations shaped by hope or dread.[54] They register our very personal interests, passions, and outlook. They are the means by which we experience other people, come to know them,[55] and forge bonds with them.

At the same time, they are vulnerable to bias and distortion, and as much as we wish to be fair and balanced, our judgments can be brutal, crude, and blind. Most people have a shrewd gauge of this vulnerability and take on, as part of the work of being human, the job of questioning, testing, and refining judgments. We probe the views of family, friends, and colleagues to enlarge our understanding and to assess and revise initial responses of who deserves praise and who deserves blame. We mull over our judgments as we read novels and watch plays or TV soaps, as we listen to political debates and watch news programs. Our conclusions are sometimes more and sometimes less intelligent, sometimes more or sometimes less subtle, sometimes more or less biased,[56] but, as I show in this book, most of us constantly "do judgment"— whether addressing moral concerns or the broad appraisals we consider throughout the day, every day. This is why it is crucial to understand how our judgment meter works and how we might harness our efforts to ground our judgments in feelings that define rather than defy our values.

2

The Chemistry, Psychology, and Economics of Praise

THE FIRST JUDGMENT we experience in our interpersonal world is likely to be praise from a parent's curiosity, delight, and wonder.[1] Praise goes far beyond specific compliments or formal assessments. The first entry for praise in the *Oxford Dictionary* is, as a verb, "to express warm approval or admiration," and, as a noun, "the expression of approval or admiration." Praise conveys the message that we are a source of delight. Hence, praise becomes part of our world long before we understand the words "Well done!" or "You're wonderful!"

Praise and the Release of Social Chemicals

Praise is essential to the growth of a healthy brain. The brain grows by forming new networks of interconnected neurons, which are the basic elements in the brain's communication system. Certain hormones provide essential fuel for building new brain circuits. The most important of these hormones in early brain development are oxytocin, sometimes referred to as "the bonding hormone" because of its role in pair bonding, and the endorphin compounds that release naturally occurring opiates that give us a high (very similar to the high of opiates such as heroin). When a parent's face conveys praise with the message, "I want to see who you are, and I admire you," the infant's brain is awash with both oxytocin and endorphins. These pleasure-giving hormones encourage the friendly, steady gaze [2] that promotes intimacy and understanding between parent and child, and which provides additional brain fuel. These hormones also underlie the comfort we feel in the presence of someone we love and our impulse to reach for someone's hand when we are frightened. [3] The presence of a familiar person is not only emotionally soothing; it also seems to reduce physical pain [4] and explains the kiss-it-better effect.

As a neuromodulator, a chemical that affects how the brain functions, oxytocin influences our judgments. [5] With moderate to high levels of oxytocin flowing in our brain, we are more likely to trust others and more resilient to disappointment or betrayal. [6] Moreover, children for whom praise is commonplace show greater accomplishment at the age of three years and again at the age of ten years, [7] while children deprived of everyday praise show blunted responses in brain networks, particularly those associated with learning and motivation. [8] Praise is an essential building block of the healthy brain and we never outgrow our need for it.

Mimicry and Praise: How Babies Praise Parents

Praise is rarely one-sided, and children, even as infants, have many ways of praising grown-ups. Even before babies can smile—a very effective way of reciprocating praise—they have an arsenal of techniques to make the adults around them feel very, very good. A baby's smell, particularly the smell emitted by glands at the top of the infant head, induces a chemical high.[9] More important, however, babies convey the powerful message that their parents are admired by imitating them.

Mimicry is basic to learning, and basic to the social life of humans. It involves an extensive network of mirror neurons that fire up *both* as we ourselves do something and as we watch someone else do it,[10] so through imitation the infant not only learns how to behave like other people but she also begins to experience what other people feel.[11] Within an hour of birth, an infant's undeveloped muscles work at imitating the facial expressions of an adult within her vision.[12] This intense focus provides the adults who care for a child with a sense of being important and interesting.

I remember the shock of pleasure I felt when my eight-month-old daughter opened her mouth, pushed her head forward with rhythmic jerks, and made chugging noises directed at the piece of egg she grasped in her hand. I realized that she was imitating my efforts to cool the egg before offering it to her. This mundane action suddenly took on enormous significance. I was someone to model, someone whose movements were packed with meaning. The drudgery of constant childcare fell away as my daughter told me that she looked up to me.

Mimicry demonstrates trust and confers authority. It shows faith in the intentions and knowledge of the person mimicked. When someone imitates you, he expresses admiration and a desire to become like you. Watch two people in conversation, and you can gauge their admiration for one another by the level of imitation. Does one person move her hands in sync with the other's movements? Does one shift posture in response to the other's gestures? When one leans forward, does the other do likewise, or is there a backward movement, however subtle, in rejection of the other. Does one person's voice match the volume and inflection of the other, or does one resist the other's influence? That unconscious flow of mimicry—known as the chameleon effect—creates rapport.[13]

Even so, we are highly sensitive to the nuances of mimicry: a slight change in emphasis can turn praise into derision. Exaggerate something just a little, make it deliberate, and the implicit judgment is no longer praise; it becomes aggressive and mocking.[14] We learn to make such fine distinctions because others' judgments are crucial to our social survival.

Praise: Parents' Power Tool

So important is praise that the history of parenting, the history of character building, and the history of educational psychology can be traced through changing fashions and assumptions about how to praise a child.

Haim Ginott, a pioneering teacher and child psychologist working in the 1960s, noted that praise generally had more positive impact on behavior than any kind of blame and punishment. He was under no illusion, however, that praise was simple or straightforward. "Praise," he writes, "like penicillin, must not be administered haphazardly. There are rules and cautions that govern the handling of potent medicines—rules about timing and dosage, cautions about possible allergic reactions. There are similar regulations about the administration of emotional medicine." [15]

Praise can change the way we think about ourselves. It can inspire and motivate us but also can issue a reminder of what is expected. It can confuse and irritate. It can come across as insincere or patronizing. Three decades after Ginott warned that praise was powerful and also potentially dangerous, the psychological world was rocked by the discovery that certain kinds of praise could actually damage a child's pride and lower her motivation.

Theories of Praise: Old and New

When I first began my research on children's development more than twenty-five years ago, the prevailing theory was that there could never be too much praise, and it did not matter what praise was for. Any task a child undertook, however simple and inconsequential, should be praised. Any effort, however half-hearted and feeble, should be praised. A child should be praised simply for showing up. In some schools, the daily assembly contained a routine instruction to children to give themselves a hug and praise themselves for being smart and beautiful and wonderful.

This praise immersion theory grew from the belief that children built their self-concept on what others said about them. If parents and teachers praised children for being smart or clever or talented or thoughtful or kind or good, then children would internalize these labels. They would then live up to their own and others' expectations.

Sufficient doses of praise, it was once argued,[16] would provide a vaccine against all social ills. A child who had been vaccinated with esteem, it was supposed, would not succumb to the temptations of drugs or alcohol, and would not engage in risky sexual behavior. Children fed a steady diet of praise and told that everything they did was splendid or great, it was supposed, would come to view themselves as successful. They would acquire the confidence that characterizes many successful people and become successful themselves.

Some evidence did support the belief that children live up (or live down) to others' expectations. When teachers were given the names of so-called smart students and so-called not smart students, the students who had been labeled as smart achieved significantly better academic results by the end of one semester than did those students labeled as not smart. This was true even though the students had not actually been assessed; the labels "smart" and "not smart" had been assigned at random. The teachers' *beliefs* about the students' abilities, not the students' actual abilities, probably explained the different levels of academic achievement.[17]

This transformation is called the Pygmalion effect, after the mythical sculptor who fell in love with his own ivory statue of a beautiful woman, and who, through prayer and offerings, was then able to bring the woman to life with his kiss. (George Bernard Shaw's play *Pygmalion*—better known in its musical version as *My Fair Lady*—tells a similar story: the educator Henry Higgins sets out to transform an uneducated, unpolished woman into a high-status lady.)[18] The story of Pygmalion conveys abiding truths about the mysterious interplay between ourselves and others' judgments of us,[19] but praise immersion practices were ultimately found to have a number of troubling consequences.

Diminishing Returns of Praise

Praise that arouses delight and pride in a baby and toddler can have very different effects on older children, particularly in the classroom. When Roy Baumeister studied the effects of praise, he found that it generated more anxiety than pleasure[20] in school-aged children. Children accustomed to the background hum of praise seemed to become dependent on praise to initiate any activity.[21] A child who was accustomed to classroom praise spent less time focusing on a project and soon stopped working to wait for a teacher's assessment. Praise seemed to hinder concentration, too. Children's absorption in a task (often called *flow*) seemed to be disrupted by the reminder that someone was watching. When they were singing or playing an instrument, swimming or hitting a ball, or doing anything that involved deep skills run on autopilot, their performance was particularly badly affected[22] by praise.

When I interviewed teachers for a study on children's shifting levels of confidence,[23] I heard similar stories. "Some of these kids cannot do anything until they are praised," notes third-grade teacher Sammi Vickers. "They start something, and then just freeze, waiting for you to tell them it's wonderful." Most poignant to me in watching a class of eight-year-olds was how a child's voice would change in a praise-saturated environment. The spontaneous speech of an eight-year-old has an engaging melody; it seems to flow directly from the pulse of her mind. All this is lost when she hears the constant hum or purr of praise. Instead, there is a distinct self-conscious inflection associated with seeking out praise.[24]

The discovery that praise could lead to lackluster work in the classroom[25] was so puzzling, and so counterintuitive, that many psychologists simply refused to believe it. Eventually, a series of studies led by the psychologist Carol Dweck shifted, probably forever, the paradigm of praise.

Testing the mind-shaping power of praise, Dweck studied two groups of young schoolchildren. In each group the children were struggling at school, and seemed discouraged and demotivated.[26] The first group was given a series of very, very simple tasks, and, whenever they got something right, they were praised for being smart. According to praise immersion theory, these children would live up to the praise. Convinced they were smart, they would behave like smart children; they would apply themselves, rise to challenges, and progress in their work.

Initially, this approach seemed promising. When children were given rudimentary tasks and praised because they succeeded, their spirits rose, and they approached the next task positively, their anxiety and reluctance apparently dispelled. Unfortunately, however, praise buoyed the children only as long as the tasks remained very simple. As soon as the tasks became more challenging, the children lost motivation and once again were reluctant to engage in schoolwork. Soon the children in this much-praised group were back where they started.

A second group of schoolchildren, equally demotivated by their lackluster achievement, were given progressively more difficult tasks. When they succeeded in solving the more difficult problems, they were not praised for being smart; instead their attention was drawn to *the link between their efforts and achievements*, and they were praised for these efforts. These children, praised for persistence and effort, were likely to sustain their motivation and hard work even when the going got rough because they were inspired by the possibility of *growing* their abilities.[27]

Each and every day a child looks beyond the things she can do to the things she cannot yet do.[28] How we praise her will shape her vision of what's possible—and how she views her potential is as important to her confidence as how she views what she can do now.

Conundrums Beyond New Theories of Praise

The illuminating research that focused on hard work rather than inborn ability has had enormous effect in educational psychology, changing the way children are praised in a class-room. The message is: if you want a child to succeed, if you want a child to embrace challenge, then praise her effort, her hard work, her persistence, and not her intelligence or talent or ability. The confidence a child needs for life success is not confidence in her inborn ability but confidence that working at something will be a good investment.

Everyday praise, however, is more difficult to pin down, because the meanings of praise arise within complex and highly individual relationships. Throughout life, that earliest form of praise—admiration for a child's existence and intense curiosity about who she is—can be as welcoming and replenishing as rain in a desert. Statements like "You're the most wonderful kid in the world!" and "You're the best!" defy the new rulebooks on praise,[29] but remain an essential base of esteem. The actual rules according to which praise has a positive or negative effect are complicated and exacting.

So one of the most surprising things I have learned from observing children's developing relationships with parents, siblings, and friends, is that praise from people we love can in some contexts be extremely irritating. In one of my studies,[30] five-year-old Maeve bursts into tears when her grandmother looks at her school workbook and proclaims, "It's brilliant!" while seven-year-old Steve pounds his fist into the newly made clay figure when his mother praises it as "beautiful."[31]

Maeve is confused and irritated by her grandmother's over-blown enthusiasm. "What does Granny see that I don't?" she wonders, and, "How can I achieve this again, when I can't see what's so good about it?" Steve wants a focused response from his mother, not this formulaic enthusiasm. He sees some good things about the model but struggles with the overall form. His mother's praise seems more appropriate to a toddler's first efforts than to his concentrated aims, and its warm fuzziness [32] marginalizes his aspiration.

Teens' responses to praise can be even more confusing. The parent's global admiration, once so sustaining, now seems, to the teenage daughter or son, outdated. Parents believe that somewhere inside the surly teen is that lovable child with whom they exchanged mutual praise, but the teen wants his or her new self to push into the foreground. "You don't really know me!" teens protest in face of a parent's praise, and, "You are in no position to judge me!"

The teen's vehement rebuff often confounds parents. In the time I spent observing and recording parent-teen interactions, I was amazed, when it came to analyzing the transcripts, how often praise fueled arguments. When Pamina tells her fourteen-year-old daughter, "You look gorgeous," Aisha hisses, "You are just stupid!" When her mother, visibly hurt, leaves the room, Aisha takes deep breaths, fighting her own tears. When her mood seems more settled, I ask her whether we can talk. (Aisha knows that after a session in which I observe teen and parent together, I meet with each individually.) So Aisha and I sit side by side and piece together her scattered emotions. She explains, "How can she praise me when she doesn't know who I really am?" After a pause, she adds, "Besides, if *she* thinks I look 'lovely' then something's wrong. I must look too young, too sweet, and not at all how I want to look." [33]

Part of the teen's job—in the teen's view—is to shake her parent out of the tired old habit of seeing the teenage daughter as a little girl the parent thinks she knows. [34] To prove that her parent does not know her, she may change her hair, her friends, her interests, to those her parent will not call "lovely." Well aware of its power, teenagers are highly ambivalent about a parent's praise. Though they retain the child's high standards for appropriate praise—and crave it—over time they grow increasingly uneasy about their dependence on it.

Our wariness of a parent's judgment lasts long after the intensity of adolescence subsides. Whether the praise lacks enthusiasm or sincerity, or highlights something we ourselves do not value, praise that does not seem just right to us signals, "You don't really know me."

"My daughter is twenty-seven," reflects Marianne, "and there's still that bridle and buck when I dare say anything about anything she does, even if it's a compliment." [35]

"Well, there's a history there," laughs Marianne's daughter Leslie. "When I was a kid Mom praised me for being 'just so neat and clean,' and I'd make sure my room was neat as a pin before I went to bed because I was worried I wouldn't keep getting this praise. Then she told me I was *so good* at taking care of my little brother, and that turned me into a goody-goody even when I wanted to kick that snotty kid. Basically, compliments are her way of controlling me. So why does it come as this big surprise that I don't glow when she praises me? Her praise gets under my skin; it's like a caress that sort of feels good but you also hate it."

We constantly assess praise for sincerity, proportion, and focus. We also gauge the motive—and it is her mother's underlying aim in offering praise that irritates Leslie. This sensitivity to praise's motives also takes on special importance in couples. In 2015 and 2016 I had the opportunity to engage in research with couples along the lines of research I had previously done with parents and teens.[36] I spent time—usually two days—with them in their homes, trying to be as inconspicuous as possible. While it is impossible to be a fly on the wall, the aim in such observational research is to be as neutral as the family dog.[37] I was astounded by how often praise was resented. Sarah, thirty-five, enjoys what she calls "the truly impressive career" of her husband Steve who, at age thirty-four is often invited to give keynote papers alongside older, far more established academics. "He's so sweet," Sarah tells me. "He's quick to praise me when he gets accolades." But something other than pleasure shows on her face. She pauses and bites her lips. She seems to be engaged in an internal debate about what to say before she actually speaks. "Ok," she begins, "he's sweet." Now her words have a new hardness. "He tells me what an asset I am at conferences. But these conferences eat up my time and energy. I'm 'there' but I'm not in the conversations. I feel so uncomfortable—and bored!—and when I try to tell him this, I just get his usual spiel: 'You're such an asset. You're great!' When I get praise like that, where it's sweet, maybe, but it's also downright manipulative, I feel this wormlike anger—

oh, it's a really squeamish rage. But it's hard to know what to do with it. It's praise that makes me feel awful—and guilty."

Frances and her husband Gary are in their late twenties and, living in rural East Anglia, have a very different lifestyle from the big city academic lives of Sarah and Steve, but sensitivity to the motives behind praise plays a similar role in the quality of their partnership. Having been married only six months, they are still, Gary explains, "getting the hang of living together." Frances snorts good-humoredly at Gary's words. "It's getting the hang of how not to be just man and wife, but also how to be us." Gary nods, and they seem in accord, until Frances's voice breaks the harmony with its harsh tone. "You tell me, 'No one makes sandwiches as good as you do.'" Gary's eyes widen with bemusement as his wife's voice cracks. "That's bad? That I think you make good sandwiches?" "Yes!" she insists, and before Gary finishes his dismissive I-give-up gesture, she explains: "Of course I'm pleased. But it's more than about making the sandwiches and getting your lunch ready. It's also a way of leading me by the nose, making me add that extra thing to the awful morning rush. Sure, I want your praise. But I don't want to feel duped. And that kind of praise really is a way of getting me to do stuff. It pushes me into a role we really agreed we wouldn't do to each other."

I am all too familiar, from my own experience, with that squeamish anger in response to praise that seems like an attempt to trap you in a role. When my mother-in-law praises me for "doing an excellent job ironing [my husband's] shirts," I feel a tight grip locking me in a traditional housewife's role.

She interprets my puckered forehead and labored breath as embarrassed pleasure, but it is nothing of the kind. I swallow rage not pleasure as I am praised for something that has no value to me. Praise feels like a tool used to shape me into someone I do not want to be.

Neither Sarah's nor Frances's husband, nor my mother-in-law, is likely to have any idea that the praise conferred is controlling or patronizing or demotivating. Each would protest that they meant well: after all, how could a compliment be intended in any other way? Each would accuse the person who so ungraciously receives the praise of being touchy or contrary. But we can all be touchy and contrary when it comes to praise because, as Leslie says, it gets under our skin, promising pleasure but potentially exerting an unseemly power that silences our own judgment.

Unsatisfactory praise is like bad sex: the words are associated with pleasure and arouse expectation, but somehow they let you down. Good praise, on the other hand, makes the pulse rush, expands hope, and warms us with esteem.

The Hidden Economy of Esteem

The need for praise, and the esteem it brings, has such profound meaning that some philosophers believe praise is a driving force throughout our lives, both private and public. Geoffrey Brennan and Philip Pettit describe "a hidden economy of esteem" that flows beneath our more obvious motives and goals. In a market economy people value—and do things to acquire—money largely because of its power to purchase goods and services. In an economy of esteem, others' good opinions become underlying incentives for being a cooperative worker, inventor, entrepreneur, politician, or good neighbor.[38] Like the Gulf Stream that forms a distinctive river-like body of water within the ocean's network of torrents and currents, the desire for esteem, hidden in the deep and wide waters of our interpersonal lives, layers our motivation, often even guiding our aims and actions.[39] Our interests and pleasures and goals are wide-ranging and varied, but these are often shaped and channeled via the importance of others' judgments.

Day to day, living among other people, we have a shared awareness of what others are doing, which we register with our judgment meter.[40] We share concern "about whether others think well of us in certain ways, even if they say or do nothing to express this . . . even if they do nothing or say nothing it is often obvious . . . that some others see and think well, or see and think badly, of what one of us does."[41] Equally important is what people *might* think about what we *might* do.[42] So, even when we are not being judged, the possibility of being judged in the future will influence behavior.

"Esteem," more commonly referred to as pride or positive self-regard, is the emotion that allows us to hold our head up as we walk among others. We each value esteem, or warm approval and admiration from others. Likewise we each shrink from others' "disesteem" —a word Brennan and Pettit use to describe the absence of esteem, an absence that ranges from indifference to condemnation and derision. Our constant mindfulness of others' judgments, Brennan and Pettit argue, is a real force in our lives, alerting us to the potential pain of disesteem and the potential pleasures of esteem.[43] Others' judgments have a firm foothold in our minds and are constantly at hand to prod and adjust our behavior.[44]

How Our Mind Works Sometimes Deviously to Secure Praise

When something is as important to us as praise and as painful to us as any form of blame (which includes disapproval and disesteem), we will do our utmost to secure the former and avoid the latter. The persistence and ingenuity of the mind's hold on self-praise fascinate today's psychologists, and over the past three decades an inventory has been made of many ways, every day, the mind performs impressive gymnastics to protect esteem.

One of the first studies a freshman in psychology is likely to read exposes the most common human bias—the belief that we are better than most other people. This standard study explores responses to the question, "Do you think you as a driver are average, below average, or above average?" Of the people sampled in the United States, 93 percent rated themselves as above average in skill, and 88 percent assessed themselves as above average in safety.[45] Given the meaning of average—by definition, most people are average—the people sampled were clearly overestimating their skill.[46] In academia, where people are trained to assess critically the implications of their claims, the same principle of illusory superiority reigns: 68 percent of academics believe they are in the top 25 percent for teaching ability,[47] while 87 percent of MBA students at Stanford rated their own academic performance as above the median for their class.[48]

Whether people compare their ability, their effort, their achievement, or even their health and the quality of their relationships to others, they are likely to rate themselves as better than average.[49] This common phenomenon is sometimes known as the Lake Woebegone effect, after Garrison Keillor's fictional town in which "all the children are above average,"[50] but in psychology it is known as the *superiority illusion*.[51] Under the sway of the superiority illusion, we believe we deserve more praise than others. In many cases, too, the less likely we are to be praised—because we simply have not earned it—the more strongly we believe we deserve it—probably because, in such circumstances, we need more self protection.[52]

Over and over again, our views of events, their causes and contexts, are shaped according to whether the story protects esteem or leaves us open to disesteem.[53] The superiority illusion is only one of many self-serving biases. In a study in which people were told arbitrarily, with no reference to their actual performance, that they did well or badly on a task— such as solving a puzzle, or taking part in a game, or starting up a conversation with a stranger—a new self-serving bias was apparent. When asked to explain their success, they were likely to attribute it to ability and effort. "I'm good at puzzles," or "I gave it my all," they were likely to say. When a different group was told, again arbitrarily, without any reference to their actual performance that they did badly on the task, they were likely to see some external impediment (distracting noise, a poor night's sleep, badly worded instructions) as having stacked the odds against them.[54] Or, if the task had involved working alongside others, they were likely to blame another's failing ("The team never pulled together," or "He didn't listen to my advice").

When a colleague neglects to mention my contribution to raising funds for a teaching post and cites only her own efforts in clinching the deal, or when a colleague is praised for work to which I also made a contribution, I immediately spot *their* self-serving bias at work. In all likelihood, neither of my colleagues is intentionally cutting me out of praise. It is more likely that their memory works to preserve their esteem and has less concern for mine. What is humbling is that when I try to think of cases where my self-serving bias has been at work, where my memory delivers a clear recall of my contributions while others' lurk in the shadows, I struggle to find an example. Perhaps I am meticulously fair and there are no such cases. It is far more likely, though, that like most people I find it easier to see bias in others. I, too, fall prey to the blind spot bias[55] that protects our esteem while endangering the quality of our judgment.

I frequently come across the self-serving bias in my own research on close relationships. I first observe people interacting with one another, mostly in pairs but sometimes in groups. I then invite each person, on her or his own, to describe the relationship. I ask them about good times and bad times, and about gratitude and grudges. In one instance, a forty-seven-year-old woman, Gabriel, described her crystal-clear memories of her mother hitting her with the side of a brush, pulling her hair, and pushing her into a doorframe. When I interviewed Gabriel's mother and asked her to recall any heated conflicts during her daughter's childhood, she said, "Gabriel was always stubborn. I know she complains about me, but she's never been a grateful person. But I never, ever laid a hand on my child."[56]

When daughter and mother read, as previously agreed, each other's interviews, the daughter challenges her mother's version, "Oh, come on, Mom!" She cries while her mother flares in denial: "I never did that! How dare you say that? You made that up!" We may be able to shrug off minor pricks to our esteem, but at the big ones, a self-serving bias springs into action. As psychologist Cordelia Fine notes, "The bigger the potential threat, the more self-protective the vain brain becomes."[57]

THE eighteenth-century Scottish philosopher Adam Smith[58] wrote: "Nature, when she formed man for society, endowed him with an original desire to please, and an original aversion to offend his brethren. She taught him to feel pleasure in their favorable, and pain in their unfavorable regard. She rendered their approbation most flattering and most agreeable to him for its own sake; and their disapprobation most mortifying and most offensive."[59] The "original desire to please" is not a sycophant's urge to cater to others' wishes or to curry favor. It is a feature of our evolution as social beings.

When Adam Smith spoke of the original desire to please, he imagined an "impartial spectator" aligned with our own best judgment and reflecting our own values, similar to but more extensive than a moral conscience. The impartial spectator bridges our own inner judgments and others' views by representing to us what *people we respect* would think. Through this, we distill and refine the praise others give us, and the praise that confers esteem, according to our own needs and values. This remains one of the most important activities of our judgment meter.

Haim Ginott's metaphor of praise as a powerful emotional drug, not to be administered without following "rules about timing and dosage, cautions about possible allergic reactions"[60] remains true to this day. Praise occurs in what Ruthellen Josselson calls "the space between us,"[61] the web of connections between parent and child, between couples, between friends, between colleagues. These are dynamic and mutable relationships, for which we are likely to have high expectations. High up on the list of those expectations is being praised for who we want to be and being protected from the onslaught of disesteem, or blame.

3

Blame: The Necessity and Devastation of Guilt and Shame

PRAISE IS A KIND of glue. It triggers the flow of bonding hormones, increases trust, and makes us more willing to cooperate. Blame, the counterpart to praise, jolts us with fear of ostracism and exclusion.

In early childhood we cannot yet distinguish between guilt, or remorse for something we've done, and shame for who we are.[1] Throughout our lives, the emotional heft of blame fuses the two somewhat different concepts of guilt and shame. Blame can trigger a sense of guilt. Even when we are convinced we are innocent, blame sends the message, "I disapprove of what you've done," or, more strongly, "I disapprove of you." Blame can all too easily cascade into messages that shame us: "You are defective, deficient, inadequate."[2]

The feelings blame arouses are so painful that we often protect ourselves by stubbornly denying our mistakes, finger pointing or blaming others, or transforming our memories to make a more palatable version of events. Yet nothing is more important in navigating the negative judgment system than a willingness to accept blame and absorb lessons from guilt, while resisting shame.

Necessary Lessons

It is impossible to imagine a society that has no use for blame. Blame is the earliest teaching tool in a child's social and moral education. "I can do it myself!" can be a thrilling expression of pride and competence, but there is another side to this: you can be held accountable for your actions and their consequences. Blame conveys the message, "You should feel bad about this." It opens questions about whether, and how, to punish or exclude someone from the warm circle of relationships.

Blame may seem a strong word to cover ordinary disapproval, particularly disapproval that lies outside the moral realm,[3] but our experiences of blaming and being blamed extend well beyond universal moral principles. We blame others for their feelings and attitudes and little annoying habits: "I expected more sympathy from you," "You should show more respect," "You are so irritating," and "Why are you really unwilling to give me a hand here?" We may blame someone for not listening, for failing to offer support or comfort, or not caring enough about something we value. We may blame someone for shutting us out of her thoughts or refusing to tell us about his feelings. The people we blame in our everyday interactions, usually, have committed no crime and broken no commandment, yet we believe they should feel guilt—and they often do, because the message underlying blame is, "I am looking at you with disapproval," which, in a close relationships indicates, "You are not what I think you should be."[4]

The link between disapproval and blame, between doing something that offends people close to us and being wrong, is forged by our earliest relationships of profound dependence.[5] A cross word, a scolding, or telling off transforms the child's world: The child whose body was singing with joy suddenly crumples, tenses, and droops. The alert and eager face is cast in gloom. The bright gaze dims, wandering uncertainly to the parent's face, watching for the storm to ease. Meanwhile, the shoulders hunch, the mouth pulls down, and the child keeps still—a version of playing dead in the face of danger.

Blame, Exclusion, and Evolution

The vibrating alarm activated when we hear someone proclaim, "This is all your fault!" or "You are useless!" or "You are such a disappointment!" is familiar to most of us—not necessarily because we experience it often, but because we have deep memories of those experiences. Blame triggers a primitive shudder[6] in the amygdala—the small, archaic heart of the emotional brain where memory and emotions congeal, where quickly triggered responses attach either positive or negative value to what we see.[7] Lawyers, prosecutors, judges, jurors, and philosophers may apply clear, cold logic to parsing blame in legal and moral terms; but when we are blamed in our everyday lives, we are likely to lose equilibrium and proportion, and experience something much more basic—a visceral dread of others' disapproval. Disapproval and exclusion hurt as much as being cut or burned or hit, and, just as we draw away our hand when it touches the hot oven almost before we are aware of the pain, so too does our fast-thinking system react when we are threatened by blame.[8] The emotional pain we experience in the face of blame serves a purpose. It warns us that we are in danger of being rejected.

Exclusion is very different from the solitude many people enjoy when they sit alone, reading a book, listening to music, or following the course of their own thoughts. There can be great pleasure in having time alone, setting one's own routine, and tending one's own needs, only. Even those who value close friends and family and partners may find emotional and imaginative richness in solitude. In fact, many people need solitude to restore their equilibrium after intense social interaction.[9] But solitary pleasures occur within an underlying human infrastructure, not in enforced isolation.

Our human ancestors lived in social groups, dependent on one another for information, food, and protection. Exclusion from one's group would have been synonymous with death. This is one reason people who have experienced solitary confinement describe it as an extreme and devastating punishment. Shane Bauer, who was imprisoned in Iran in 2009, reflects, "No part of my experience—not the uncertainty of when I would be free again, not the tortured screams of other prisoners—was worse than the four months I spent in solitary confinement. . . . I needed human contact so badly that I woke every morning hoping to be interrogated."[10] Similarly, Nelson Mandela, who spent twenty-seven years in prison under the South African Apartheid regime, said, "Nothing is more dehumanizing than the absence of human companionship."[11]

Even ordinary social isolation puts our mental and physical well-being at risk. When we are lonely, we become more vulnerable to viruses, including common colds and flu.[12] Isolated or alone, we are at greater risk of psychological illness, too. These negative effects of isolation are encoded in our genes. In 2007, researchers at UCLA discovered that people who experience long-term loneliness show a very distinctive genetic pattern in their immune cells. They were not born with this genetic pattern. Isolation altered the behavior of their genes, just as physical injury does. And just as a physical injury activates genes that drive inflammation and lower our immune responses, isolation increases our susceptibility to viral illness, heart disease, and cancer. "Loneliness," the researchers concluded, "causes a yearning for social connection in the same fashion hunger makes us crave food."[13] A subsequent study in 2013 found that the likelihood of death increases by 26 percent when people suffer social isolation.[14] We have evolved to react strongly to the danger of being cast out of our group,[15] and hence we have evolved to fear blame, which warns us of possible exclusion.

Blame, Pain, and Empathy

The power of blame arises from another source, too: empathy. Humans are programmed to experience empathy. In fact, being affected by others' emotions was crucial to our evolution as a social species,[16] and this sensitivity emerges at birth. The chorus of wails in the neonatal room of a hospital does not start because babies all feel hunger at the same time; the infants cry together because they are responding to the crying of another infant.

When researchers explored empathy in babies between the ages of eight to sixteen months, they found signs of both cognitive and affective responses. That is, in addition to having an emotional response to the sound of a distressed wail, the babies showed understanding of what would cause pain and what would ease pain. When babies saw their mother (pretending to) hit her finger with a hammer or to bump her knee, even the youngest registered their own pain with a downturned mouth and furrowed brow. The older, sixteen-month-old babies, who were more mobile, approached their mother, patted her, or uttered soothing, cooing sounds.[17]

Empathy may start with the people we are closest to, but it does not end there. By the age of one year, a child tenses when she sees another child fall in the playground; feeling the other's pain, the one-year-old tries to soothe herself by sucking her thumb or pulling at her hair.

A month or so later, just after her first birthday, that child will pat or stroke the fallen child. She may offer her own favorite toy in an attempt to comfort or soothe him, particularly if he cries. With a sibling, she may draw on a wider range of techniques, distracting her sib with funny noises or shaking her face close to the sib's sightline and making a silly grimace or performing any of the tricks that in the past elicited squeals and laughter. It is only when she herself causes the infant's distress that she reverts to the passive, frozen empathy more characteristic of a younger child.

By the age of two years, her sensitivity to others' feelings will draw on more sophisticated cues. Her friend will not have to fall down or cry to trigger empathy; she will pick up cues that someone is sad from a voice, facial expression, or gesture.[18] Her own mood will also change, for empathy makes emotions contagious. By the age of five years, she will know, without needing any cue, that her friend is unhappy because her mother is leaving and that her brother feels bad when he breaks something. By the age of seven years, she will understand that certain conditions, such as being driven out of one's home or having one's city bombed, would be a source of long-term distress. Now empathy joins forces with imagination to forge new levels of interpersonal connection. By this stage, a child is capable of empathy for an entire group of people; she may want to take steps to improve their conditions, even if doing so comes at the expense of her own comfort.

Empathy Hurts

If we were able to see inside the child's brain when she experiences empathy, we would observe mirror neurons activated alongside the neurons that, from birth, accompany recognition of emotional expressions.[19] Feeling bad *for someone* involves feeling bad oneself; we imagine what others are feeling, but more than that, our brains register others' pain along the same pathways that register our own pain. In our brain's world, we really do feel others' pain.[20]

Imagine, for example, that we see a pedestrian hit by a car. We feel the nausea and shock to the system of the person who has been hit. We would have liked to prevent it[21] and feel anxious because we have not, and so we feel bad on that account, too. We may even—however illogically—experience something that feels very much like guilt. We think, "It might have been me who was hurt." That notion is frightening, yes, but something else goes on that disturbs us in a very different way. The neural response to witnessing pain has a strange physiological kinship to the neural activity of imagining ourselves *inflicting* pain.[22] So observing someone being harmed spreads the alarm that somehow we might be susceptible to blame.

The intuitive and powerful link to others' pain is fundamental to our judgment meter: "Have I hurt someone or have I pleased someone?" I ask as I assess my own behavior. "Has he or she pained or pleased someone," we ask when we appraise others. Empathy and pain for others underpin the human sense of right and wrong[23] and lay the groundwork for the sociability, for concern about others' well-being, and for the care we usually take not to hurt others.[24] However, guilt and empathy trigger, as all pain does, efforts to avoid pain, and many of these efforts cause havoc in our relationships.

Blame Avoidance

Blame is an effective teacher[25] because it is painful, but sometimes we cause further damage as we try to avoid blame. We
may laugh knowingly at a child who grabs a toy from a sibling,
and then, when the sib cries in outrage and appeals to the
parental judge, defends herself by insisting, "I had it first!"
We shrug in weary disbelief when a child says, "I didn't hit
him hard. I didn't really hurt him." We think this automatic
defense is particularly feeble, and we see through it easily; yet
adults, too, fall prey to the same flawed judgments. We sum-
mon up every emotional ploy and imaginative device to run
from blame. Ironically, defensiveness can be more destructive
to our relationships than the original fault—another example
of the cover-up being worse than the crime. Yet it is all too
easy to panic in the face of blame; instead of thinking things
through, we cling to any available defense, however implausi-
ble and whatever the future cost.

Threat-Rigidity

Just as the human mind has self-serving ways of enhancing
esteem, it has developed a range of defenses against blame.
Confronted with the threat of being in the wrong we are quick
to condemn the person who makes the negative judgment:
"Who are you to talk?" and "Who cares what you think?"

    If the accusation continues to rankle, we reach further into
our toolbox of defenses. We revise accounts of past behavior,

trace new causal paths through familiar stories, and cast blame elsewhere, all in an effort to defend ourselves from blame. "Are you saying that this is *my* fault?" or "You're shirking *your* responsibility for your actions!" are familiar exchanges in the daily minefield of judgments.

Even when we are clearly in the wrong, we have ways of simultaneously admitting and denying culpability by highlighting other causes and others' responsibilities: "I only did this because of what you said." Sometimes we revise history: "You were the one backing that policy; I only backed it because you said it was a done deal." Sometimes we vary cause and effect, turning what someone sees as our fault into something caused by someone else: "I fell off the wagon because of you." Underlying these maneuvers is a simple denial: "I did nothing wrong," "I am blameless," "You are exaggerating the damage I did," and even "*You* are to blame for thinking *I'm* to blame."

Denying that we are to blame and casting blame on someone else may provide relief, but this relief is likely to be temporary, and it is likely to have unfortunate consequences. In a defensive state, our brains close to others' perspectives. We no longer listen to what others say, so intent are we to elaborate reasons for our own innocence. This stubborn state arises from the natural fear of being blamed, and so it is termed *threat-rigidity*.[26]

In this state, we are unlikely to learn from our mistakes. Our energies are focused on self-defense; we are angry and planning our counterattack.[27] A tense lower jar and widened eyes signal to others that they continue to blame us at their peril. But even in the grip of threat-rigidity, a small part of our mind remains alert to our bad behavior, and this makes things worse. Still primed to defend our esteem, we are likely to see our bad behavior as proof of the far worse behavior of the other person;[28] we may magnify *their* faults in order to justify *our* behavior.

Most of us, I believe, find this drama is enacted on a daily basis. I get a message complaining that I have not submitted a student's reference, and I feel a blame jolt that generates the thought: "I am in a position of responsibility and let a student down!" But such an omission on my part is inconsistent with my belief I am reliable and responsible.

This inconsistency, our holding on to two contradictory beliefs, is known as cognitive dissonance. Dissonant beliefs tend to protect our esteem from negative judgments. They uphold self-justification and self-righteousness.[29] They allow us to believe things we may know are untrue. So I insist, "No one told me there was a deadline for the reference," or, perhaps a vague image that seems like a memory floats across my mind's eye and I offer, "Surely I did that a while back, and my secretary just didn't send it off?" In short, I may admit that a mistake was made, but not by me.[30] If I stick to this mindset, I may deflect blame and protect myself from the awful feeling of being in the wrong, but I also am likely to generate a negative cycle of interaction.[31]

This impulse to counter being blamed by blaming someone else occurs even when there is no one else I can blame. I knock my toe against a bedframe and feel a spasm of anger toward that mean metal frame. Ridiculous though this is, most of us, at least some of the time, go to inordinate lengths to avoid admitting that we have made a mistake, and absurd distortions of thought appear perfectly acceptable. No one is harder to reason with than the person who projects blame. As Carol Tavris and Elliot Aronson reflect in their extensive review of defensiveness, "Aggression begets self-justification, which begets more aggression." [32]

Finger Pointing

Finger pointing is another avoidance strategy that a child picks up quickly, usually by the age of three years. In my work on siblings, I looked for opportunities to observe small children during the odd moments—usually less than five minutes—a parent left them on their own in one room while she prepared a meal, or used the bathroom, or simply took a few minutes' break. When three-year-old Leah and four-year-old Jared kick and punch one another, each is quick to insist, on the parent's return, "He/she started it." They can even cast the blame elsewhere: "The baby spilled my juice," Leah declares, pointing at her not-yet-mobile baby sister.

Finger pointing is a sophisticated maneuver for a child who is only just beginning to grasp that other people form beliefs on the basis of their individual experiences, which may be different from the child's. However, the impulse to blame others is so basic that it can be seen in other primates, too. Francine Patterson reported that when Koko, the western lowland gorilla she had coached to use sign language, was asked how a toy cat had been damaged, Koko (who had indeed broken the toy) signed, "The nighttime attendant did it." [33]

"Mistakes were made, but not by me," is, as Carol Tavris and Elliot Aronson note, a common maneuver to mitigate the terrifying force of blame. We often harness the complexity of causes and effects to protect ourselves from blame. Actions, their causes, and their consequences are not connected with simple links in a simple chain. Hence, they are subject to manipulation and revision.

Even a question apparently as straightforward as, "Who started it?" can raise dispute. Was it the brother who hit his sister, or was it the sister who teased and taunted the brother, goading him to strike? Was it the older child who snatched the toy from a toddler, or was it the toddler who grabbed the toy being used by the older sibling? Did a careless child cause the messy spill or was it the fault of a wobbly table? Heated exchanges about sins of omission, sins of commission, faults and failings of character, motive, intention, and responsibility begin from a very early age, and they continue throughout our lives. We are opportunists when it comes to making use of the intricate causes of events in order to save ourselves from blame.

Self-Serving Memories

Memory often seems like an objective record of the past. Through our memories we all too often relive events we would rather forget: An old grief floods us as if it were brand new. We tense with regret over something we once said, and squeeze our eyelids shut as the memory rises up, as it were, before our eyes. But common sayings suggest how easily memories, particularly for painful things, can be lost. The cry "Never forget"— never forget those who died and never forget what harm some people can inflict on others—implies a general understanding of how atrocities are easily forgotten.

While we work to keep history's memory alive, to avoid the catastrophes and tragedies that have marked the past, we can easily forget our own mistakes. As Cordelia Fine notes, "Memory is one of [our] ego's greatest allies . . . Good things about ourselves tend to secure a firm foothold in the brain cells, while bad stuff . . . has a habit of losing grasp and slipping away."[34]

Having served on many appointment committees, I have often been struck by how slow candidates are to answer the question, "What is the biggest mistake you made in your last job?" while they are quick to answer the question, "What achievement are you most proud of in your last job?" Here memories of achievements march to the fore and offer a wide choice; but memories of mistakes seem lost. Even when they genuinely search for an example, they cannot think of one. They may not be intentionally hiding anything from the committee; their self-serving mind does the work for them.

At one time, memory was seen as a recording device, like a video we played when we recalled events: we press a start button and past events unfold, just as they did at the time we experienced them. But psychologists studying the intricate processes of memory have found that we store memories as piecemeal impressions packed with our own meanings, and when we go back to retrieve memories (when we "remember" something), we reshape the gist of past experience to fit it in with our sense of the world.[35] Our minds put in a lot of work filling in holes, generating coherence, and drawing on our wider knowledge of the laws of time, physics, and probability. Memory is not a replay but a construction: every time we return to a memory we revise it, molding the memory fragments into a comfortable fit.[36]

Stories about our past are powerful. They give meaning and coherence to our lives. When other people's stories about shared experiences and intersecting histories challenge ours, we feel that our very identity is under threat. In much of my research, I engage with people in intimate relationships—parents and children, siblings, friends, couples—and different memories, particularly those that involve blame, are always a flashpoint.

Before publishing any study, I offer participants the opportunity to read over their words as I present them, and also to read what another family member has said about them. This process reveals just how different memories of relationships are. "How can you say that! I never laid a hand on you!" we heard Gabriel's mother insist, as she reviewed her daughter's memories of their stormy relationship. "That's not what happened!" Annabelle protests when she reads her younger sister Leah's account of a time Annabelle once locked her out of the house. When Nina reads her younger sister Stacey's account of "the times they got into trouble," she protests, "I didn't break Mom's precious vase. It was you. I took the blame to cover for you! And now you've written over the real story." Couples, even when dealing with very recent events, find memories become blurred or distorted to protect their ego: "I wasn't the one who forgot to insure the car. It was you." No one is lying, yet neither is seeing clearly as each blames the other.

The memories we construct and the memories we omit are crucial to calming the storms set in motion by our responses to blame. Yet the more we engage in blame avoidance, the more rigid we become. Some of these defenses are vital to our well-being because they operate on the assumption that we are basically good and lovable, even in the midst of our faults and failings. Self-enhancing memories provide assurance that we are praiseworthy, and this belief helps us regain equanimity after a jolt of blame. Hence, self-illusion, in moderation, fosters resilience. But defensive responses to blame also pose serious risks, preventing us from learning from mistakes, closing our minds to others' views, and even setting us in opposition to people we love.

Blame and Self-Blame

While most people have an impulse to avoid blame, some absorb it all too quickly. It remains lodged within them, palpable and persistent. Self-blame is an emotional and physical burden that greatly increases the risk of mental health difficulties. It is a stronger predictor of mental issues than genetic risk, social environment, or personal crises, such as the death of a relative or close friend, divorce, or losing one's job.[37]

Many therapists I have spoken to in the course of my research tell me that the most common problem presented by patients is a form of self-blame that contains feelings of guilt, but is far more diffuse. Someone feels guilty for a specific act, such as having cheated on an exam or lied to a friend. Even when we do something unwittingly, we may feel guilt: perhaps we were clumsy and broke a vase, or reckless and hurt someone, or irresponsible and lost something. But the diffuse feelings of guilt in self-blame do not focus on a specific action or omission. If we are in the grip of self-blame, we suffer from the belief that the people we care about would be better off without us.

The psychoanalyst Alice Miller observed, "No argument can overcome these guilt feelings, for they have their beginnings in life's earliest period, and from that derive their intensity."[38] No argument can overcome such feelings because they do not arise from what we do but from how we are treated.

Self-Blame and Shame

James Gilligan is a psychiatrist who understands fully the tragedy of extreme self-blame, or shame. In exploring the disturbed minds of violent criminals, both in prisons and in mental hospitals, Gilligan heard how many inmates and patients had been abused verbally, emotionally, and physically throughout their childhoods. Some were subject to sexual abuse and some to life-threatening neglect, starved or abandoned by their parents.[39] They lived, Gilligan realized, in a state of shame.

Why does someone else's behavior shame me? Why does a child feel terrible about herself or himself when beaten or sexually abused? Parental abuse, Gilligan explains, is "the clearest possible way of communicating to the child that the parent does not love him (or her)." As he listened carefully to his patients, trying to piece together the broken shards of their thoughts, he heard his patients use words over and over again: "empty," "numb," "zombie," and "robot." They felt that their personalities had died long before they became criminals. Being threatened with punishment for assault or murder was meaningless because, for them, everything had already been lost.

Speaking in the metaphorical language of the psychiatrist, Gilligan says, "When the self is not loved, by itself or by another, it dies, just as surely as the body dies without oxygen."[40] For the neuroscientist, these words ring true: shame causes actual damage to the brain and the nervous system. Shame is likely to make us more vulnerable to disease and to worsen any existing disease. It leads to increased secretion of cortisol, high levels of which suppress the immune system and the proinflammatory system—the system of checks and balances that aid recovery.[41]

Being shamed, repeatedly and persistently, changes the physiology of the brain, reducing resilience and self-control. Shame affects our genes, too, and can activate aggression by switching on the so-called warrior genes, genes initially identified in research on a family with a high number of violent members. At first it was thought that these few genes—the

MAOA and CDH13 genes—in themselves resulted in violent behavior. Further investigation found that many people who show no tendency toward violence also carry these genes. In fact, warrior genes are switched on only when a carrier of those genes also suffers the shame of childhood abuse.[42]

Once shame takes root and alters the brain, the most minor slight can activate a catastrophic defense. For most people, being jostled on a train, losing a small amount of money in a dispute, being the subject of a passer-by's sneer, or having a driver speed past with a rude gesture are little more than annoyances. There may be a flash of anger and ripple of humiliation, but the status quo, where you are a person whose feelings are respected, whose opinions carry weight, and who has reasonable access to esteem, soon returns. But someone with prolonged experiences of shame has no buffer against humiliation. The slightest facial expression, tone of voice, or gesture is interpreted as a personal affront that can issue a reign of terror.

The neurobiologist Antonio Damasio, whose work has been so important in understanding links between emotion and physiology, explains, "Once the brain is properly tuned up by repeated experiences of such emotional conditioning the brain areas that monitor these bodily changes begin to respond whenever a similar situation arises."[43] It is not surprising that shame is sometimes called the "ugly" emotion,[44] for it makes us feel ugly, and, in some circumstances, makes our actions ugly.

Shame, Violence, and Self-Harm

The extreme shame of Gilligan's violent patients may seem a far cry from our ordinary experiences, yet most people are familiar with the experience of "being mortified" when a flaw or failing has been exposed, when we feel we have revealed ourselves as inferior, and when, instead of being held in others' esteem, we are held in contempt. The word *mortification* is derived from the Latin *mortis* which means "dead," and *facere* which means "to make." Mortification suggests an inward crumbling, along with the wish to die or disappear. Profound and persistent mortification is shame, and shame is the death of esteem, which, Gilligan explains, is the death of the self.

Anyone who faces this death of the self will make some effort, however clumsy, however reckless, to restore some semblance of pride. Gilligan found that those who had been, over time, crushed by shame—unloved, unvalued, unpraised—were willing to risk everything, including life and liberty, to rescue their esteem. Yet they knew of no other way to build themselves up than through inflicting terror—for example, by pointing a gun or punching a face. Shame transforms the child's innocent need for attention to a vicious, raging demand to be given "respect," which may simply mean being noticed.[45]

Our vulnerability to mortification changes over time but never fully subsides. In childhood, we do not question the legitimacy of others' negative view of us: if people we love have no admiration for us, then we believe we are not worthy of admiration. In adolescence, there often seems to be no meaningful life beyond one's peer groups and finding acceptance with them. Teens, with their raw self-consciousness, are exquisitely sensitive to others' taunts. A bully can strip away a teen's esteem and leave the self dangling from a thread. Social exclusion, often an effect of bullying, is the major risk factor in teen suicide, which itself is the leading cause of teenage death.[46] We can read about fifteen-year-old Lewis, who gave up football after being pushed and jostled in the locker room, and who shot himself in 2013, leaving a note explaining that he had taken his own life because he was bullied,[47] or seventeen-yearold Gregory Spring with Tourette's syndrome who was teased relentlessly over a period of years, and who, having broken up with his girlfriend—the one relationship that protected him from social exclusion—took his own life.[48]

Adults who "lose face," or see their social identity destroyed, may also view suicide as the only possible resolution to their shame. Living without esteem seems impossible, because esteem shaped their identity, and without it they are no one, or nothing. Lady Isobel Barnett, who appeared regularly on British radio, who in her daily life enacted the role of aristocratic lady, who was thought to embody "British decency, uprightness, and charm"[49] was transformed from someone enjoying social status to outcast when she was convicted in 1980 of stealing two small items—a can of tuna and a carton of cream—from a local shop. Four days later she was found dead in her bath, fully clothed, with an electric heater immersed in the water. In 1998 Admiral Jeremy

Boorda shot himself just before a scheduled interview with *Newsweek* journalists who were challenging the legitimacy of two of his medals.[50]

None of these people was subject to physical torture or even hardship, yet shame left them without any sense of proportion, without hope, and without a sense of self. As Gilligan observed, death of the self, or total loss of esteem, is "more tormenting than the death of the body could possibly be."[51]

Shame is something only a very social creature can feel. It arises from thwarted longing for others' esteem and exclusion from society's vital heart. When people on the street freeze as we pass, either because they expect us to be dangerous or because we are repugnant to them, when they ignore us because we are of no account, when our voice is boxed into a bell jar with a label of "liar" or "dangerous" or "insignificant," then we either flee or fight for recognition. As developmental psychologist Bruce Hood reflects, "It may be no surprise that people prefer social acceptance, but what is surprising are the lengths that some will go to become members of a group— and the terrible retribution they can wreak when they are excluded."[52]

Shameless Exceptions

It is impossible to imagine a human society in which praise and blame do not shape behavior, yet a small proportion of people live as outliers, impervious to guilt and shame.[53] These emotional aliens look upon others' pain with a cold curiosity.[54]

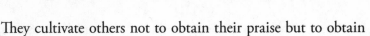

They cultivate others not to obtain their praise but to obtain power over them.

Those who inhabit this troubling and exceptional category have no difficulty reading emotional and social cues. Hence, they are very different from people with any form of the Asperger syndrome. Someone with this condition lacks an intuitive lexicon for social signals but may well be fully capable of empathy, sympathy, and true affection,[55] whereas these outliers are excellent mind readers but incapable of empathy. They are quick to note the small shifts in face and voice and posture. They catch the fleeting look of need, and they are adept at inspiring trust. Mindsight, for them, means knowing how best to manipulate others.

These "shameless exceptions" are thought to constitute approximately 1 percent of the population, and they are commonly referred to as psychopaths.[56] Psychopaths are capable of inflicting severe pain, sexual violence, and murder without any qualm of conscience or remorse. While they are often assumed to be criminals, and while many criminals are thought to be psychopaths, the overlap is relatively small. In fact psychopaths—callous, impulsive, thrill-seeking individuals—form only 25 percent of the prison population.[57] The shame-ridden patients James Gilligan describes are not psychopaths. They are violent not because they are indifferent to others' judgments, but because they feel oppressed by them and lack any positive way to regain esteem.

Just as not all criminals are psychopaths, not all psychopaths are criminals. There are many high-functioning psychopaths who live among us, inconspicuous, law-abiding, and successful. Charismatic, good at getting his or her own way, adept at befriending people who are useful and discarding them when they have served their purpose, psychopaths are drawn to positions of power, where impulsive risk-taking may be lauded as courage and imagination.[58] Because psychopaths tend to be good actors, it may be that the telltale signs would emerge only from a brain scan. We would then see that their neural responses to words that for most of us carry a dark emotional charge—words such as *kill* or *rape*—cause barely a ripple in their neural responses. To a psychopath, words associated with violence and pain register in the same way as neutral words such as *chair* or *tree*.[59] Even the prospect of their own danger leaves them unmoved.[60]

Most people, with their active judgment meter, find the psychopathic mind frame impossible to imagine. Whether we are a surgeon, with someone's life literally in our hands, or the guardian of a child, or a neighbor, a friend, a spouse, we routinely pose questions to ourselves: "Am I taking good care of others?" "Am I being fair?" and "Am I sufficiently thoughtful, or considerate, or helpful?" For most people, the need to see themselves in a positive light is paramount, and this includes having a positive impact on the people around them.

Shame has been called a "necessary" emotion[61] because of its role in regulating social and cooperative behavior; it functions in most people as an internal police force to remind them what is expected and what is acceptable. But, in every social species, and in every society, there are exceptions. These cheats and freeloaders—and psychopaths—benefit from the norms of a cooperative society but do not follow them. If more than a few people were so impervious to shame, though, the entire fabric of cooperation would collapse.

The Original Story of Human Shame

The links among blame, guilt, and shame were drawn long before professional psychologists studied human nature. The Bible's Book of Genesis shows the terrifying impact of disapproval: when Adam and Eve displease their God, they are expelled from their home and, for the first time, experience shame.

This foundational story serves as a reminder that we live with the risk of disapproval, guilt, and shame, and that a core human task is managing these risks. We try to avoid disapproval from those we love and respect, but we can never do so completely. Sometimes we fall prey to temptations from our own poor judgment, and sometimes others judge us unfairly through their own errors or bias. We cannot live in a blame-free haven, but we can learn to manage both the blame we inflict and the blame we receive.

As I look more closely at blame in specific relationships—parent and child, friends, spouses, colleagues—the problematic nature of defensiveness emerges again and again, along with examples of more constructive ways to manage negative judgments. Keeping an open mind when someone blames us can seem as hard as keeping our hand over a burning flame. Yet remaining open to another's perspective can reshape a negative judgment ("You are to blame") into something positive ("This is what I can do in the future to avoid your blame, or my guilt, and to gain approval, either from others or from myself").[62]

It seems counterintuitive that accepting blame reduces the risk of shame, but there is strong evidence of this. In assessing the well-being of a group of Harvard graduates over six decades, the psychiatrist George Vaillant found that people who blamed others for their misfortunes adjusted less well to the inevitable changes they confronted in their lives.[63]

Many other studies, too—77 percent of those done on this subject—show that when we blame others we are worse off emotionally and physically.[64] Blaming others, and being unable to forgive them, imposes health-threatening stress.[65] Blaming others may offer temporary relief, but it implies that what happens is out of our control. If our circumstances are someone else's fault, then they are also in someone else's power, not in ours.

Fortunately, we also have techniques for making amends. The child bows her head, and the display of utter misery and humiliation shows remorse, a sign that she feels bad for doing bad. Soon she will learn the power of apology. Saying "I'm sorry" assures others that we acknowledge our fault, accept that we are to blame, and enlist them in our desire to be absolved of guilt. Even more important than regret, however, is the assurance we offer in giving an apology: we show that we value the person who has been offended by our actions.[66] This explains why every society and every relationship benefits from something comparable to days of atonement, confession, and penance—rituals that manage the terror of blame, allowing us to regain approval from those we love and depend on.

4

Family Judgments, Family Systems

EACH FAMILY HAS unique habits and rules for praise. In one family, praise is long lasting, as solid and sweet as a giant gumball rolling on one's tongue. In another family, praise's sweetness dissolves quickly, leaving no trace and offering no satisfaction. When one person responds to praise with a rush of pride, while another feels anxious and wonders, "Did they really mean it?" and "Are they still pleased?" it is likely that their families expressed praise in very different ways.

Each family also has unique practices and rules about blame. In some families, blame is short-lived, quickly overridden by praise. In another, blame is set down indelibly in the family record, frequently referenced as an enduring measure of low worth. One person takes blame in his or her stride, shrugging it off: "It was a mistake anyone could make." Another bristles defensively, "It wasn't my fault," or "Your view doesn't matter to me." A third is immediately flooded with self-abuse: "Yes, I really messed up; I always do that; it's all my fault." Such very different responses are linked to the ways blame is meted out and expressed within our families, from infancy through midlife.

Systemic Differences

Families are more than clusters of individual people who share a home. Family members interact according to recognizable patterns that are regulated by an implicitly shared, carefully monitored family judgment meter.[1] A parent sees one child feeling left out as his younger brother is being lauded for his good school report. She leans close to the older child and says, "I saw the train set you built in your room. It's wonderful. Well done!" An implicit rule that everyone deserves praise is followed. Another child sees his parents locked in a quarrel: "You never listen to me," says one and "You don't talk to me; you just nag the whole time," says the other. The child then spills his drink or hits his sister, drawing his parents' attention away from their argument. The child has learned that his parents' blame and counterblame can be resolved only by presenting them with the opportunity to blame him.

Psychologists compare the sensitive feedback loops in family judgments to a central heating system where a drop in temperature, below a preset level, sends a signal to the boiler to switch on and run until the normal temperature is reached.[2] The family's coordinated responses and feedback loops normally ensure the comfort and well-being of family members. Sometimes, though, the system maintains profoundly uncomfortable patterns, and these patterns are referred to as "dysfunctional." Whether the judgment system works well, or whether it is dysfunctional, depends on how rigid or flexible it is, and how responsive or intrusive.

Judgment Systems: Rigid or Flexible?

Every family requires some rigidity in its judgment system. "You may think this is ok, but I do not!" a parent, reasonably, says to a three-year-old who is taunting his baby sister. Parents exercise necessary authority by taking charge of praise and blame.

As children learn family rules governing praise and blame, they explore and test them: "Why am I blamed for taking her toy?" and "You should blame her. She's not sharing." In a responsive judgment system, these challenges are acceptable (even when there is no agreement) and explanations are given. In a rigid family system, these questions are offensive. "Because I say so," puts an end to the matter. If a child presses further, he or she attracts blame: "Just do as I say!" or "Stop being such a pain."[3]

Children use this family lexicon of praise and blame to their advantage. When they inhabit a responsive family judgment system, they adopt and adjust parents' explanations for their own purposes. "I gave her my toy! I am sharing," and "I ate all my supper," they announce to elicit praise. They spin descriptions of their behavior to avoid blame: "I'm playing with her. I'm not teasing her." Or they finger point: "She started it!" and "He was mean to me first." In a flexible family system, children are likely to get a hearing, even if the child's version is then challenged. In a rigid system, however, a child who says he or she is "just playing" (rather than "teasing") is blamed for "lying" or being "sneaky." The underlying message from the parent is, "I am in control of true judgment, and your judgment means nothing."

Balancing flexibility versus rigidity takes on even greater importance—and becomes more difficult—in the teen years. Teenagers thrill to their new powers of critical thinking, which they use to hone their own, very individual judgments. Teens constantly test the power of their judgments against those of a parent, and, in the process, challenge balance, fairness, and reason.

How Teens Challenge a Family's Judgment System

Over a period of nearly three decades I have participated in research of parents and teens that included daylong observations in their homes, in malls, and on journeys to and from school. In the course of this work I recorded and analyzed many, many arguments.[4] Common points of conflict included questions as to who is judging whom, who is in the right, who shows respect to the other. Even the most carefully moderated family judgment system is likely to be sorely tested by a teenager's arguments.

In the Maryland home of thirteen-year-old Gina, her ten-year-old brother Jose, and her mother Roberta, I saw a minor tiff between Gina and her mother Roberta[5] over the daughter's daily schedule escalate to global blame about her attitude and behavior: When Roberta reminds Gina that she has a swim session later that day, Gina barks, "I don't feel like swimming!" Roberta balks at her daughter's attitude ("A little respect would be appreciated"), and then reminds Gina that she signed up for swim class and concludes that her daughter is failing to organize herself and manage her time. Gina defends herself, insisting her mother's blame is unfair: "I have all this covered!" But once the blame dynamic begins, each is invested in defending her own position. Roberta highlights her daughter's underlying character flaws of disrespect and irresponsibility, while Gina counters with accusations that her mother is intrusive and distrustful: "You think I can't do anything without you breathing down my neck." They wage a battle to secure the other's good opinion, but the result is that each feels increasingly condemned by the other.

In the Washington, DC, home of fourteen-year-old Alex, her older sister Jess, her mother Peg, and her father Chris, preparations for a night out become a heated moral debate. Peg hesitates as Alex emerges from her room, her hair in glossy curls, her face smoothed and defined with makeup, her party dress and all accessories in place. "You don't like it!" Alex scoffs, interpreting her mother's hesitation. This charge seems to make Peg defensive, and she explains, "I'm worried about the message it gives." "What message!" Alex presses, and Peg shrugs. "Slutty?" she suggests. Her father Chris, having just come into the room to catch only the last exchange, tries both to support his wife and modify her remark: "Some people will think, looking at you, that you have some real shallow values." Alex reddens and protests: "This is how *everyone* dresses. And you have to be pretty stupid to judge someone's values by how they dress." Alex pauses, and refuels her rage: "You are so backward-looking!" she shouts. "And you are really, really mean."

The following day I speak to Alex privately. (This is routine: a debriefing interview after a quarrel is crucial in uncovering what meaning it had for everyone involved.) Alex, still upset but no longer fuming, complains that she is "boxed in and boxed out" of her family. She is boxed in by their judgments that are fixed and final, and she is boxed out of influencing their judgments. "You can never, ever get them to see things your way," she complains. Later, when I speak privately to her mother, Peg believes it is Alex who blocks real discussion: "I only have to hint that I'm not pleased with something, and she has her teeth at my throat."

Teens are quick to judge others, heatedly and passionately, and they are slow to return to a calm, reflective baseline. Arguments consisting of blame and counterblame are an exhausting but inevitable feature of the teen-parent relationship. Cool decision-making, calm observation, self-control, and forward planning do not come easily to teens, and there are physiological reasons for this. While teens' heated arguments are often attributed to hormones, it is actually the teenage brain that is the culprit. The teenage brain is a rapidly growing organ, capable of abstract thinking and sophisticated reasoning, and as an intellectual powerhouse it equals the adult brain. The teen's *social* brain, though—how it perceives and responds to others—is far from mature.

The human brain was once thought to reach maturity at puberty, but recent imaging techniques[6] reveal two important ways in which the teenage brain is very different from an adult brain. The wiring changes taking place in the teen brain mean that it has to work harder than either a young child's brain or an adult's brain to process social information.[7] Mindsight—the inferences we make about other people's intentions, emotions, and judgments—is, during the teenage years, biased toward heated and negative interpretations. A facial expression that an adult would interpret as uncertainty or fear, a teen is likely to interpret as anger—a heated form of disapproval.[8] So, for example, when Alex's mother expresses anxiety about her daughter's clothes, Alex interprets this as anger; in response, she becomes defensive and angry herself.

In addition to teens' skewed interpretations of so many feelings parents express toward them—anxiety, doubt, fear, uncertainty—are challenges presented by the teenage pre-frontal cortex. The functions performed by this part of the brain include what are called the executive functions such as impulse control, forward planning, and emotional regulation.[9] With the brain's gray matter growing at a rapid rate, with new neural connections proliferating daily, the teen's brain can be seen as an unpruned thicket, dense and jammed.[10] Not until the age of twenty-four years will the brain's wiring be pruned of the excess connections and run an efficient prefrontal cortex. For the time being, it functions like an overheated circuit board. In particular, the teen's prefrontal cortex is slow to send that all-important calming message to the amygdala: [11] "Shh; it's okay; you're not in real danger." Until this radical pruning takes place, which normally occurs in early adulthood, teens are quick to take offense to anything they perceive as blame.

Parental Management and Mismanagement of Teens' Judgment

For many parents, a teen's condemnation is terrifying. Not only is it hurtful, as all blame is, but it threatens a parent's control and influence that, generally, is intended to protect a child. Mira, as a single mother of fifteen-year-old Kylie, whom she describes as "a soft child who's acting like an overactive spike, always piercing me," said she volunteered for my study of teens and parents so I could "see what [she is] up against." Mira feels worn down by her daughter's constant blame: "I hear one accusation after another, day in and day out. What this girl, all set against me, doesn't realize is that my biggest nightmare is her getting hurt. She thinks this is a power struggle, and she wants to show she's stronger than me. If she really proves that then I'd be the happiest mother in the world. What I'm terrified of is that those monster friends of hers will pick her bones dry."

Rejecting a parent's judgment and blaming a parent for being judgmental call into question a parent's effectiveness in the most important investment he or she is ever likely to make: raising a child. There are high stakes in being an effective parent. The message, "Your judgment is worthless. I am not influenced by your praise and blame," is tantamount to saying, "We have no real relationship."

Yet for all their bluster, teens value parents' responses. They challenge the family judgment system, seeking out its weak points, pushing patience and empathy beyond any reasonable limit, because they want parents to register their transformation from the child the parent once knew so well, who was once dependent on parental approval,[12] to the one who now seeks approval for her own emerging judgment meter.

Blame Avoidance, Teen Style

When family arguments become too painful even for a teen, when a teen feels frustrated and hurt by continuous disapproval of her friends, her plans, or her values, she may disengage from the judgment wars by *appearing* compliant. In my research on adolescents and families, I shuddered to see how adept some teenagers get at lying. Jenny, mother of fifteen-year-old Senka,[13] said, "The only way to deal with this teenage nonsense where she's the only one who knows what's right and who's to blame is to lock things down." Jenny found her arguments with Senka "simply awful . . . I thought they would kill us both. I just had to take charge." As her mother becomes more strict and authoritarian, Senka describes herself as wearing two faces, one real and the other fake. To avoid "hearing the list of my faults read out every time I ask permission to do something, I just pretend I'm doing stuff she approves of. . . . Lying gives me a mask to wear so that mom is not always condemning me."

Family arguments usually start as dialogues, however heated, in which each responds to the other's views. When dialogue is prohibited ("Don't you dare say another word!"), the teen faces unsatisfactory options: Either the teen accepts that a parent is right and that he or she is at fault, or the teen sits in cold opposition to a parent. At this point, the relationship is shaped by anger and rebellion or by deceit, where the teen hides her opposition, disguises her real self, and covers her own judgment meter by pretending to adopt the family judgment meter.

This impasse is likely to generate guilt on both sides. Because we are a species so closely bound to other people, one of the most painful things we can blame ourselves for is damaging an important relationship. Rather than admit we have done this, we deny that our shouting and scolding, our unkind verbal venting, is hurtful: "Everyone shouts," Lois insists, after her seventeen-year-old daughter Margot speaks to me about the dread she carries with her, anticipating the next onslaught from her mother that "splits her head in two.[14] Alternatively, a parent insists that the son or daughter is solely to blame. "I have no choice," Jenny says when she becomes an authoritarian parent. "She made me into this monster." The teen may put on a display of fierce opposition and insist she does not care about a parent's judgment, but the dissonance between teen and parent is likely to generate a discomfort that feels very much like guilt. For this discomfort, each is likely to blame the other.

Psychologists have found that one very common way people justify their own poor behavior, and avoid self-blame, is to magnify the faults of the person we offend.[15] So, when Gina argues, in effect, "I have only forgotten about swimming, but you are being so nasty about it," Roberta defends herself by magnifying Gina's faults with the accusation that she is *always* disorganized. Gina and Roberta soon reclaim a reasonable conversation as each listens to the other; but extreme cases of stress, frustration, depression, or disappointment can leave a parent heavily invested in justifying her blame. The vehement condemnation that, in the heat of the moment, seems appropriate actually makes the argument far worse.

Praise and Blame: Labels or Guide?

Each family has distinctive ways of using positive and negative words. In some families they are used like labels, pinning a final judgment on someone. In others, they are guides and prompts, and look positively to the future.

When four-year-old Finn grabs a toy from his playmate, his father says, "You have to learn to share," but when five-year-old Stella pulls a train away from her brother, her father says, "You're a selfish kid." When thirteen-year-old Ella is late for supper, her mother says, "You've kept us waiting. That is inconsiderate," but when thirteen-year-old Vito is late, his mother says, "You're rude. You're also ungrateful. You only think of yourself." For fourteen-year-old Kirsty, missing her curfew signals doom: "No one will ever want to trust you," her mother predicts, "You'll get nowhere." As Kirsty explains the specific circumstances behind her lateness, Kirsty's mother counters by listing past offenses: "This is just like the time I offered to take you shopping and you left me waiting for half an hour," and "It's like the time you 'forgot' I was picking you up from school."

In some families, blame describes an action; in others it defines a person. When blame points the way to correction ("learn and make an effort") it is a positive lesson; it can even feel like praise as it sends the message, "You can do better." When blame defines a defective character ("You are selfish/ unreliable"), the message is purely negative.

Using one negative judgment as a lens for an entire person is called globalizing. We respond very differently according to whether blame is specific and contained, or global. When we hear blame that is focused on a particular fault, the initial jolt soon subsides—particularly if we hear suggestions about how to avoid such blame in the future. When we hear globalized blame, our anger mounts.

What is surprising is that the person who delivers the blame is similarly affected. We feel angrier when we make a global accusation than when we make a specific one.[16] This is not only because we are more likely to engage in global blame when we are very angry, and more likely to blame a specific fault when we are less angry. This is because the physiological effects of globalizing reinforce anger and cloud our perception.[17]

In this aroused state, our brain is quick to perceive wrongs and threats, but is not good at sifting evidence. Anger fires up the amygdala before the cortex, the part of the brain that considers and weighs judgment, gets a foothold in our thoughts.[18] While it is often said that expressing anger releases it and reduces pressure, like a kettle emitting steam, anger in fact is self-reinforcing.[19] Emotions often drive our thoughts, and in an angry state, we fish for reasons to justify our feelings. We remember all the times the person we blame has done something wrong and let us down, and we forget the times he or she was reliable and considerate, because those memories do not fit our mood. The more vehemently we blame someone, the more entrenched is our sense that he or she deserves blame.[20]

Thirteen-year-old Laura describes her experience of this escalating blame storm: "It starts from one thing: I forgot to pick up some groceries on the way back from school. Or I didn't clear something away when I made myself a snack. Suddenly I'm careless and disrespectful, and then a whole bunch of other things, and she's ready with the list of all my crimes, past, present, and future. My mother is like a hurricane when she is angry. Everything that gets in her path is destroyed. . . . I feel so angry myself. I want to explode in her face." [21]

For parents, judging a son or daughter negatively is a double-edged sword.[22] They want to strike hard, to drive the lesson home, but they also wound themselves through empathy with their child's distress. In addition, they anxiously reflect on their own part in her behavior. "Am I responsible for her being like this?" and "What will her life be like if she doesn't overcome her faults?" they may ask themselves. Parents want to see a child's faults in order to help her correct them, yet they want to think well of her, to offer praise, and to enjoy the love that thrives on mutual praise. The challenge is to frame blame positively, directing it toward small and specific actions, to see this child, with her highly individual interests and desires, walking into a proud future.

Praise: Generous or Meager

In some families praise is a generous resource: everyone is seen to deserve some praise, and praise is easy to give because there is much to go around. In other families, however, praise is in short supply. "Your sister is so beautiful/smart/helpful/funny," carries, in the first family, a warm and inclusive message: "We are all pretty great." In the second family, the praise of one member implies disapproval of another; the underlying message is, "Your sister deserves praise, but you do not."

A family that issues praise guardedly and meagerly often explains that it has "high standards." To deserve praise you have to be superior to others. For tiger parents—those who believe it is their child's duty to win prizes and come out on top—praise is competitive and failure to win ruptures the relationship. The parent's message is, "I need you to get more praise than anyone else, and your failure to do so leaves me bereft. You should be ashamed to hurt me like that."[23] In this judgment system, praise puts a child on a knife edge.

For many years I worked in a university whose students came from those who had been "the best" in high school.[24] Linda cannot understand why I praise her weekly essay when, in response to her question, "What percentile is it in?," I tell her it is well above average. "So I'm stuck with everyone else," she protests, and her eyes fill with tears. She hears my praise as contempt; anything less than praise for being "the best" is worthless.

Ivy, in her freshman year in college, tells me she wants to give up math because she is only a so-so student, where, in high school, she was always "the best one." Now she feels "discouraged, really rubbish, because there are so many people better than [she]." If praise is only for being the best, Ivy reasons, it is safer to keep your circle of reference very small, and avoid new challenges.

The demand to be the best ushers in a cascade of anxieties. There is the anxiety of seeing another person praised and wondering how another's excellence affects our place in the praise hierarchy. There is the anxiety over retaining first place, when we have no control over how well others will do. There may also be an unwholesome grudge against others' successes, because in a judgment system where praise is competitive, both parent and child are likely to feel threatened by others' accolades.

When praise is so scarce that it has to be rationed among siblings, each child lives with the threat of exclusion. While being singled out as "the good one" may offer temporary comfort, a "bad sibling" haunts every child in the household. "When will it be my turn to be the bad one?" each child wonders. Each is very likely to feel sorry for the one targeted by blame and to feel guilty for hoarding what seems like a limited supply of praise.

Gavin, at twenty-nine years, reflects on being the "best" son. "I kept thinking it was my fault that my little brother was being punished." Stan, three years younger than Gavin, was "always annoying" his mother. His occasional school detentions were seen as an indication of a bleak future. "I just froze when Mom shouted at Stan and called him names and reminded him how inferior he was to me. I've never been easy about praise, and I avoid it as much as I can. Whenever Stan messes up I know it's my place to sort stuff out for him. It's a dreadful thing, feeling that your little brother is getting [criticized] because of you."

The idea that the favorite child will feel especially blessed, that, like Joseph with his coat of many colors, he will rise in the world with a princely aura, is countered by the distinctive syndrome of self-sabotage among "Mom's favorite" [25] that is well documented by psychologists.[26] The favorite child may try to assuage guilt and anxiety by undermining his or her own successes. The favorite child loves, but feels distant from, the rejected child. For Gavin, even in adulthood, praise is a burden, and he blames himself for his brother's mistakes. In this distorted judgment dynamic, praise makes him feel ashamed.[27]

Judging Emotions

Every family evaluates emotions. In an intrusive judgment system some emotions are considered to be bad and, when expressed, a child is told some version of "You deserve blame for feeling this." In a responsive judgment system, some feelings flag problems and invite questions: "Why do you feel like this?"

Emotions toward each other may also be a focus of judgment. Affection and respect for one's family, particularly parents, are generally the norm. Disrespect, dislike, and disdain toward other family members are generally deemed unacceptable, which does not mean they do not arise but that when they do they can attract blame. Families also monitor members' feelings toward neighbors, teachers, colleagues, and friends. Fury, envy, and hatred are in many (but by no means all) families considered unacceptable, and children are then reminded of the importance of patience, fairness, gentleness, and forbearance. Most of us nonetheless feel all these "unacceptable" emotions sometimes. How others then respond—with the condemnation or dismissal of blame, or the curiosity and interest linked to praise (even when approval for those emotions is withheld)—will be either shaming or liberating.

One day during the parent-teen study, Betty explains that she and her daughter, thirteen-year-old Robin, will have to draw the session to a close because Robin has to visit her cousin who is convalescing after a course of chemotherapy. "I don't want to come with you! I hate these visits!" Robin protests. Her mother seems astonished: "That isn't like you. You're always so good with her. You're so patient and kind."

"It's not like you to say such a thing," and "I can't believe you would want to do that," suggest that the darker, angry, and rebellious aspects of a child are unacceptable, and that a parent needs her to feel only positive emotions. Her mother's praise reminds Robin of what she *should* feel. However well founded, the underlying message ("You should be willing to spend time with a cousin who has been having a rough time"), implies that her real feelings are shameful.

In some families, any emotion other than happiness is unacceptable. Sam, who participated in my midlife study, said that her mother "emitted a spray of anxiety whenever I felt blue. She wouldn't look at me, and she'd fill in the silences by humming. I felt angry and ashamed." Any parent would be disturbed to hear a child speak in a very negative way about his or her life ("I feel useless," or "I feel as though I'm about to sink," or "I don't know how to go on"). Some things a child says are hard to hear; some things a child says signal a problem; but refusing to hear what a child feels by insisting, "You can't really think that!" or "How can you say such things?" sends a message of blame.

In other families, positive emotions are subject to blame. Emotions such as excitement and delight are seen as an affront to those family members who cannot experience joy. Peg Streep, in her book *Mean Mothers*,[28] describes her family's judgment system, in which joy was prohibited. Streep's mother was angry and offended by her daughter's happiness:

"If I am frustrated and disappointed, then no one else should find life so enjoyable," she reasoned. Similarly, Carlos, who is the first person in his family to attend college, expects his parents, Bob and Maria, to share his excitement on being awarded a scholarship; but Maria thinks "everything comes easily to Carlos, so he thinks he does it all by himself. He's not grateful for what we've done." And Bob says, "He can't wait to get away from us." [29] Bob and Maria condone one another's anxiety and resentment by condemning Carlos's happiness. Bob says, "He doesn't know what it will be like. He shouldn't get so excited." Maria concludes, "He's always been inconsiderate. He should think more about the stress you're under at work, and not flaunt himself right in your face." For Bob and Maria, Carlos's success threatens their bond with their son, and hence they feel that Carlos's excitement implies rejection, criticism and blame toward them.

Managing an Intrusive Judgment System

"You *shouldn't* feel this," or "You are wrong to feel that way," present a daughter or son with a relational dilemma. What can a child think when blamed for these feelings? As John Cleese and Robyn Skynner note in their amusing and insightful book, *Families and How to Survive Them*, "Our dependence on love gives us a moral attitude towards our feelings and thoughts . . . if the family thinks (or behaves as though) anger is destructive and deadly, [t]hen you feel bad, sort of morally, because the assumption is that you are hurting, disappointing people with your [feelings]." [30] A child then has to make a choice between silencing and suppressing such emotions or suffering the blame.

Yet emotions help us discover who we are and what we need. As Martha Nussbaum argues in her powerful and illuminating book *Upheavals of Thought: The Intelligence of the Emotions,* [31] emotions anchor us to the world; they give us points of reference to things we love and loathe. It is not surprising, then, that as parents try to mold their children, they monitor emotions as carefully as behavior and may be as quick to subject each other's emotions to praise and blame.

The paradox we confront when we are blamed for our feelings—whether positive or negative—has been beautifully described by Carol Gilligan in *The Birth of Pleasure.* The only way you can preserve a relationship in which you are blamed for what you feel is to move out of a real relationship into a "cover" relationship. [32] You opt for approval at the expense of genuine self-expression. You disguise who you are in order to gain approval for how you appear. You may even feel guilty because you believe your emotions are hurting people in your family, people you love and upon whom you depend. You then may silence your emotions: "If they see what I want and what I desire, I am going to be judged as worthless, and I am going to be shamed."

The conundrum that arises from seeking approval from those we love and adhering to our highly individual judgment meter (when our deepest emotions and desires are not respected by those we love) gives rise to what Donald

Winnicott called a "false self:" "Other people's expectations can become of overriding importance, overlaying or contradicting the original sense of self, the one connected to the very roots of one's being." [33]

The Over-Eye

Understanding our family's judgment systems is essential to making sense of our inner world. The internal judge, that private spectator monitoring esteem and disesteem,[34] self-praise, and self-blame, is an amalgam of the judgment system we grew up with and the judgment meter we use and hone, day by day. There are the judgments rooted deep within our being and the judgmental voices that have been imprinted on our minds. A major clash between these two spheres of judgment can badly distort our measures of praise and blame.

Every internal judge has a personality of its own.[35] We might envisage it along the lines of the personal daemon Philip Pullman describes in *His Dark Materials*, a manifestation of the inner self, but a complicated and volatile one, capable of speaking both one's own thoughts and representing the urging of others.[36]

Most people, buoyed by a resilient esteem, protected by a range of positive feedback, as well as a moderate dose of self-serving bias, have an internal judge that is inclined to praise and to soften the blows of blame. Genial and lenient, it casts a warm eye on our gestures, words, and motives, supporting us, for example, as we give a public presentation, with whispers of "Good! You're doing well." In other people, however, the internal judge breathes the chill of suspicion, constantly picking apart our words and actions; it roars at us, demanding: "Why can't you speak without stumbling over words?" and "Why did you ask that stupid question?" and in other contexts—when, for example, we may have to cut short a visit to a grieving friend—it hisses, "How can you be so selfish?"

This internal judge that resides within the negative judgment system focuses on every shortfall and magnifies every failing. It is busy putting us down without pointing the way ahead. Its leaden voice can overpower the gentleness of normal self-love as well as the listening beat of our own intuitive judgments. It has the power to countervail praise. Since those who are quick to feel guilt are also particularly sensitive to facial expressions and other microindicators of disapproval,[37] a negative internal judge is self-reinforcing: we interpret others' responses to us through its accusing eyes.

The psychologist Dana Crowley Jack called this version of the internal judge the over-eye.[38] The over-eye embodies parental or cultural norms that replace our sensitive, searching judgment meter and "silence the self." Crowley Jack's term provides an illuminating model for the tense internal dialogue between praise and blame that can continue throughout one's life.

When I did research on how women negotiated changes from youthful adulthood to midlife, I heard a great deal about this internal dialogue between the shadows and whispers of blame and the natural urge to achieve esteem.[39] In many cases, the shadows of blame arose from early family dynamics, when a child's notion of who she is can be so easily shaped by how others treat her. Dora, now in her fifties, stands out among the participants as someone whose many successes, both personal and professional, seem overpowered by what she calls a "diffuse guilt that is always dancing on the surface." She understands that this guilt arises from an internalized voice, a ventriloquist for her mother's disapproval: "It is not a measure of who I am, but it's a constant judgment, and I try to argue it away, but I'm never outside its reach."

From the age of two years, Dora was labeled "naughty." The toddler was "naughty for touching other children's toys." The child was "spoiled" and "willful" and "stubborn." Scuffing her shoes, staring, wanting a snack, and being slow to wake in the morning were proof of character defects. Throughout childhood Dora tried to avoid blame and to please her mother, but she never achieved this, either as child or adult, despite her distinguished career, her reliability, and her integrity.

The blunted responses Dora has to praise, and the highly sensitive responses she has to blame, are likely to arise from the neurological circuits set down by her family's judgment system. For over three decades Richard Davidson has worked in affective neuroscience—the study of the brain mechanisms that are activated in our emotional life. He and his research team discovered that people vary by as much as 3,000 percent in brain sensitivity to positive experiences such as praise, and there is a similar variation in individual responses to negative experiences, such as blame.[40] The person who shrugs off blame easily and the person who is unmoved by praise would have very different activity within the pleasure and pain centers of the brain. But Davidson subsequently found that the story is more complicated: variations in how the brain registers positive and negative experiences turn out to be far less important than the *conversations* that take place within the brain.[41]

The brain starts building circuits for its distinctive conversations from birth. Repeated transitions from alarm to calm, facilitated by a parent's attention and care, provide a model for managing emotions.[42] Normally, the primitive brain areas (particularly the amygdala) that register our initial responses to praise and blame are influenced by the more reflective brain areas (the left prefrontal cortex).[43] Before we are aware of what we feel, one part of the brain converses with the other: a prefrontal cortex that "knows" we deserve esteem will signal something like "Shh, calm down," when confronted with blame. But when a child experiences sustained disapproval in any form (including neglect or abuse), high levels of the stress hormone cortisol impede those calming conversations. When our prefrontal cortex thinks blame is natural, or appropriate, then it cannot buffer the amygdala's alarm.

Throughout childhood, we build and refine our model of relationships, how much praise and blame they are likely to contain, and how to navigate these. Early experiences are particularly important in shaping this model because brain development in infancy and childhood is so rapid, but the brain remains capable of change throughout life, especially when we are able to name what we want to change. The punitive over-eye is stubborn but need not be a permanent feature of our internal judge.

Auditing the Effects: Family Judgment and Self-Judgment

A personal audit for assessing whether an internal judge is likely to be uncomfortably out of sync with your own better judgment can begin with identifying the judgment system that operated in your own family.

RIGID VERSUS FLEXIBLE. Did praise and blame seem to be allocated with a divine authority? Were you able to explain yourself and negotiate more comfortable judgments from parents, or were your efforts to express your own judgments seen as offensive?

GLOBAL VERSUS SPECIFIC. Did you experience a family judgment system in which blame was globalized? Did a single word or action trigger blame for past offenses and ingrained character defects? Were dire predictions uttered ("No one will ever like/trust/admire you") when you made a mistake?

These dynamics in a family's judgment meter give everyday blame a very different force from the everyday blame in a family where judgments are specific and the fault is concisely described: "You are late for supper this evening," versus "You are inconsiderate and thoughtless and lazy." The former blame is pragmatic; the latter is, to a child, utterly alarming.

If you experienced a rigid family judgment system, particularly if negative judgments were globalized, you are likely to have a heated response to blame. This may result from the belief that nothing you say in your defense will be heard or, even worse, that attempting a defense will activate further blame. Furthermore, you are likely to expect blame to escalate from one specific thing to the roots of your being.

DEFINING VERSUS GUIDING. Did family judgments identify "good" and "bad" members, or did they simply note acceptable and unacceptable behavior?

If you grew up in a family judgment system in which "good" and "bad" defined character, then you may find it difficult to distinguish criticism from blame. You may find that you become too anxious to focus on a specific criticism. Instead, you anticipate a full-blown attack when anyone says something negative about anything you've done.

You may also see criticism as fixed and final. Instead of guiding you toward considerations about correcting some deficiency or omission, your attention freezes on the negative implications of criticism.

GENEROUS VERSUS MEAGER. Was praise always competitive, so that praise for someone else excluded you from approval? Was there only one praiseworthy person at any given time?

If this was your family judgment system then you may feel anxious when someone else is singled out for praise. You may struggle with feelings that might be called envy, but which is really fear that praise for someone else is a sign of your deficiency.

When you receive praise, you may also feel anxious, because you expect it to be transient, or easily usurped by someone else, who will soon be seen to be more deserving.

RESPONSIVE VERSUS INTRUSIVE. Was the rich subjectivity of your internal life respected or were your feelings scrutinized with suspicion?

If you experienced an intrusive judgment system in your family, your internal judge may be hyperactive. You may accuse yourself of being stupid or useless whenever there is any hint that something has gone wrong, however minor. You may feel ashamed of your emotions, and worry that you are disappointing others by not feeling what you should. You may continually question your own preferences and desires: "I shouldn't feel like this," and "I should/shouldn't want to do this." This suggests that a negative over-eye is regulating your judgment meter.

Balancing needs that stem from what Winnicott calls "the very roots of one's being" against the importance of gaining praise is a lifelong challenge.[44] We cannot change our past experiences, but research in psychology shows that being able to make sense of our feelings empowers us to repair the disruption and so move forward in a positive direction.[45] Understanding our own emotional histories and how these may shape our day-to-day responses—often referred to by psychologists as reflective functioning—not only feels liberating. It also calms and strengthens neural activity, and opens a mental space wherein we can assess our thoughts and desires.[46] But it is not only families that contribute to our ability to navigate—with either ease or difficulty—our judgments. In our wider social worlds, too, particularly our friendships, we experience the enormous power of praise and blame.

5

Just Friends: Praise and Blame Between Peers

WHATEVER WE LEARN about praise and blame in our families is only a prelude to testing ourselves in the wider social world. Within friendship we satisfy our hunger to explore others' judgment systems and their unique maps of praise and blame. In childhood and adolescence, friends become mirrors and models. We engage in intense friendship work to express ourselves so that we can see ourselves through the eyes of a friend. We hope that the "real me" will be admired, but we learn there are risks in self-exposure: we may be judged deficient and ousted from the warm circle of friendship.

The costs of such exclusion are high. A child without friends is at greater risk of being shunned by peers or targeted by a bully. Teens without close friendships face higher risks of depression, suicide, disengagement from school, early pregnancy, drug use, and gang membership.[1] Throughout our lives, friendships continue to provide measurable health benefits to both physical and mental well-being; friends are quite literally good for the heart.[2] But relationships with friends, as with parents, lovers, and colleagues, expose us to both pleasures and pains. We are tasked with navigating others' judgment systems in which we may be neither flattered nor comforted. In the process, we exercise, test and develop our own judgment meter. We also learn what we need to be to earn praise and how to avoid blame. This includes learning about loyalty, friendship ideals, and acceptable expressions of gender, or what it means to be a proper male friend or a good female friend.

Praise and Blame, and Gender

In childhood, praise is a common currency[3] of friendship and strict rules apply. A compliment is normally reciprocated within two minutes of its being given. Raising their entwined hands toward her face, Shelley tells Fran, "You have lovely skin," and Fran tells Shelly, "You have the prettiest eyes in the world." Such exchanges are basic marks of belonging: I praise you and am confident that I will be praised by you. Above all, friends are trusted not to condemn or mock one another.

While boys are less likely to walk together with arms entwined, stroking one another's hair, as girls do,[4] they exchange praise, even in apparently competitive games. They praise one another's humor by being quick to laugh at a joke and then repeat it with obvious pleasure. They praise one another's skill: "That [goal that you hit] was from way far away," or exchange looks of amusement and sympathy for a missed goal. Even as they wrestle and roughhouse, boys frequently acknowledge a friendly opponent's skill: "Wow, that hurt!" is more likely to offer praise than blame. Whereas boys are sometimes said not to be so sensitive to gossip, they are highly invested in reputation as it affects respect or esteem.

Girls and boys experience different judgment cultures because their friendship groups, from middle childhood through early adolescence, tend to be highly segregated. Girls choose girls; boys choose boys. If boys try to join a group of girls, they usually mean to cause trouble. If a girl tries to join a group of boys, she is very likely to be rejected. [5]

Sex segregation in children's friendships seems to be universal; it is found across culture and class.[6] Adults often encourage girls and boys to play together, but the children themselves stick to their own group. This may be linked to the greater interest children show, from birth, in children of the same sex,[7] or it may be because they have different styles of playing and interacting. Boys and girls like playing with different things.[8] Boys enjoy physical roughhousing and engage more directly in competition with one another (50 percent of their playtime versus 1 percent of girls' playtime).[9] It is often said, too, that girls are more cooperative with friends and boys more competitive,[10] but this is a matter more of style than substance. Conflict between girls is often disguised, as a girl pursues her own ends but placates her playmate with promises to take turns or claims that she wants something for someone else: "It's Mary who wants me to have this now." [11] Cooperation among boys is common and their friendships are rich with intimate emotional exchanges, but these are often obscured by jokes or simply kept very, very private.

Some of these differences seem inborn. Melissa Hines at the University of Cambridge has fascinating data on Rhesus monkeys, male and female. Hines shows that young monkeys demonstrate toy preferences similar to those of human children: the males pick up the cars and trains, and the female monkeys pick up dolls and cooking pots.[12] Though these findings may be specific to Rhesus monkeys, they suggest deep, evolved preferences; but in girls and boys the majority of gender differences—by far—are not hardwired.[13] A great deal about what it means to be female or male is learned through praise and blame, and the judgment of friends provides intensive schooling.

Children see gender everywhere. Every toy, every game, every story assumes one gender or the other. Rarely is anything gender neutral,[14] though gender in their toys is not fixed. The action figure, marketed for boys, easily becomes a child in need of care to a girl, and the teddy with a pink bow becomes an astronaut to a boy. Children still see many activities as "right" for girls or "right" for boys. While teachers and parents often monitor films and TV shows to guard against such gender stereotypes, it is all too easy to overlook the power children exert over other children through their judgments.

Girls' Friendships and the Fragility of Praise

When a girl praises another for being a good friend, it is likely that she means her friend understands her. This means that her friend will have a favorable view of her looks, her thoughts, her feelings, and her behavior. Understanding, within friendship, includes praise.

In our study of girls' and women's friendships, Ruthellen Josselson and I found that girls, particularly in late childhood and adolescence, use friends as mirrors to reflect a self that can be admired.[15] As girls speak on their phones, shop together, and just talk, they confirm their attachments by constantly praising one another. Gabriella, age sixteen, assures her best friend Shelley that her skin is "just fine," while another girl marks a very different relationship when she says with faux sympathy, "Oh, hard luck, I see it's breakout time." Teens, unsure of who they are and what they look like, rely on friends to piece together a favorable image of themselves, but it is all too easily shattered in the rough and tumble of their social lives. Gabriella says, "When someone says something about my wretched acne, I feel I'm falling to pieces, until a friend tells me I'm not hideous, and I feel whole again."[16]

Kelly, another sixteen-year-old participant in our study, says that her best friend will ask "a hundred questions" when she is describing a situation with her family. "I like that she's so interested, but the best thing is when I worry if I messed up, and she'll say, "No, no, you did just the right thing. I don't see how your mom can say you're inconsiderate. You're one of the most thoughtful people I know."[17] Her friend helps her defuse her parent's blame with "narrative praise"—a description of her actions that highlights valuable and valiant qualities.

A friend is expected to help with blame management. She reveals your "real" reputation, reports what others really think about you, and has your back, which means rising to your defense when she hears negative gossip about you. She even shapes your life story, however messy, into a good and decent one.

Our Friends See Judgments We Try to Hide

Knowing who is drawn to us and who is drawn to others are essential to social navigation. So children's mindsight develops along with their friendships, as they decode judgments implicit in even minor interactions: What does her smile say about me? If he turns away, what is he turning away from? Am I easily liked? Which groups welcome me, and which shut me out? Among my in-group, am I praised? If so, what am I praised for?

This social education begins in childhood but it does not end there. Throughout our lives, across a range of interactions, we identify who has others' approval and who does not. This sophisticated skill involves tracking who looks at whom, whether looks are exchanged, and whether mutual looks are synchronized. It involves noting whether one person holds the other's gaze and whether each feels comfortable in the exchange.[18] It also involves detecting judgments people may think they are hiding.

Hiding our judgments is a necessary social skill, and it is called politeness. The rules of politeness dictate that negative judgments be disguised to prevent us from damaging someone's esteem. But one of the most intriguing things about our interpersonal life is that our disguises are predictably flawed. We get a sense of who really thinks well of us and who doesn't think we're up to snuff, even when they do not voice their thoughts. We often forget that we, too, leak information about our judgments to others.

Erving Goffman, the sociologist who popularized the concept of self-presentation—the steps we take to shape how we appear to others—highlights our unspoken agreement not to reveal that we see what other people want to hide. We look away, or pretend not to notice, when someone spits food as he speaks, or wipes his nose, or scratches his crotch. [19]

We also pretend, following the rules of politeness, that we cannot detect someone else's disguise of his or her feelings. When we see a false or insincere smile, we usually proceed as though the smile were genuine. When someone loses his temper and then apologizes, we say, "Forget it," or "Bygones," even when our judgment of the person is radically damaged. When someone talks about himself and his successes, we feel irritated and bored, but we say, "Well done!" or "Fantastic!" or "Wow!" When someone feeds us lines like "I'm so stupid," or "I'm so sorry to trouble you," which, according to the rules of politeness, require reassurance, we say, "Not at all," and "I don't mind," even though we may find her both stupid and tedious.

The rules of politeness do not diminish the force and flow of judgments. I register that the person with the forced smile is unhappy or insincere or cold. I decide that the person whose outburst I forgive is not such an admirable friend after all. Stuck with the egoist sitting beside me throughout a dinner party, I am likely to enthuse over his successes and awards, but I carefully file my judgment: "This person is a conceited bore." Perhaps I tag this as something to run by others whose judgment I value: "What do you make of Jeff?" I might ask, testing my own assessment.

Positive judgments also come under the sway of our social censor. We may want to suppress our arousal and fascination with a beautiful face by assuming a neutral mask. We amplify our enthusiasm when someone solicits praise. "That's fantastic!" I say when my friend tells me she has been promoted. I feel pleased but not necessarily thrilled, and within minutes I'll be going about my ordinary business and my ordinary concerns or perhaps brood over my own disappointments. My effusiveness is not false but it measures how pleased I think she has a right to be, rather than how pleased I in fact feel. Exaggeration is accepted as social ritual and, of course, exaggerated pleasure sometimes masks strong negative feelings, such as envy.

Sometimes we scold ourselves for our judgments. We engage in complex internal dialogues about what we do feel versus what we should feel. In our research on girls' and women's friendships,[20] Ruthellen Josselson and I witnessed persistent efforts to be fair to a friend, to avoid being mean, to make a judgment that "makes sense from [my friend's] viewpoint." Fourteen-year-old Amy, whom I interviewed in her school just outside Cambridge, wonders whether her judgments are consistent with being a good friend: "Lucy's my friend and she's won this big essay competition and it's not only the teachers, but everyone, it seems—her parents, my parents—are ooh-ing and ahh-ing all over the place, and I plaster my face with this big grin that really hurts, but feel knives in my stomach. Wham! Wham! Am I a bad person because I'm not pleased for her?"

Thirty-two-year-old Linda, also in our friendship study, shows that these efforts to balance praise and blame of friends continue in adult friendships. "I know I *should* be on Clare's side," Linda muses, "but when she goes on and on about the awful things her ex-partner is saying to her, I say, 'Oh, that's so unfair,' but I'm thinking very different things. He says she's no fun to be with. She's a pessimist. She's constantly fussing. She's disorganized and she's controlling. And I secretly think, 'Actu-ally, that's Clare all over.' So here I am, blaming the friend I'm supposed to support."

When I recently embarked on a study of male friend-ships, inspired by new work that exposes old biases about how different these are from women's friendships,[21] I heard twenty-two-year-old Martin reflect, "Jed has been my friend for years. I mean, *for years*. It was always easy. We did stuff together, and we talked, and we just hung out. But lately, I don't know, maybe with his flashy job, or what, he spills stuff about his girlfriend, and other girls, and I think, 'This guy is a creep.' I don't know what to do with myself when—you know, when I'm thinking, 'You jerk. You big jerk.' I don't know where to *look*. I think he thinks I'm impressed. I have to get up and walk around. I look at my phone. I do anything to escape this weird sense of thinking such bad things about him, while he's right there, all proud and happy, and thinking I think he's so impressive."

We struggle with our own judgments, and worry whether the way we praise or blame others makes us deserve praise or blame. We try to manage our judgments when we blame a friend. "Anyone can let you down once," we may say. Or we chide ourselves in private, "Don't be so quick to condemn her." Or we reason, "I'm annoyed because I'm tired and had a really bad day." When I listen to a friend's outpouring of her woes, I may feel unsympathetic, and I may be eager to get away; but I remind myself how important the friendship is, and how showing my real feelings would damage it. I reach for a chocolate; I shrug my shoulders, shift my position in my chair, and try to dampen my irritation. All the while, following social codes, I listen and nod, and show interest and sympathy. But am I as good as I suppose at hiding my disapproval?

The judgments we *think* we cover up are likely to leach into our compulsively communicative face. Sylvan Tomkins, who developed several foundational theories about emotion and self-presentation, declared with provocative humor that the human face is like a penis.[22] What he means is that a penis shows whether it is aroused, or not; it cannot pretend. In that respect, it is surprisingly like the face.

The psychologist Paul Ekman was inspired by Tomkins as well as his own work as an anthropologist to develop a lexicon of microexpressions.[23] These are fleeting facial movements, lasting only a fraction (between one-fifteenth and one twenty-fifth) of a second and express emotions someone tries, either consciously or unconsciously, to conceal. Microexpressions are generated by the effort to hide responses from oneself or from others. These are different from false expressions that deliberately feign emotion; these are fleeting expressions of disdain or disgust or anger or fear or desire. Microexpressions reveal the judgments that insincere or fake expressions mean to hide. Sometimes, too, they express judgments that we hide from ourselves or that lurk beneath the radar of consciousness.

We pick up these microexpressions, often without being aware of how it is we are seeing beyond a person's words and peering into her or his judgment meter. Then we ourselves reveal more of our real judgments than we intend: tension in the mouth shows anger or disgust, dilation of the pupil or widening of the eyes signal arousal. Our face betrays our judgment, and this in turn influences others' judgment of us. These partially registered revelations keep us alert to judgments—our own and others' praise and blame—even when, following the rules of politeness, we pretend they do not exist.

Gossip, Friendship, and the Economy of Esteem

Beyond politeness lies gossip. Here we slake our curiosity about how others *really* allocate praise and blame. It is the forum in which we learn what is acceptable and what is not. By talking about other people, we share and also form judgments about others' behavior, personality, skills, motives, and even looks.[24] The emphatic tones of gossip—the excitement, outrage, and delight ("What! Really? *She didn't!*")—measure just how unacceptable certain things are. Gossip has the power to pry off a proud facade, to take others down a peg or two and put them in their place, and to call them out if they lie or cheat or pretend to be something they're not. Someone who participates in a harvest feast but has not sowed or tilled, someone who "is mean" or "who doesn't play fair" or "can't keep a secret" or "steals a friend's boyfriend," is shamed, through gossip, for hypocrisy, dishonesty, or lack of cooperation.[25] Through gossip we learn whom to befriend and whom to avoid.

The map of social judgments drawn by gossip can control our behavior even when it is not directed at us. As we hear what's said about others, we learn what counts as being stuck up or slutty, and what makes a girl nice or wonderful or perfect. Through gossip, friends monitor and punish others by sharing and disseminating praise and blame.

The word *gossip* today carries pejorative connotations—both in its content (gossip is thought to convey largely negative judgments) and performance (a "gossip" is thought to be a malicious person, usually a woman, who enjoys spreading negative views). But originally *gossip* referred simply to the activities people engage in with their "god-sibs" or close peer group.[26] And one of the most common activities within a peer group is talking—talking about other people.

The developmental psychologist Robin Dunbar looked at the ways people spend their personal time. He drew up these time-budgets from many cultures across the world. He found that humans spend 20 percent of their time in social interactions[27] and 65 percent of these social interactions focus on the exchange of social information, or gossiping. Surprisingly, in defiance of stereotypes, Dunbar observed that the amount of time invested in gossip showed very little variation across age and across gender.[28]

Girls and boys,[29] men and women, young and old engage in gossip. Dunbar, with his evolutionary perspective on behavior, argues that such an ancient, embedded, and time-consuming activity is likely to have an important purpose, one that has supported and shaped us. Gossip is notoriously problematic. Because it is informal and unofficial, its veracity is difficult to check. The information it conveys is highly unreliable. It can easily be used to serve someone's ulterior motives. The person who is the subject of gossip usually does not know what's being said, and cannot defend her- or himself from blame. Nonetheless, for all its imperfections, Dunbar believes that gossip— both now and in the past—has played a crucial role in our ability to live in larger communities, to keep track of others, to learn social norms, and to experience the costs of others' disapproval. Gossip, Dunbar concludes, "is what makes human society as we know it possible."[30]

Gossip has great power in our hidden economy of esteem, where most people care not only about what others say but also about what people *might* think about what we *might* do.[31] "That's just nasty," and "That shows what kind of person she really is," are not just behind-the-back comments on a specific person. These serve as a warning about what can be said about us and remind us how quickly we can be transformed from insider to outcast. So, when we hear negative gossip about someone else, our fear of being spoken of like that influences our behavior.

Like most activities crucial to our continued survival as a species (such as sex), gossip is enjoyable. It offers the excitement of discovery and the thrill of being in the know. As we exchange information about people who matter to us, whether because we know them personally or because, like celebrities, they play some part in a possible or imaginary life, we perform the human counterpart to the grooming done by nonhuman primates who stroke and clean one another, often for hours, releasing endorphins—those naturally occurring chemicals that create good feelings and social bonding.[32] When I hear what others are doing, I feel more at ease in my social environment because I know what's going on. When someone gives me some unofficial news, I have the sense of being particularly close to her, because offering important gossip to someone is a signal of trust.

Genuine Praise and the Risk of Self-Exposure

Stepping outside the safety zones of a friend's praise puts us in danger: "If she knows what I've done, will she disapprove of me the way she disapproves of others?" we may wonder. Yet the benefits of friendship cannot be gained without taking risks. Praise in friendship, as in the family, is satisfying only when it recognizes who we really are. In the rigid judgment system that sometimes characterizes girls' friendships, exposing individuality and rough edges and revealing bad things you've done or mean thoughts you've had takes a lot of courage. Ruthellen and I found that girls grew this courage because they wanted to make the most of what friendship could offer.[33]

As they acquire new powers of articulacy and self-reflection, self-exposure becomes a crucial activity in friendship. Girls expect a friend to listen and appreciate their tentative searching for self-expression. But in the world of girlfriends, often hedged by unrealistic ideals of unwavering approval, revealing who she really is comes with the risk of disapproval. Cautiously, one friend tests another's capacity to understand and approve of her. She monitors acceptance through cues we all recognize: nods, noises such as "mmhm" that signal "I'm following you," a sympathetic and focused gaze, a hug.

Working alongside Ruthellen Josselson, I saw how understanding could function like praise. Fourteen-year-old Karen describes to us the reassurance she has from her friend Jessica. "We got talking and I realized Jessica understood how other people could just lose it, and that didn't mean they were bad or mad. I realized she wasn't shocked by things, you know, things like . . . Well, even things like wanting, you know, *sometimes*, to murder my mom. Most people would go, 'Oooh, how can you say that? You don't really mean it.' But you do mean it, 'cause there's this mountain of anger that feels like you want, you know, to kill. Jess listened and understood. She didn't laugh or pooh-pooh it. That was great."

With another friend, Karen learns that other thoughts and desires may find acceptance. She notes how Anna speaks about her older sister: she admires her "big goals and her courage."

Karen picks up the cue that she can talk to Anna about her ambitions, without "her getting bored or silly like my other friends." So, through gossip, girls also discover safe places for self-expression and the possibility of resisting stereotypes. Gossip has the power to display a green light indicating, "It's okay to go there; those thoughts and feelings don't make you a bad person."

Two thousand miles away from Karen's home near Virginia, Amy hopes for similar comfort when she tells Josie about "stupid stuff, really private things": that she had sex with a boy who is a "loser," that her mother's drinking is out of control, that she is worried about her sister. She craves "a really good long talk" because her friend "helps me see that with all this mess I'm really doing ok, and that means I'm a really strong person." Amy says, "It's so good to talk to Josie, and feel I'm not just yuck inside, and that I'm so much better than I seem."

But a few months later, the friendship between Amy and Josie has soured. "Josie is spending far more time with Kirsty than with me. Then one girl made a joke about my mom and put her hand to her mouth, like someone guzzling from a bottle. I wanted to vomit. I knew Josie was the one who told what she promised she'd never tell. All that stuff about how I'm a really good person, really strong, was fake. The minute my back is turned I'm no longer the strong girl toughing it out, you know, getting respect. I'm the poor slut whose family is a mess, or the slut who's messing up [her] family. Things are one thing when you tell it to a friend, but things are shit when your friend spreads it around behind your back."

The volatility of girls' friendships, particularly in early adolescence, means that confidences are often broken, and what seemed admirable when spoken in private becomes derisory when revealed in gossip. The high—often unrealistic—expectation of these friendships makes them fragile. Friendship, particularly among girls, is supposed to be blame-free, and this ideal comes into conflict with the fact that girls are, as all people are, judgmental creatures. "In no other relationship are there such high expectations of harmony," Ruthellen and I realized as we spoke to girls about their friends and observed them together.[34]

Mothers and children are expected to criticize one another. Romantic partners expect to quarrel and make up. But girls seem confounded by fallings out with a friend. Nena tells Ruthellen about the terror she feels[35] at the prospect of conflict with a friend. Nena explains, "I'd rather have a fight with my boyfriend or my mom, any day, than with my girlfriend . . . I'm basically honest, upfront, but I'll say anything to get out of any argument with a friend. I'll change the whole story. I'll say I was 'just kidding' or tell her to forget it." Conflict is an admission of difference and disapproval, and disapproval threatens the ideal of a friend's perfect approval.

In most girls' view, a good friend never judges them, never bad-mouths them. This unsustainable ideal sets up a minefield. As soon as a girl's judgmental nature comes into the conversation, her friend accuses her: "You aren't a real friend." The safe haven sought in friendship, where there is only praise and never blame, cannot be maintained because it does not take into account what we are like.[36] The challenge to female friendship is accepting that we, and our best friends, all have a highly active judgment meter.

Boys' Friendships and the Guy Code

Boys' friendships are generally more stable than girls' highly volatile ones.[37] Their rules of friendship accommodate competition and conflict, so do not have the fragility of girls' problematic ideals. The tactics girls describe—excluding someone from play because she thinks too much of herself or has befriended another girl the group deems undesirable, and spreading negative gossip about her—are rarely mentioned by boys.[38] Yet boys' friendships are also fortified, or broken, by praise and blame. Typical boy-to-boy talk delivers blunt reminders of what a boy should be: "That's dumb; boys don't play with dolls," and "You're silly, that's just for girls."[39]

Listening to what he calls "real boys' voices," William Pollack writes, "Boys have described to me how every day of their lives they receive covert messages that they do not measure up, and yet they feel they must cover up their sadness and confusion about plummeting self-esteem."[40] They spend time talking to one another, and, as with girls, much of their talk is gossip. Exchanging information gives them a sense of belonging, and they get a kick out of being the one with information that interests others.[41] Like girls, they keep careful watch on their reputation; by noting what's said about them and how people speak to them, they map out who gets social approval and who does not.

Young boys are, like girls, keen gender detectives, ready to inflict social punishment—sometimes called jeer pressure[42]—on those who deviate from the boys' code; but in childhood and early adolescence, boys comfortably accommodate many contradictions between their warm and passionate inner lives and the boys' code. Boys share the same emotional complexities that girls experience, and they express their deepest thoughts and feelings to their friends. Their language of friendship is as rich with love and passion and need as is girls', with similar elements of romance; and like girls at this age, they sing one another's praises.[43] They seem adept at being overtly loving and needy on the one hand, and paying tribute to being tough on the other.

In late adolescence, however, the vice of masculine norms tightens and the tenderness of their childhood friendships is often repudiated.[44] In her remarkable investigation of boys' friendships, psychologist Niobe Way exposes how the intimate links between male friends gradually break apart. As sexuality becomes more salient, as they approach manhood, the "guy code" interferes with the intimacy of friendship. The young boy claims that he would "go wacko" without someone to talk to,[45] but as a teen he claims he doesn't need to "share things" and that he is capable of keeping feelings to himself.[46] Boys in their late teens, describing their attachments to their friends, show anxiety about how their feelings will be judged. Niobe Way found that as they spoke about their attachment and need for friends, they routinely cut themselves off, to insist there was nothing sexual in the intimacy. "No homo," [47] Way was often told, as though she might second-guess or snigger at their meanings and condemn them for loving their friends.

Niobe Way also observed teenage boys bringing a halt to emotional exchanges between them and their friends. When one friend began to speak about his attachment to the other, his friend warned him about "getting hormonal."[48] Soon, open expressions of tender feelings fell by the wayside. The boy who previously praised a friend for being "understanding" now praises another boy for toughness and independence and fearlessness.[49] The risk-taking that terrifies parents, that makes teenage boys more accident prone than any other age group,[50] is grounded in their fear of not matching up to the masculine measures that each teenage boy thinks the others use to judge him.[51]

Now, in late adolescence, the edge boys previously had over girls in dealing more directly with conflict is lost. Instead of openly processing their vulnerability and pain when a friend disrespects the friendship—by standing them up, by saying mean things—they display anger.[52] Just as girls' friendships are complicated by the belief that conflict is unacceptable, young men's friendships are starved of intimacy by fear they will be condemned for their tenderness and vulnerability.

Their shame-induced silence increases their sensitivity to negative judgments. Without a close friend to help manage blame and supply a praise narrative when things go wrong, boys develop a new thin skin. Friendship is sometimes referred to by teens as the "armor of friendship,"[53] and without it, other people appear more threatening and punitive.[54] There are always exceptions, however, and some friends, male and female, find spaces safe from jeer pressure. Sixteen-year-old Joel discovers, through cautious investigation of a friend's deeper judgments, that his frustration is shared. "I don't get it, why the guys laugh at me, and tell me I'm 'soft.' I don't think I've changed. They're the ones that are all different now. But Mike and I can still hang out, and that's great. I see the nervous smiles when we go off together—that 'nudge-nudge' stuff. But it's just, well, it's not really real to me, you know?" [55] Friendship has the power to enforce rigid rules for praise and blame, but it also has the power to revolutionize them.

Cliques as Fortresses for Esteem

Intimacy, love, and self-exploration are the bedrock of friendship, and friendships mimic other close relationships such as those of the extended family or clans. Like clans, they have their own judgment systems. Cliques—those distinctive friendship groups that start to form for girls around the age of nine years and for boys around the age of eleven years—are fortified by praise and blame. The knowledge of what looks right, what sounds right, and who is right is owned by a clique that then judges who is in and who is out. Lessons about what someone needs to be and do to remain with the in crowd are exchanged in long hours of mutual grooming: friends, male and female, shop together, share common dressing rooms, and then make preparations for a night out together. They listen to the same music, watch the same programs, and draw from a common pool of cultural references. Speech idioms, dress, hair, nails, piercings, and other accessories also become emblems of inclusion.

Once admitted to the group, they have to work to preserve their insider status. Young people carefully note the rules required for securing and maintaining approval.[56] They are highly alert to nudges—indirect messages that prod (or nudge) them toward behavior that symbolizes acceptance: "You should never wear something like that," and "Were you really talking to that odd ball?" in addition to the more direct lessons ("That's silly" and "Don't be such a *girl*"). Witnessing someone else being targeted as wrong or clueless serves as a warning to others:[57] If you defy our social rules, you too will be mocked and despised. When a parent tries to interfere with symbols of belonging ("You cannot get your nose pierced" or "You cannot cut your hair like that"), the ensuing arguments are heated and prolonged, for the young teen feels that she is fighting to save her social life.

Inclusion in a clique is far more precarious than inclusion in a family, and both girls and boys monitor their status closely. Inclusion is marked in different ways, according to age and according to gender. A girl may consider, "Do I hear important news when the others do, or am I left out of the loop?" and "Do others check that I am free before they plan an event, or don't they care whether I can join them?" and "Do they wait so I can walk to the cafeteria with them after gym, or do they rush ahead? Are they trying to cut me out?" A boy is more likely to consider, "Do they laugh at my jokes?" and "Do they ask me about things?" and "Do they follow my suggestions about where to go, or what games to play?"

The only surefire means of securing inclusion in a clique is by becoming the arbiter of positive and negative judgments, like the head of a family. When someone has the power to declare, "You are one of us, but she is not," and "We approve of you, but not him," then and only then does he or she feel securely included. As we explored the hectic dynamics of friendship cliques, Ruthellen Josselson and I witnessed girls' desperate bids for control over praise and blame. They concocted magical and mysterious criteria to discriminate those in from those out. Rules sprang up out of nowhere, arbitrary and bizarre: "If you want to talk to her, you can't play with us," and "No one should wear *that* color." [58] For boys, the rules were similarly arbitrary: "His games are boring; your ideas are good," and "You're a good mate; he's a Dodo." [59]

Peer Judgments

Once a child or teen becomes a member of a clique, the group's judgment system is quickly absorbed. Many children and teens say they have found friends who are "just like me" and who see things their way, but the process of finding a soul mate or twin is more complicated than that. Preferences and opinions are constantly processed and revised, often through conversations with friends. Children and teens shape their own judgments according to those of their friends. They may challenge a clique's views—particularly as teens practice the thrill of argument—but they are also motivated to adjust and align their views to those of a friend. In fact, some psychologists believe that when-ever people of any age discuss, argue, or gossip, "relatedness" motives—the desire to maintain a personal attachment—are at work.[60] And so it seems that if someone wants to predict what a person believes (whether about poetry or politics), he should find out what his friend believes.[61]

This does not mean we slavishly copy our friends but, whether young or old, people are social chameleons.[62] With-out always being aware of what we do, we mimic the postures, mannerisms, and facial expressions of people we speak to, par-ticularly if we like them. The more a person mimics someone, the more admiration he expresses. Mimicry, as we saw with parents and babies, is a subtle and implicit expression of praise.

Herein lies the source of the awesome power of peers. "Don't do something just because your friends do," and "Don't let someone push you into anything. Use your own good judgment," parents and teachers urge; but such adult wisdom ignores the ways in which, with friends, teens construct praise and blame. "My boy is as sound as a bell, most times," Innis reflects, but adds, "When he's out with friends he could be the stupidest kid alive. His good common sense goes out the window. His mind seems taken over by the lowest common denominator."

Innis is observing the all-too-familiar phenomenon of peer influence. It is not that her fourteen-year-old son Rob really loses his mind to others, but the depth and tenacity of friend-ship goals take priority. Others may call this peer pressure, but it is closer to a manifestation of the hidden economy of esteem. In the presence of his friends, the priority is to fit in and avoid disesteem.

Gangs: Coming in from the Cold?

Whether it was at the age of five years when a parent let go of our hand and walked away on the first day of kindergarten, or at the age of eight years when we had no one to play with during recess, most of us have experienced the scorching self-consciousness of isolation. We never fully grow out of these so-called childhood responses. Instead, we get better at managing them, usually by reminding ourselves that the exclusion is temporary. The esteem we have from elsewhere—from our families, from communities, from work—forms an armor that protects us from transient social uncertainty. But for some children and teenagers, social exclusion is a way of life. Each door they approach closes in their face. "You don't belong here," they are told, and "You are not what you should be." The judgments they receive, as they move through their social world, are negative: others fear them, shun them, and would rather not look at them. When others bully them, punch them, or steal from them,[63] no one protests, no one blames anyone other than the victim.

In searching for a place of belonging, the outcast may find a group that transforms exclusion into a badge of pride. The gangs whose influence many parents dread share many features of prestigious sororities and fraternities: formal membership, ritual gatherings, a sense of history, and pride in belonging.

The requirements for inclusion in prestigious groups—a suitable family, social status, the right accent, and distinctive attire—are different, but the purpose is the same: to secure esteem and avoid disesteem.

Low self-esteem is often a motive for joining a gang, and initially, when a young person joins a gang, his esteem goes sky high.[64] Even in the cold and violent center of the gang, a member finds esteem through acceptance and approval, and because others see them as belonging somewhere.[65] Gang inclusion implies that "We will think well of each other. Those who disrespect us are in the wrong, and our intimidation of them will be our proxy for esteem."[66]

But this esteem is fragile. After joining, the pressure to prove themselves over and over again—often by being violent or tough—leads to higher levels of depression and, sometimes, persistent suicidal thoughts.[67] The criminologist Chris Melde, who has spent the past decade studying youth gangs, found that young people join gangs as a coping mechanism, hoping to secure esteem because they were struggling with depression, even thoughts of suicide. This membership, however, with its fierce judgment meter, seldom secures the promised comforts.

According to common gang code, violence is often central to securing esteem. When you have no access to primary praise, then getting someone's attention, even negative, fear-based attention will suffice. This is precisely what Yale sociologist Elijah Anderson found in his fieldwork in ghetto areas of Philadelphia.[68] The familiar code of the street, with the rules for dress, for greeting, for stance and gait, were organized around a "desperate search for respect that governs public social relations, especially violence." Anderson notes that "At the heart of the code is the issue of respect loosely defined as being treated 'right' or being granted one's . . . proper due, or the deference one deserves. . . . [R]espect is viewed as almost an external entity, one that is hard-won but easily lost and so must constantly be guarded."[69]

The mass shootings in schools that have been rightly called "senseless"—from Greencastle, Pennsylvania, in 1764 to Columbus, Ohio, in 2016—arise from distorted efforts to counter disesteem and replace it with esteem, even if such esteem comes in the form of terror.[70] Indeed, terrorist groups thrive on the havoc people seem willing to wreak on others if they feel generally unnoticed and unappreciated. Dzhokhar and Tamerlan Tsarnaev, the brothers convicted of the Boston Marathon bombings, are a chilling illustration of exclusion converted into destructive anger, and aggression emerging from disapproval. In media posts and tweets, the older brother writes about not having "a single American friend" and says he doesn't "understand them." The younger brother tweets that he doesn't like people asking him "unnecessary questions" such as why he is sad. He resents being seen as vulnerable: "Do I look like that much of a softy? Little do these dogs know that they're barking at a lion;" "I won't run, I'll just gun you all out."[71] The need for approval is fierce. Few people take social exclusion calmly and quietly. When respect or esteem is lost and efforts to regain it fail, then, as the psychologist Bruce

Hood notes, "a much more sinister, darker set of behaviors can appear"[72] and then protests against one person's disesteem become a social tragedy.

Gangs: Esteem and Resistance

Anita is fifteen years old, with diamond black eyes in a face hard-set with a sullen mask signaling, "Don't mess with me." After I had given a talk at her southwest London school and invited her class to speak about their friendships,[73] she followed me to the exit, drawing my attention with a sharp, "Hey, you!" When I turned, she shut down. Her shoulders squeezed into her body, as though with cold, and her legs froze, though I could see the nervous tensing of her kneecaps through her tight leggings. She was silent for a full minute, and I had the sense that she wanted me to be intimidated. I felt she was waiting for an embarrassed smile or some sign that her belligerent stare rattled me. Eventually she said, "What about loners? What about not wanting friends? You going to leave me out of your *study*?"

Some people of course are comfortable spending time alone, entertained by their own thoughts, engrossed by solitary activities. But Anita was not one of them. She talked about her "off-putting manner" and her intolerance "of all these guys who look down their noses at me." She gave one of the best descriptions of a disorganized family I have ever come across: "I mess up because people say I don't know how to behave. Well, I know a lot more than my mom who gets things by crying, or my dad who thinks he's so smart but is in jail for fraud, *again*. No one's around to teach me those peachy lessons about how to behave, and I do just fine myself."

When I returned over a year later, Anita was no longer friendless. She sported an edgy, shoulder-jumping walk, and was surrounded by "friends" who, like Anita, wore a uniform of body piercings, with a quarter of their heads shaved in a zigzag pattern. Anita was now part of a gang: "Some change, huh?" she asked with a proud smile, indicating with a spread of her arms the four friends that flanked her as she approached me.

Anita explained that she had never felt so comfortable in her own skin, and she felt "her gang's" presence even when she walked alone. Though her gang was associated with a specific boys' gang, with overlapping territories and some shared financial dealings, they were all, she said, "up to here"—and she drew a line above her head—with what their male peers expected of "their" women: "We don't look up to anyone, and sure as hell not because they're male. And we don't listen to anyone who thinks they know better about any female code."

Resistance is an unexpected but common strength of gangs. In exploring girls' gangs in New York City, Anne Campbell, an evolutionary psychologist and professor at Durham University, found that the girl gangs she studied rejected the terms of inclusion to more acceptable female groups.[74] "Girlfriend," "nice girl," "sexy woman" all seemed, in the experience of minority inner city women Campbell interviewed, versions of female martyrdom. Instead of being victim to male control and abuse, the girls joined forces whereby it was acceptable to be as aggressive and edgy as the men. Within gang membership, they devised a space to take charge of praise and blame, outside the gendered norms.

THROUGHOUT our lives friends offer a sense of connection, solidarity, and self-worth. In adult friendships we continue to test the waters to see how much we can reveal and sometimes we face a dilemma: Do we speak truthfully and search for an authentic voice, or do we prioritize approval, disguise our real feelings, and construct a false self?

At its best, friendship provides a place in the interstices of personal and social judgments where we extend the listening power of praise and manage blame through understanding and empathy. We look to friends to judge ourselves: Are we making reasonable choices about work, romance, parenthood? When we experience setbacks, whether personal or professional, we benefit from friends' assurances that such disappointments do not diminish our fundamental value. When we have difficulty with a partner or a child, we run the story by a friend who may offer advice; but more important is a friend's assurance that we are a good person and we are not in the wrong.

Friends become allies in our continuing efforts to explore the boundaries of what is right, acceptable, and desirable. As we make new friends we extend our notion of who is like us. We find that, after all, we share a great deal with someone we once found strange or foreign or totally different. The education of our judgment meter is—or should be—a continuous enterprise. With *good* friends, judgments become a joint enterprise, just—as I show in the next chapter—as they do in a good marriage.

6

Intimate Judgments: Praise and Blame Within Couples

THE WORDS OFTEN USED to formalize marriage speak of a "joyful commitment" of two people brought together "in delight and tenderness."[1] Such joy and delight will last "from this day until the end of days"[2] only when praise is sustained and blame is carefully managed. A marriage without mutual praise is a bitter, weary partnership.

"I'm looking for love, and to me that's also total acceptance," Roger explains, while Rachel playfully challenges him: "I want someone who thinks I'm great, always, even when I'm not, and even when I don't think he's so great." Roger, cupping Rachel's right hand in his own two hands, kisses her fingers and says, "You are always great, and so am I."

Roger and Rachel, both in their midthirties, are among the twelve couples[3] participating in an eighteen-month project looking at the rhythm of day-to-day judgments during the first years of marriage.[4] Like many couples, they put praise and appreciation, and a blame-free haven, at the heart of their relationship.

Married for less than three years, Rachel and Roger tease one another about their high expectations, yet share a warm confidence that these expectations will be fulfilled. Many marital therapists, however, deal with couples who have buried their positive expectations and who seem bonded by mutual blame. In the first session with a couple seeking professional guidance, a therapist may invite each person to tell the story of how they met and what initially attracted them.[5] This shifts focus from the complaints and countercomplaints that tend to be at the forefront of the couple's mind when the couple enter the therapist's room; and, in most cases, this process calls up warm remembrances of past appreciation. It also alerts the therapist to what each partner once admired in the other and where disappointment may lie.

In the group of couples who had agreed to participate in my research (which did not include therapy), the effect of this invitation to tell the story of their coming together was the same. "He really *got* me, you know. I was always the sensible one, and everyone in my family relied on me. Ying could see something else in me, that I wanted to have fun, and it was possible for me to grow, even though I'd been playing at being grown up for ten years." Ying says that Sophie "fit right into my heart. Every time we met up, she looked at me in a way that washed clean all the hassle and complaints I get at work." As they lean into each other, the smile of each is reflected in the other, their shoulder movements and laughter in sync. They seem to have discovered their perfect soul mate but their story is about the creation of two new selves. They became "perfectly matched" as one elicited from within the other, through admiration and praise, a previously unrealized persona.

Sophie's mother died when Sophie was fifteen, and she looked after her little sister, coaching her to study hard and guiding her through friend and boyfriend troubles. Ying is an immigration lawyer, dealing every day with, as he puts it, "heart break, deception, and abuse." Each has discovered a new vibrant self through the other's praise.

Valerie, aged fifty-eight, and Julian, aged sixty-two, are preparing a big celebration for their first wedding anniversary. Valerie's past was "a real bumpy ride." She reflects, "I was a widow with three children at twenty-two, and I was on one rollercoaster, and then another, in my businesses and in marriage. I thought I was done. Sure, in my fifties, with my children grown and my business established, I could now catch my breath, but I seemed at some end point. That was me, done. I never thought someone as wonderful as Julian could ever find anything in someone like me. But here we are!" For recently widowed Julian, this new relationship "is bliss." He explains, "My first marriage was a long, long history of faultfinding. [My wife] was a great woman, but she was a faultfinder, never could get to the end of her blame list. Val sees a totally wonderful me. Each day she discovers something else to admire." With only a whisper of self-mockery, he concludes, "And she's very convincing."

Beth, thirty-nine, having just married Douglas, aged thirty-seven, says, "He's the most grounded person I know," and Douglas says, "I can't tell you how many women think I'm boring. Beth knows my real worth. It's a blessing."

Each couple, each person within a couple, praises different qualities, but there is a common theme: one partner brings to life in the other, through praise, a new or neglected admirable self. Such praise is often implicit. Exclamations of delight at a partner's humor praise his or her unique take on the world. "You're so understanding," offers praise for acuity in grasping his or her inner thoughts, and for being a helpmate. "What would I do without you?" are all part of a steady flow of reinforcing praise.

It is the fragility of necessary praise, rather than any diminishment of sexual attraction, that poses the greatest threat to marital harmony. For in marriage, as elsewhere, people automatically evaluate every human transaction on a positive or negative scale. Each monitors the other's actions and feelings and judgments with these questions in mind: Do you appreciate who I really am? Do you treat me, and our relationship, with respect? Are you the person I expect you to be? Do I still admire you? If not, is love being destroyed by disappointment and blame?

How praise is sustained and how blame is managed are the most important variables in a marriage's success or failure.[6]

Key Discoveries in the Power of Marital Praise and Blame

Very little was understood about the mechanisms of marital praise and blame until a small handful of psychologists realized they could go no further with either the large survey and statistical data available to them, on the one hand, or the tiny number of clinical cases on the other. The only way to improve their understanding of the deep dynamics of marriage was to engage in the time-consuming, messy, and costly business (in research terms) of observing couples talking and arguing in their daily lives.[7]

One of these psychologists, John Gottman, now draws on four decades of such time-consuming, "messy," costly—and fascinating—studies. He has closely observed interactions of over 3,000 couples, many of whom he followed over a period of years. He set up a marriage lab, complete with a fully furnished apartment where a couple discusses both neutral topics and a topic that they consider to be "an area of disagreement." The naturalistic, homelike setting is well equipped to monitor each interaction: cameras and recorders capture visual and verbal information, including posture, fidgeting, foot tapping, and eye movement. Additional equipment records physical and psychological information, including heart rate, perspiration, and adrenaline flow; even the blood flow from the heart to the earlobes and fingers is measured. The marriage lab began producing data in the 1970s. The analyzed data have made enormous contributions to revealing "the often invisible forces that hold a marriage together or tear it apart."[8]

The carefully observed and ingeniously coded[9] interactions in the marriage lab were then compared with a couple's survival rate: Did they remain together or did they separate?

After collecting and correlating these data, Gottman tested the results to see whether it was possible to use the marriage lab material to predict which couples remained together and which divorced. After decades of collecting further data, Gottman showed how *one variable* was a reliable predictor of either divorce on the one hand or a continuing committed marriage on the other.[10] The key variable is not whether a couple quarrels or whether they have interests in common, or whether the sex chemistry is sustained; the key variable is the role praise and blame play in their relationship.[11]

Some couples have a tolerance—even enjoyment—of high drama. Their routine arguments are punctuated with shouts and tears and slammed doors. But these couples may also show a great deal of love, appreciation, and humor. They laugh together more than they shout. They break off an argument with convulsive giggles. Their heated disagreements segue into animated discussions. They challenge and probe one another's views.[12] Yet not the number, nor the volume, nor the temperature of their quarrels predicts divorce.

There are more emotionally quiet couples who exchange few expressions of appreciation, but whose expressions of criticism or contempt or any form of blame are also minimal. They are careful with one another, each sensitive to the other's sensitivity. An observer might see such relationships as boring or empty, but it would be an error to predict that these couples are likely to divorce.

What matters is not whether couples quarrel or don't quarrel. What matters is the amount of praise compared to the amount of blame. Blame carries more weight than praise, arousing more emotion and sticking more firmly in memory,[13] so a higher ratio of praise to blame is needed to absorb the damage caused by blame. Analysis of Gottman's data shows that a marriage in which interactions involving praise outnumber those involving blame by 5:1, is likely to thrive; this is now known as "the magic ratio" and it marks the probability of a couple's survival.[14]

Praise: Necessary, But Not Always Positive

The chemistry of romantic love is very similar to the chemistry of parent-child bonding, and summons up similar feelings of rapture at being seen, understood, and admired.[15] Praise is as essential to marriage as it is to parent and child, and can, in high doses, be an antidote to blame. This powerful tool can be used to reassure our partner that she or he is admired and approved, that he or she is the one or the right person or the love of our life.

Yet just as parents' praise of children is both necessary and complicated,[16] praise within marriage can ignite problems as often as it can cool them. Couples, like families, use praise in many ways, and some are at odds with a partner's goals and values. Issuing compliments, saying nice things, and uttering adjectives such as *best, fantastic, gorgeous,* or *brilliant* may fall wide of the mark. To be effective, praise has to be a good fit with a person's own judgment meter.

Praise has many functions. It can be used to exert power, to assign roles, and to usurp the other's judgment meter. When praise shuts down its listening function, when it is no longer responsive to the other's desires and needs, it becomes authoritarian praise—patronizing, controlling, and sometimes even menacing. Jenny and Gil, Alex and Graham, Beth and Douglas, three couples in my group, experience the confusing tensions that arise from authoritarian praise.

When Jenny presents Gil with a suit she picked up from the dry cleaners just before his business trip and Gil says, "You're so organized! I completely forgot about this. You're always so thoughtful. I'd be in a fix without you," he is showing appreciation and expressing the warm, emphatic gratitude for small gestures that is so important in marital praise. At the same time, his message outlines a role he wants her to play: Jenny, he notes, is thoughtful and helpful and protects him from his own disorganization. This may be a legitimate division of skills, but when "You are so thoughtful" is reiterated, again and again, it may serve as a reminder of whom Gil expects Jenny to be, and whom he needs her to be. When, the day before his next trip, Jenny tells Gil, "There's a bunch of dry cleaning to collect before you pack," and Gil says, "Can you pick it up? You're so thoughtful," he is dumbfounded by her outburst. "I hate it when you say that!" she cries, for praise, in her view, has become pressure rather than appreciation.

When Alex suggests to her partner Graham that they get a full-time nanny for their three-year-old son, she presents a well-reasoned argument. She calculates the increase in income she would receive if she worked longer hours; she notes how having someone to help in the early evening would ease her evening tension and fatigue. Graham listens, looks at the figures, mulls things over, and then says, "But you're such a good mother. I cannot imagine anyone being as good as you. You're the best person to care for our child."

This is high praise for a highly significant quality. Who would not be pleased to be the best person to look after her child? But the praise also dismisses Alex's perspective. The cost-benefit analysis prepared by Alex collapses as Graham's praise summons up emotive references to a child's well-being and evokes the full cultural whirlwind surrounding motherhood.

The power of praise and blame within a marriage often links forces with cultural norms. Each partner knows the other well enough to activate his or her over-eye [17] with a single phrase. The over-eye's repository of shoulds, scolding us until we comply with others' ideals, is often a third party in marital judgments. Gil's praise of Jenny's thoughtfulness and Graham's praise of Alex as mother, for example, are underpinned by familiar gender norms.

Each couple negotiates compliance and resistance with cultural norms in its own way. A similar discussion about child care between Sue and Mark focuses on practicalities. Mark's judgment that "you're the best Mom in the world, the kids might miss out," is balanced by Sue's declaration of her strong feelings: "But I'm as frustrated as hell, and I feel I'm missing out." Since, in this marriage, Sue's feelings become essential to

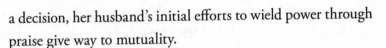

a decision, her husband's initial efforts to wield power through praise give way to mutuality.

Another version of authoritarian praise signals dangerous deviation from the implicit marital contract. Beth tells Douglas, "You are so good at looking after me. I can always depend on you." When Douglas loses his job, and feels listless and depressed, Beth reminds him, initially, "You're strong. You've always been strong. I know I can depend on you to sort things out." When, after some months, the depression bites further and Douglas stops bothering to look for a job, Beth does not complain outright. She does not say, "You disappoint me. I can't rely on you." She simply reiterates her ideal: "You're strong. You'll be fine. You've always taken care of us." With this praise, she is a heartbeat away from saying, "You are not being who I need you to be."

Authoritarian praise can instill as much guilt as outright blame. It pressures one partner to comply with the other's ideal. Since partners and their needs change in the course of a marriage, this ideal may no longer be appropriate (if indeed it ever was). Douglas may need time to be weak, but Beth, with her rigid praise, shows that she cannot tolerate his weakness. Douglas then faces a dilemma: Do I challenge her image of me and risk disappointing her, or do I neglect my own needs and pretend I am someone I know I am not?[18] If he opts for openness and honesty, he takes a big risk: If I disappoint or defy her, I am damaging the marriage.[19] Praise's failure to match a partner's needs, desires, and goals can create unease, guilt, and disharmony.

Power Through Judgment

Whether a person decides to comply with the messages conveyed by authoritarian praise or resists (and tries to change) a partner's expectations depends a great deal on the lines of power within the marriage. Power within marriage has been analyzed in many different ways. Some believe that the partner who earns more money or has more wealth holds the greater power. Some believe that the wider society determines the status of each; this may be the social status of a person's family relative to that of the partner, the professional standing of one person relative to the other, or the assumption that one gender is, in the couple's culture, positioned as decision maker.

All these factors shape a couple's relationship, but a distilled definition of power in a marriage is the ability of one person's emotions to affect the partner's emotions.[20] One measure of this is whose praise and blame have the greater impact.

Does mild praise from a partner fill the other's day with a warm glow or is it received with indifference, perhaps even contempt and mockery? ("Who cares what you think?" or "You just had to say that, didn't you?") Does one person fear a partner's blame and anxiously monitor a partner for any negative response? Is each interaction conducted on a minefield, where any word or deed might activate an explosion of blame? Is one person indifferent to a partner's outbursts?

Like all interpersonal power, the relative power of each partner within a marriage is negotiated and enacted in day-to-day dynamics. We have seen how praise can be used to exert power; the fivefold power of blame is far more difficult to counter and far more damaging.

The Dangerous Dynamics of Globalizing Blame

The common pitfalls of blame—globalizing, finger pointing, rigidity, and self-serving stories[21]—are particularly destructive in marriage, not only for the pain they cause to a partner but also for the impact they are likely to have on the trajectory of disagreements.

For some couples, disagreements over which washing machine to buy, where to eat, what to wear, or what time to arrive at a party barely register negativity. These are practical issues that come, inevitably, with living together. In some couples, however, minor issues rapidly and routinely escalate into major conflicts. The difference is not how much the couple care about the issue they discuss, but whether they focus on who is to blame.

Blame is globalized when a single problem or dispute becomes a peg on which to hang other far more general complaints; here a partner's mistake or omission is seen as a profound character deficiency. The destructive nature of globalizing emerged in one of the earliest observational studies of marriage where a couple were discussing which television show to watch. Suddenly, apparently out of nowhere, came a full-blown attack: "Damn it," exclaimed the wife. "You always watch what you want to see. You're always drinking beer and watching football. Nothing else seems important to you, especially my wishes." [22]

It is sometimes said that we can be blinded by anger. I have found, though, that people can be acutely observant in the throes of anger. Within seconds we grasp the sweeping arc of a verbal attack and feel each word's meaning. Here, the hard opening ("Damn it") expresses long-term contempt; the message is, "I've been fed up with you for a very long time." The complaint is global: he always gets his own way; he is selfish; he is a freeloader; he contributes nothing to the marriage; he is indulgent, lazy, and uninteresting—"always drinking beer and watching football." In a speech lasting less than thirty seconds, one partner utterly condemns the other.

Globalized blame is contagious. A partner who is attacked often retaliates in a similar vein: "You always put me down. You're always complaining about me." Sometimes, when we inflict exaggerated blame on someone we love, we gasp at our own unfairness and catch our moral breath. Some couples get to this point and look at each other in amazement, appalled, sometimes amused, by the ridiculous course the argument has taken. "I don't really mean this; you don't mean this either," each finds a way of saying, and the argument suddenly disappears. But our automatic defenses against blame can take over reason and leave us with the conviction that our anger is proof that our partner is to blame. In these heated moments, when terrible words come out of our mouth, we deny that we are being unfair and believe we are simply responding to the gross unfairness of our partner.

Fritz Heider, one of the first psychologists to look closely at blame within marriage, called this pattern the "fundamental attribution error,"[23] though it is now more commonly known as the actor-observer bias. Under the sway of this bias, we blame a person's unseemly behavior on her or his character, whereas our own bad behavior is attributed to some external influence. For example, Ruth tells her husband, "You always blame me. It just shows how mean and ungrateful you really are," but when she reflects on her own unkind words she thinks, "I said those awful things because I was tired and hungry and I've had an awful day." Her spouse is blamed for being hurtful because his character is defective; she, on the other hand, is hurtful only under the sway of temporary, external influences.

When we are on the receiving end of the attribution error, no part of us remains protected or respected. We are not being blamed for a specific mistake or for a slip or for momentary lack of judgment. We are being blamed for who we are. How can we make amends for that? How can we repair the damage? How can things ever improve if I need to become someone else for my partner to admire me? Being criticized for who we are, rather than for something we did or said, evokes a profound sense of helplessness.[24] In the midst of the bewildered helplessness comes shame: "If I am blamed for who I am, then the only thing I can do to escape blame is to hide or, even better, disappear."

Finger Pointing and Biased Memories

Another dangerous use of blame involves finger pointing. The couple have a problem, but instead of focusing on a solution, one blames the other—or, in many cases, each blames the other—for causing the problem. This is so common that every couple in my group was quick to describe a recent argument in which at least one partner used finger pointing. When the Chus' car engine spluttered and died, Sophie and Ying discovered their membership to AAA had expired. Ying immediately blamed Sophie for being "disorganized and unreliable." When the leaking pipe in the Hirsh home resulted in a flood, Rachel blamed Roger for putting off the renovations they were planning and opting for piecemeal repairs: "You want to do everything on the cheap! No wonder it flooded." When the value of the Menkens' investment portfolio plummeted, each blamed the other: Julian blamed Valerie for "not keeping [his] eye on the ball," and Valerie blamed Julian for "trusting that stupid financial advisor."[25]

Finger pointing is sometimes no more than a momentary eruption. "It sure is difficult to keep track of all this *stuff*. We should set up an automatic payment," Ying says, and the argument over the AAA renewal ends. "Thank goodness it's only money," Valerie concludes as she puts aside the portfolio summary. The accusation is withdrawn and quickly forgotten.

Finger pointing, however, can easily escalate into a brutal battle about who is to blame. The closer we are to someone, the easier it is to cause offense and to induce guilt. One partner defends him- or herself by using the initial accusation as an arrow to shoot back to its sender: "You say *I'm* disorganized. Take a look at yourself!" and "Are you saying *I'm* the bad guy here?" or "How dare you say that to me! Just think of all I've done for you!" Here, each spouse views him- or herself as a victim of the other.

The underlying pattern runs something like this: "I know I am hurting you by blaming you, but I am forced to do this because you are so awful; you disappoint me; you do not show me proper respect or care enough about my feelings. I am not a cruel person so I would not hurt you unless you truly deserved it. Your negative personality is making me act like a bully (or shrew)." Under the sway of the fundamental attribution error, we see our own unlikable behavior as transient, while our spouse's problems are persistent.

At such points of conflict, self-serving memory springs to our aid, albeit to the detriment of the relationship. A biased memory, fueled by our ugly mood, supports our conviction that our partner is at fault. We remember all the times we have been thoughtful and generous and supportive, and we remember all the times our spouse has been withholding or selfish or indifferent to our needs.[26] Memories of a partner's kindness, thoughtfulness, support, and generosity lie buried, and instances of behavior that made us as angry as we are now, come to the fore.

Mind Reading

One of the most confusing forms of marital blame involves mind reading, where a partner second-guesses the other's thoughts and motives. This is the dark side to understanding. Instead of a soothing, "I know how you feel," the intimate knowledge of a partner becomes a leering accusation: "I know you," and "I know just what you're thinking." [27] One partner claims to expose the other's real motives: "You wanted to make me look bad!" or "You're trying to make me feel sorry for you." [28] The mind reader presumes to be an expert on a partner, and refuses to listen when the other protests and corrects this ugly view; the partner whose mind is read becomes a silent and helpless text, at the mercy of what the reader finds there.

As arguments escalate, each confronts the terror of rejection and the shame of being cast out of the relationship. Shame, as we have seen, makes us reckless, willing to destroy even those upon whom we depend. The social psychologist June Tangney observed that a shamed spouse tends to strike back with the bitter accusation: "You *made* me feel this," and "You are a terrible person to want to make me feel so bad." [29]

When a couple gets to this stage, the very purpose of quarrels shifts. Now the couple no longer seeks a solution to their problems. The aim becomes "to wound, to insult, to score." [30] Each partner summons a firestorm of blame toward the other. Each partner reasons, "I am a nice person and would not hurt someone close to me unless I had a really good reason for doing so. Because I (a good and fair person) am hurting my partner, he or she must really deserve it." The narrative praise that most friends, parents, and partners offer, whereby each looks at the other's life and character in terms of complex challenges and valuable efforts, becomes a blame narrative in which each depicts himself or herself as a victim of the other.

This mutual blame destroys a marriage. One flame is lit

as a couple move from "You've hurt me," to "You're hurtful." Another is lit as one partner demands of the other, "Why should I compromise or negotiate when the problem lies with you?" Then another is lit as a partner confronts a wrenching dilemma: either accept blame for who you are and remain with me so I can punish you, or leave me because you are beyond the pale. And thus runaway blame destroys a marriage.

Counterproductive Fear of Blame: Stonewalling

Just as partners in love find their way around one another's bodies and needs and habits, partners learn the routes an argument between them is likely to take. In some marriages, arguments etch patterns into the fabric of a couple's interactions. Every exchange falls into one of the grooves and then follows a set path. Some couples learn to anticipate blame every time a conversation presses forward, every time a difference arises, every time an issue is raised.

A stalemate is reached even before the argument begins. If they discuss childcare arrangements, if they discuss the mortgage on the home, if they discuss a child's unsatisfactory school achievement, if they plan renovations in the kitchen or a summer vacation, they face the dreadful possibility of discovering that, somehow, in the other's eyes, they are deeply at fault. When they confront any of the inevitable practical glitches of daily life, they come up against the routine response: "It's your fault!" For some people, the worst thing about marital blame is their own chaotic and alarming response to the other's blame.

Tom and Aisha, who participated in my couples study, agree that there is "a lot of dry tinder" in their relationship. "There's no point in arguing with Aisha," Tom says, and Aisha counters, "There's no point in arguing with *you*."

Tom says he feels "a bell is clanging in [his] head," when his wife starts "on at [him], like a dog with a bone." He explains, "She's an intelligent woman, so I guess she must be making sense, but I only hear loud noises. I know she's telling me something is wrong with me, but I can't see what I'm supposed to do. I hate that she's angry, but the worst thing is how angry I get. That's the worst thing . . . and what I can't deal with." Yet Aisha says that Tom seems to "feel nothing when [she's] upset." She continues, " I get zero response from him. He zones out, like I'm not even there. This is the first I've heard about how *he* suffers when I'm angry."

High levels of emotion in marital arguments often lead one partner to stonewall—a technique used to shut down receptors and turn our body and mind into a wall of stone when confronted by feelings we can neither name nor control. Stonewalling is a response to flooding, or diffuse physiological arousal.[31] Our heart races; our adrenaline levels spike; our blood pressure rises. Our entire physiology screams, "You are facing extreme danger." In this condition, we cannot process our experience. Our ability to hear decreases and our vision is constricted. We cannot think straight because the blood, instead of serving the brain, protects the organs that feel endangered and alerts the muscles to fight or flee. Our priority becomes managing the chaos within ourself rather than understanding and empathizing with our partner. Withholding the usual tracking sounds ("Hmm" and "Ah") and gestures (nods, head shakes, eye contact), we seem impervious to the other's emotion, yet are defending ourselves against the stimuli that deluge our system.

Approximately 85 percent of people who stonewall are men.[32] Women are sometimes said to find criticism more difficult to take than men; it is said that they cry more easily, for example, or get more "emotional" than men. On the whole, however, women manage heightened emotion and interpersonal conflict more robustly than men. In marital quarrels stress levels in men rise much more quickly than in women. Hence, men are more likely to suffer emotional flooding.

This difference in tolerance for strong surges of emotion accounts for a common complaint women make of a male partner: He becomes cold, stonelike, withdrawn in an argument; he refuses to engage with or discuss personal problems; he "disappears." In other words, he stonewalls. From a man's point of view, this shutdown provides self-protection against the emotional and physiological onslaught brought on by the conflict.[33]

Stonewalling is not meant to be offensive; it is self-defense. But to a partner, stonewalling conveys disapproval, icy distance, and even smugness.[34] In a close interpersonal context where not listening and not understanding are profound insults, this sends an offensive message: "I don't want to engage with you," or "You're too ridiculous or insignificant for me to notice you," or "I don't care about your feelings."

The terrible irony is that a woman is likely to experience

emotional flooding when her partner stonewalls. As she witnesses her partner's emotional shutdown, she experiences the physiological onslaught—the racing pulse, the perspiration, and the jarring adrenaline rush in the face of threat—that a man tries to avoid by shutting down. From her perspective, the refusal to listen or respond empathically leaves her bereft and isolated. Each blames the other for his or her awful feelings.

Infidelity Feels Like Blame: The Context

A marriage can be destroyed not only by how the couple praise and blame each other, but also by whom they praise outside the marriage. When a partner is not the only recipient of that primitive praise we experience in sexual intimacy, then the marriage's scaffold of praise collapses.[35]

There is a strong evolutionary basis to our powerful responses to infidelity. Sex is never just sex, whatever minimizing language may be used in self-defense. Human sex goes far beyond its reproductive purpose. One of its functions is to establish bonds between a couple, and it does that admirably. When humans engage in sex, they enter a profoundly altered state, both neurologically and physically. The areas of the brain associated with pleasure and reward[36] become extremely active; the "bonding hormone" oxytocin[37] and the natural opioids that give us a druglike high[38] are triggered while the areas of the prefrontal cortex involved in *critical* appraisal shut down. The rhythms of our pulse, breath, and blood pressure quicken. The entire pelvic area seems to expand, as the tissues swell with increased blood supply. The normal dislike we have of physical intrusion becomes thrilling.[39] We experience what Maggie Scarf has described as "the inchoate, rapturous feelings of being engulfed in the safe and intimate world of early infancy."[40]

However casually partners come together, their brain chemistry mimics the brain chemistry of love. The stroking, touch, and smell associated with sex are also associated with love and connection. As each holds the other, each receives intimate information about the other's experiences; each registers the other's muscle tension, perspiration, heartbeat; each hears and responds to minute, semiprivate vocalizations. The overpowering sensations of sex become associated with our sexual partner. When these associations become embedded in memory, they generate praiselike emotions of gratitude, trust, and admiration. They also generate expectations about future behavior. The bonds feel full of promise. The intimacy feels safe and exclusive.[41]

Monogamy is rare across the 4,000 mammalian species, and some researchers have concluded that human monogamy is "unnatural";[42] but in most human societies sexual fidelity plays a crucial role in a marital relationship.[43] Though the norm of fidelity may be cultural rather than instinctive,[44] fidelity nonetheless shapes our expectations and emotions. We expect, generally, that we will be the only sexual mate our partner needs, or that the value he or she puts on our intimacy will outweigh transient attractions.

The most reliable predictor of whether someone will have

an affair is the measure of negative comparisons between his or her partner and other potential partners.[45] Statements like, "I could do better," or "She's better at understanding me," or "I feel happy/more relaxed/more interesting/more attractive with someone else" post red flags to marital therapists.[46] They imply contemptuous blame and reveal a disturbing lack of commitment. They become justifications for betrayal. The partner having an affair often thinks, "My spouse's reflection of me is not sufficiently positive," or "She/he does not know my worth," hence, "She is not worthy of my commitment."

Why Infidelity Feels Like Blame: Three Messages

We trust a partner not to make negative comparisons between us and someone else. However, the most common reasons a married person gives for having an affair are "I want someone to make me feel good about myself," or "I wanted to feel I was attractive again," or "I needed someone who noticed me," or "I was overcome by admiration and desire for someone else."[47] It is in this context that infidelity sends the first message of blame: "You are not enough for me," or "You are not as good as someone else," or, even, "You are fundamentally inadequate."[48]

The lying that almost invariably accompanies infidelity gives the second message of blame. While an unfaithful partner often justifies deceit as protecting his or her partner and, perhaps, preserving the marriage, deceit destroys the admiring, listening threads of marital conversation. One partner listens not to enjoy emotional and psychological intimacy but to

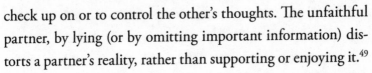

check up on or to control the other's thoughts. The unfaithful partner, by lying (or by omitting important information) distorts a partner's reality, rather than supporting or enjoying it.[49]

Two couples within my group of twelve[50] were torn apart by infidelity. Karen, aged thirty-eight, noticed that her husband Tony's "mind was elsewhere." She explains, "He was coming home really late. He said things were 'crazy at work,' and I believed him. Totally. When he didn't do stuff in the house, and I reminded him, he'd bark at me: I didn't understand the pressure he was under. When I tried to talk about this, and what it meant to me, he told me I didn't understand, and when I told him I was really worried about him, he told me that I was 'imagining things.' So for all those months, I bought his story that I was the one to blame. I was the one who was damaging the relationship. I was a nag. I was too stupid or neurotic to understand him. When I discovered the real story . . . well, 'angry' doesn't do justice to what I felt. I'd been fooled into thinking I was the one to blame."

Lying quickly becomes more than an avoidance strategy. It becomes an attempt to shift the blame from the unfaithful partner to the one who is deceived. "You're imagining things," sends the message, "You are damaging the relationship, not me." A partner's lies create a "gaslight effect."[51] Drawn from the title of George Cukor's 1944 film[52] in which a husband gradually manipulates his wife into thinking that she is suffering a psychosis, the gaslight effect arises when one partner usurps the other's reality and tries to cheat the other into taking the blame.

The closer we are to someone and the more we have trusted him or her, the more intense our blame when we feel betrayed.[53] Therapists who work with couples in the aftermath of affairs say that the most salient and intractable issues are about blame and guilt.[54] Karen says, "I sometimes want to kill him, but then I also want him to live so that he can own his guilt, and suffer from it." Tony insists the guilt lies at least in part with Karen: "She was as much to blame as me. I felt frozen out by her." As Karen feels betrayed by the collapse of her partner's protective praise, and as Tony realizes he has shattered Karen's admiration of him, positive feelings seem to drain from the relationship.[55] Their marriage has become a constant and bitter argument about the allocation of blame.

Infidelity conveys blame, thirdly, by disrupting the couple's privacy. Couples inhabit a very private world. Their intimacy is built up of shared references and responses, common interests, and daily domestic engagements with children, with finance, with housing. Each expects protection from harsher, external judgments, whether these come from friends, neighbors, or even other relatives. When Douglas learns that Beth spent a weekend with an old boyfriend, he broods over their conversational intimacy: "The worst thing is her telling some other guy about us. And complaining about me, you know, justifying to him why it's okay to cheat on me. What hurts most is that she pretended to respect me and she was dishing out the dirt on me." The intimacy that made self-revelations safe and exclusive is now shattered.

Rejection Reinforces Blame

Whatever challenges we experience within a marriage, we expect our partner's view of us to be held together by a scaffold of praise. This means that we trust our partner to reflect a positive image of our personal history, our motives, and our character. Divorce dismantles this scaffold. It is the ultimate rupture, the ultimate form of spousal rejection, and the ultimate form of blame. Many couples find it impossible to retain any positive feelings toward one another. Their friends and family look with horror at the vindictiveness of a divorcing couple: How have two normally sensible and reasonable people become so angry, petty, and mean? Divorce sends a whirlwind of bitterness through each partner's judgment meter.

Few divorcing couples say, philosophically, "Things just didn't work out," or "We gradually grew apart." Instead, each seeks to assuage his or her esteem by judging the other negatively: "He (or she) must be to blame for the breakup," or "He (or she) must be unworthy for me to want to leave." This process is sometimes called "dissonance reduction"[56]—a way of reducing the tension between two inconsistent beliefs, such as "I am behaving badly" and "I am a nice person." Blaming our partner allows us to avoid blaming ourselves for the marriage breakup: "I am leaving you, hurting you, and disrupting this family unit; therefore, you must be an awful person. You are the one to blame for this breakup and deserve nothing."

"My ex-partner is to blame for everything," underlies the familiar battles over every piece of property, from dinner sets

and beach apartments to child custody. Every point in the set-
tlement becomes an opportunity to continue the battle over
who deserves the most blame. Each feels that hurting the
other will alleviate the shame of rejection.

All couples exchange both praise and blame as they negotiate their individual and often competing goals and desires.
Many marriages founder not because each is with "the wrong
person" but because the dynamics of blame take over and
praise disappears into thin air. A successful marriage is only in
part a matter of finding "the right person;" it requires motivation to work as partners who, together, find patterns of interaction that maintain the scaffold of praise.

Managing the Praise/Blame Ratio

The premise that each partner is basically good and admirable
even when one has upset or offended the other is the premise
of a successful marriage.[57] It underlies a commitment wherein
breaches can be easily repaired and forgiveness granted. The
premise that a spouse disappoints us because he or she is basically bad (inconsiderate, irresponsible, selfish) is the premise of
an unhappy marriage. When a deep character flaw is thought
to underlie problems, then making up is difficult. Apologies
twist and break and propagate additional complaints: "I'm
sorry, but you really make things so difficult for me," or "I'm
sorry but I need someone who understands me." Each imputes
negative motives to the other. Every interaction revs up anger
and conflict.[58]

Marital disruption is a devastating experience. Loss of an important relationship changes one's brain circuitry, slows the activity in areas of emotion and reward, and reduces blood oxygen levels. It is a powerful predictor of subsequent problems including depression, heart disease, and even cancer. Loss of a close relationship is quite simply bad for one's health.[59]

Does understanding the role of praise and blame help us preserve a marriage? The answer is yes. Once we identify common defenses against blame, we can no longer hold on to our accusations with such certainty and self-righteousness. Once we understand the devastating effect of blaming someone's character, and take on board the terrible consequences, we are likely to be less reckless.

But the answer to the question, Is knowing the magic ratio of praise and blame sufficient to save a marriage? is no. Just as we have difficulty managing blame or seeing how we may fall under the sway of the superiority bias (whereby we think we deserve more praise than we actually do), so too is it difficult for a couple themselves to track the ratio of praise and blame.

First of all, it is difficult to gauge whether we are actually praising a partner (and not using authoritarian praise or being patronizing) without feedback from our partner. Praise is relational; one person cannot be the final arbiter of how much praise, or blame, he or she gives.

Second, measuring judgments—our own and others—comes up against the common bias of self-serving memory. Each is likely to remember her or his own positive efforts and to minimize the negative remarks hurled at a partner. While there has to be give and take in marriage, discussions about who has given how much praise are likely to turn into arguments. Only unhappy marriages focus on quid pro quo.[60]

Focusing on who does more, who gives more, who compromises more generates dissatisfaction. Measuring your contributions as greater than your partner's implies blame: "You don't give enough." Arguments follow: "I've done more than you," and "After all I've done for you, it's only fair that you do this for me." Each may refer to some invisible referee, who always gives more weight to his or her own input and concludes that the other is to blame for not pulling equal weight.[61]

Finally, what we observe may depend on how we judge the other. When we are convinced a partner is to blame, we are less likely to notice praise, or indeed any positive overture. In fact, when couples are at odds, they have been found to notice only 50 percent of the partner's efforts to praise compared to the number noted by an independent observer.[62]

The best way to use this understanding of marital praise and blame is to respect its power. Praise, in marriage, includes admiration and interest in the partner's feelings, goals, and values, as well as an appreciative focus that precludes negative comparisons between a partner and other possible partners. When the power of judgment within a marriage turns negative, damage can only be repaired by building anew each partner's esteem. This involves the difficult task of each partner setting aside her or his defenses against blame, and taking responsibility for the offense caused;[63] it involves each partner absolving the other of humiliation and shame; and each offering the other praise for these efforts toward reparation.[64]

Perhaps what is needed is a revised relational contract. Instead of "We shall love each other unconditionally," each might accept something more realistic: "I know we will judge each other, but we shall do our best not to ignore what is positive in the other or to exaggerate what is negative. When we feel overwhelmed by negative judgments, we will try to negotiate a way through and avoid casting persistent, contemptuous blame on the other. When one of us really messes up we shall offer one another comfort, empathy, and support. We shall ensure that negative judgments focus on specific things, while positive judgments focus on deep character traits. We also know that sometimes we will fall under the sway of the many biases that protect esteem but threaten the relationship. That is what we have to deal with because we are human." Of course, it is not only within a marriage that we deal with the tricky balance of praise versus blame, as we see in the next chapter, which looks at how our judgment meter impacts relationships in the workplace.

7

Professional Dues: Praise and Blame in the Workplace

WHEN WE ENTER our workplace, we may leave behind the intense intimacy of our relationships with family and close friends, but not our judgment meter. In meetings we listen to our coworkers and respond to the substance of what they say, but we also assess their character and motives: "I can see why she was promoted. She's very effective when she speaks. And she seems genuinely concerned about this issue," I think, and note how others nod as my high-powered colleague speaks. I see that others share my appraisal, and I feel proud to have such an impressive colleague. "He likes the sound of his own voice," I think as another colleague drones on. I pitch in, hoping to move the discussion forward; I see someone fidget with her rings and then look around the room. I wonder whether I am boring her. Ten minutes later, there is a new voice across the table. I note the self-serving tone and think, "This is not news; I said the same thing five minutes ago, and now he is just taking credit for it." I exchange a knowing, amused glance with a colleague, and we bond through our shared judgment.

Judgments—ours of others and others' of us—play a key role in job satisfaction. After working for over a decade in a variety of organizations, the psychologist Ben Dattner concluded that pay and promotion usually matter more as signs of esteem or disesteem than for their material benefits. The crux of most job dissatisfaction actually involves "outrage about not getting fairly [praised] or resentment about getting unfairly blamed."[1] Unfortunately, such unfairness seems to be common in the workplace. When Wayne Hochwarter and his colleagues at Florida State University College of Business asked 1,200 people about their immediate supervisor, 31 percent reported that their boss exaggerated his or her accomplishments and achievements, and 27 percent reported that their boss bragged to others in order to get praise.[2]

Feeling unappreciated at work is one of the most common reasons for leaving an organization.[3] In one study, 37 percent of people who left a job said it was because a boss failed to give them credit when they themselves believed they deserved it, while 23 percent said they left because a boss blamed others to cover up his or her own mistakes.[4] Those who stay on in an organization that fails to praise them appropriately, or blames them inappropriately, suffer extreme stress and low morale. Since stress and low morale are contagious,[5] understanding how praise and blame function in the workplace is important for each worker and to each organization.

A Personal View of Workplace Judgments

The academic setting is often referred to as an "ivory tower"—a biblical reference to noble purity.[6] The term implies that those who devote themselves to intellectual work are untainted by personal vanities such as praise and blame. For fifteen years I worked in a college as dean[7] of both students and academic staff, while my research took me into the heart of very different workplaces[8]—a hospital, two schools, a law office, and a large manufacturing corporation. As I gathered my research findings and reflected on my own experiences, I concluded that academia is not a safe haven from ordinary judgments but a rather good place to begin an exploration of praise and blame dynamics in the workplace.

Academics, far from being removed from a personal judgment meter, are obsessed by it. The academic workplace is full of what the psychologist Oliver James calls "office politics"[9] and Ben Dattner calls "the blame game,"[10] whereby people position themselves to be in line for praise, protect themselves from blame, and all too often do their utmost to prevent coworkers from getting praise.

Academics pride themselves—rightly—on nuanced and informed judgments. They appraise the quality of others' research; they can be obsessed with ranking others' intelligence; they also assess others' contributions to the field, carefully monitoring their colleagues' status. This can be difficult when the gradations are so varied and tiny and the rewards, often, inconsequential. The discrepancies that appear minor to others are magnified within the ivory tower. This follows Sayre's law, whereby the interest in esteem is inversely proportional to the magnitude of the reward. According to Wallace Stanley Sayre, "Academic politics is the most vicious and bitter form of politics, because the stakes are so low."[11]

Listening was central to my role as dean. I engaged in extensive discussions with academics, both junior and senior, about their careers. Along with other senior college staff, I was struck by how these independent-minded people brooded over others' judgments of them, their worth, and their work. The brooding cast such a long shadow on morale that a decision was taken to review faculty well-being in the workplace. As part of this review, I noted the themes faculty raised in their discussions with me, and logged the proportion of time devoted to status and esteem anxiety. When staff came to see me, I explained that I would be taking notes, and that, along with the principal and vice-principal, I was looking at areas where people felt dissatisfied at work.[12] The records taken over the course of one academic year showed that issues about praise and blame took up approximately 55 percent of the conversation time.

Gemma comes to see me to request a reduction in her teaching stint, but underlying this practical request are issues about praise and blame. Now in her late forties, she believes her research has suffered as a result of her dedicated teaching, yet feels that her teaching contributions are not appreciated: "I find it so discouraging that the excellent teaching I do doesn't even register in the university's assessment exercises. These days you have to show off your research to get acknowledgment."

Gemma is not praised, as she deserves to be, for her teaching, and she is blamed, inappropriately, for her low research profile.

Alastair comes to see me to ask for a reference in the senior promotion exercise, but most of the meeting is devoted to complaints about the lack of praise he is given here, in his home institution: "I go to these high level conferences, and people want to hear what I have to say. The paper I gave [abroad] was to a packed audience. I mean packed, with standing room only. Here my colleagues think my popularity is a sign of shallowness. They put it down to mere flair. Oh, you know what that means. They think it doesn't have substance unless they're the ones fanning their peacock plumes. I know part of the game is hyping yourself over the person in the next office, and doing him down, but this is wearing on me, and if I don't get promoted soon, I'm going to leave."

Chiara comes to see me about enhanced secretarial support, but the underlying issue is esteem as much as workload: "Most of the hard work I put in is invisible, and sharing a secretary doesn't make it easier. I don't mind when people ask me to do this and that. I'm happy to help. But I mind that they're asking because they look down at me."

I often hear that we should be satisfied with knowing our own worth. If we value ourselves, why should others' judgments matter? But they do matter. We may have high respect for our internal judge, and we may give particular weight to the judgments of people we value (personally or professionally), but rarely are we impervious to the judgments of others.

When the psychologist Bruce Hood looked at the evolution of the human mind, he realized that we have a "domesticated brain" highly sensitive to others' views. In fact, Hood concludes, "Humans are such social animals that we are completely preoccupied with what others think about us. No wonder reputation is paramount when it comes to feeling good about ourselves. The social pressure to conform involves being valued by the group because, after all, most success is really defined by what others think." [13]

This does not mean we passively accept others' views of us. Gemma, Alastair, and Chiara try to manage their sensitivity to others' views. They also confer with their internal assessor, drawing on their very personal measures of praise and blame. Resisting, negotiating, and naming the terms on which praise and blame are allocated are constant workplace activities, and they continue in our thoughts, in conversations with partners and friends, long after we leave the office.

Mapping Judgments in the Workplace

The workplace provides a theater in which we are both audience and actor in the drama of everyday judgments. Modern work brings together people who might otherwise choose to ignore one another, people who, we feel, are not like us and whom we would never chose to see socially. Often we have to find common ground, follow their instructions, and accede to their arguments. This presents us with the challenge of monitoring and assessing people we don't easily read.

When we need to read or assess people who puzzle us,

when job survival depends on knowing whom to trust and how to work alongside someone we find difficult, we may seek help from someone whose judgment meter seems aligned to ours. "What do you think of Joel's work?" and "Do you have trouble getting through to Emily?" and "Is Garth always like this or is he just having a bad day?" we ask. So common is this practice that Oliver James found, in his study of workplaces, that "hardly a day goes by in which colleagues are not explicitly or implicitly asked for opinions about the personality and competence of each other." [14]

These informal exchanges, or gossip, create alliances. Someone who shares our judgments seems a kindred spirit. When we seek someone's opinion of a coworker, and we meet with a brusque or guarded response, we realize we have misjudged *that* person's judgment of us. "Ah, I see he isn't willing to be open with me," I note, and steer clear of gossip in the future. But when a long conversation ensues, when I hear, "Yeah, he's always like that, and you have to watch out when he's on your team," I not only receive important information, I form an alliance based on pooled judgments.

Personal judgment in the workplace can have a huge professional impact. For a manager seeking feedback on an associate's leadership skills, hearing, "She always messes up something in a presentation," can shift a not-yet-formed judgment of that coworker to a decidedly negative one, while hearing, "Wasn't that interesting! I like the way she goes off-script," can sweep away the doubts about the less polished part of her presentation. Similarly, a competitor may try to get the edge on a coworker's projects by feeding the coworker misinformation about what is expected in a presentation. He or she can instill suspicion by casually warning others, "Don't believe his forecasts. He's always confident and always mistaken." In skilled hands, workplace gossip is a speedy, efficient, and devastating vehicle for praise and blame.

Such judgments, repeated over and over with an aura of authority become embedded as if facts, and are then very difficult to challenge. The coworker who is described as "always mistaken" might protest, "My forecasts are usually right. No forecaster will get it right every time." But if he does not know what is being said about him, if he does not know that others have been primed to look out for his errors, then he is ill-equipped to defend himself.

We may not hear negative gossip, but we feel it. Sometimes it has a positive effect on our work: knowing that our coworkers will gossip about us increases our motivation to collaborate and cooperate.[15] But often, when we catch the microexpressions of our coworkers and the glances exchanged among them as we speak, the workplace becomes a dangerous place, hedged with whispered, shapeless accusations. Neuroscientist Richard Davidson found that "if you cannot interact with coworkers without picking up silent messages being transmitted between bitter competitors, for instance, you might very well have trouble functioning at your undistracted best."[16] What begins as unfounded gossip can become true: we lose concentration and confidence, our ability to perform suffers, and we prove the negative judgment right.

Competition and Praise Scarcity

Managers are often trained to use the sandwich technique in giving negative criticism. First, you praise the worker: "You are a hard worker and good in a team; you were helpful to Jerry in last week's presentation." Then you deliver the negative judgment: "The presentation you gave to the client was really not good enough. [The client] was clearly unhappy, but you didn't listen to him; you just repeated your initial idea." Then, to soften the impact, you focus on the future: "This should be a good learning experience; use your talents with a team to try things out with others before you go to a client. We'll get someone to give you deep background on the client, so you'll be better prepped." Focusing on the future can keep criticism within the positive judgment system because it shapes ideas about how to deserve praise.

The principle underlying the sandwich technique is that praise is a plentiful and useful resource, and criticism should not be blame; it should be constructive and focus on the future. However, when profits fall, when client numbers contract, when people feel that their jobs, their status, and their value are under threat, praise is guarded like a hawk and all criticism is transformed into blame.[17]

Some years ago I took part in research on work-life balance in a midsized law firm and manufacturing firm,[18] both of which were undergoing restructuring. I rapidly learned that everyone was focused far less on what their workplace offered than on how they were judged at work. Glen, aged twenty-nine, tells me, "Whatever policies there are about well-being or work-life balance, count for nothing. What matters is whether people here think you're the go-to person, or whether you're useless. You have to show everyone that everyone else thinks you're wonderful, and you do that by showing how busy you are. Some guys do this with that faux complaint, 'Oh, I wish I could just take some time off. But there's so much to do.' And then they'll list all they've been asked to do, while my in-tray is getting really low."

Ajit, aged twenty-four, says, "You can't believe how hard it was to get an offer for something even on the bottom-most rung here. In law school we spent hours and hours on self-presentation: 'You have to give a strong interview. You have to show them what you're made of to get an offer,' they said. Now I'm here, I'm in, but the game is just as fierce. Every day is like a brutal interview. Convincing the partners that you are going to be great is more important than any work you actually do."

For Kelly, age thirty-two, the priority, day in and day out, is to avoid blame in an environment in which she is ever more closely scrutinized because, in current conditions, blame is useful to the organization: "I know they want to slim down this department. Any little slip up is an excuse to give you some kind of warning. You miss a deadline, you lose a client, you fail to shine in a meeting, and the higher-ups will just go for you."

At every level in Kelly's firm, in every department, the employees, threatened with blame, are quick to cast blame on others:[19] "I did my part, but the accountant totally messed up, and his double counting made nonsense of my targets," complains Adam, Kelly's manager. "We designed a wonderful product, but the sales team just fell down on their job," explains Arun, Kelly's teammate. Caught in the blame game, Kelly's coworkers devote their energy toward finding scapegoats and convincing each other that they are not to blame. Kelly realizes, though, that the higher-ups have control over the judgments that really matter. Once again, power is expressed through judgment: whose praise and blame matters, and whose does not.

Narcissism, and the Manipulation of Praise

In everyday usage a narcissist is a person with a big ego. In psychology, however, a narcissist is someone with a fragile ego and a façade of grandiosity, who compulsively bolsters his or her esteem by demanding admiration from others. These demands can have a devastating effect in the workplace. Narcissists drive forward initiatives that attract personal praise—such as high-risk investments—but play havoc with the well-being of the organization. Narcissists aggressively fight off criticism and bully those who disagree with them. With their bluster and apparent confidence, they are often very successful in the workplace. Some psychologists estimate that approximately 4 percent of CEOs combine narcissism with lack of empathy and a desire to manipulate others,[20] while some researchers argue that up to 21 percent of CEOs have this disturbing (some would say psychopathic) combination of traits—about the same percentage found in prisons.[21]

A narcissist is a difficult colleague for many reasons. Narcissists exaggerate their importance at others' expense. They brag and constantly solicit praise. They demand admiration and are furious when anyone fails to venerate them. They do not respond well to criticism, however necessary and positively presented. Above all, they damage the environment by shaping the workplace dynamics of praise and blame. Every encounter becomes an opportunity for them to claim praise and belittle others. The consequences of their actions to others are of no importance; what matters to them is whether they shine.

Sarah works with a senior surgeon[22] who, Sarah says, "huffs and puffs if she's asked to do something she thinks is beneath her. And if she doesn't get her way in a meeting, she criticizes the entire team and the process of decision-making and threatens to resign. She starts listing all the work she does that she doesn't get credit for. It leaves us all exhausted, and we have to think of ways to accommodate her. This can demoralize the entire unit."

Michelle, aged forty-two, an associate in a law firm, says that working alongside other people all trying to make it to the top of the pyramid exposes her to many narcissists: "I see some people warmed by the constant boasting, and poised to compete with it. Once one person starts bigging himself up it paves the way for others to match him. That sets the tone of every conversation. But I just clam up. I feel ridiculous. I hate this praise grabbing. But it's hard to ignore. You know you will be marginalized because you can't put your heart and soul into self-promotion."

The narcissist's self-assessment may be absurdly grandiose, but his or her confidence can be highly persuasive. When others see how effective a narcissist's style is, they may start to imitate the swagger and aggression. It has been estimated that between 1979 and 2006 there has been a 30 percent increase in the proportion of narcissists [23] as workplace cultures reward those with an inflated view of their own abilities. Some believe that the refusal of narcissists to reflect on and revise their own judgments, and their hostility to others' judgments, presents the greatest risk to the well-being of organizations making them far more likely to fail,[24] because they put a stranglehold on responsive, reflective, and adaptive judgments.

Metrics and Targets: Artificial Measures for Praise and Blame

Many organizations are aware of the damage caused by those who skillfully elicit undeserved praise, who deflect blame, and who make a show of being crucial to the organization's success while actually contributing very little. Many organizations are also aware that low morale can result from unfair distribution of praise and blame. To address these problems, some firms adopt more objective measures of evaluation, measures of effectiveness that are meant to bypass self-aggrandizing bluster. But can the allocation of praise and blame ever meet the terms of objectivity?

In a postmanufacturing era, without clear measures of productivity[25] such as number of gadgets produced or tubes filled or cars completed, we are, Oliver James notes, left with "a range of burgeoning professions where there are no objective metrics for evaluation of performance."[26] If I work in a service industry, such as technical support, a high number of calls may suggest I am doing my job well, but it may also suggest that customers have to keep calling back because my guidance has not solved their problem. If I work as part of an editorial team producing a monthly magazine, then how can my input be distinguished from others' input? Is it more important for me to come up with ideas or to implement others' proposals?

In some organizations the rules for praise and blame lie somewhere in the ether, present but enigmatic. Hannah Seligson, in her book *New Girl on the Job: Advice from the Trenches*, describes her bewilderment as a new office recruit. Is it helpful to be friendly or does friendliness make one look like a lightweight? Why does completing or failing to complete one task matter so much more than acing or messing up another? Why is there such a discrepancy between the job description and the actual job? Why does the official company structure bear so little resemblance to the actual locus of power? And why do others see me as failing when I am actually doing more than my coworkers?[27]

A workplace in which people cannot answer the questions, How do people think I am doing? and Why do they think I am doing well or badly? is a dysfunctional one. To avoid this, many organizations set out "metrics" for praise and blame. The assumption is that if they can present quantitative judgments—judgments that are clearly measured—then they can show these judgments are objective and fair. Moreover, quantitative judgments allow workers to be compared to one another, with higher scores on these metrics indicating better performance.

But some qualities are very difficult to measure. How can team spirit be quantified? Or creativity? How is nuance, for example, measured? Or encouragement? Or the power to listen to and develop others' creativity? When measurement takes priority, other unquantifiable qualities can disappear from evaluation.[28] Even when all qualities are measured, the measurement itself can be highly subjective. A manager may keep a beady eye on the metrics, but the score given remains a matter of judgment, and that judgment may well be shaped by the manager's like or dislike for the worker, by the worker's power to charm, or by the worker's skill at self-presentation.

One step an organization may take to correct biased metrics is to set targets; but given the nature of many workplaces, targets have to be invented. Sometimes the only purpose they serve is to set down the terms for allocating praise and blame.

Greg, aged thirty-nine, has worked in a consultancy firm for three years. He says his day is structured by "a professional version of the stickers my 5-year-old daughter gets for being good. I feel like what I really do, and how I pull my weight, disappears from the equation. There's lots of praise and blame, but no critical meat."

Sarah, as a surgeon in a large UK hospital, feels that targets are at odds with her job. "One target is the number of complications following surgery. But whether or not a patient survives surgery without complication often depends on the severity of the patient's condition before surgery. With a view to targets, some hospital administrators send difficult cases to other hospitals, so our targets for complication-free surgery won't be compromised."[29]

Setting targets by which institutions and those working there can be praised or found wanting changes the entire culture of the institution. It amplifies the human impulse to chase praise and avoid blame, without providing the critical meat Greg describes above—the need to respect the basis of others' judgments and be encouraged by them.

There is another problem. Working in an organization where targets are not in sync with our own judgment meter is highly demoralizing. The aim of these targets, to lift morale and increase motivation through fair evaluation, then fall wide of the mark. So, another process—the appraisal—is offered whereby workers can air their own judgments, of themselves and their coworkers, including their boss.

Appraisals: Judgment and Power

"I couldn't sleep for days before my appraisal," Tessa explains. "I was excited, because it's a rare treat getting attention from the upper tier, but I was also nervous, and a little angry: Hell, how do they even know what I do? So how can they judge me? I prepared lists of my achievements, and things I should get credit for, but I had no control over the conversation. It wasn't *bad*, but those 'areas for improvement' made me fume. Where did they get that? How did my successes disappear? I felt like they were talking to someone else. There was no relation between what I was told and how I actually do my job."

Appraisals—formal and documented evaluations—appeal to our obsession with judgments. In principle, they involve an exploration of a worker's judgments, but in practice they alert the worker to others' judgments of them. These include assessments of productivity (however artificially that is measured), leadership, and collaboration (sometimes called "organizational citizenship").

During a typical appraisal a worker is invited to voice self-evaluations: Where do you excel? Where do you need additional support? But this 360 degrees principle— that is, the principle that the appraisal is a joint enterprise and each participant's judgments get a hearing—ignores the balance of power. In a workplace it is clear that one person's judgment carries far more weight than another's. Formal appraisals may impact pay and promotion for the person appraised but not for the appraiser.

As in families, as in friendships, as in couples, power emerges in the question, Whose judgments matter more? Tessa reflects, "I guess I put so much energy into these appraisals beforehand because I know I'm not really going to be heard. How is my evaluation going to trump management's? It can't, and it never does."

Appraisals: His and Hers

Duncan, aged twenty-eight, is a buyer in a grocery business. Two days after he had an appraisal from his head of department, Leslie, Duncan predicts, "Six weeks max will see me out of a job. The problem is that I'm smarter than my line manager, and he's basically insecure. One of these guys who smile all the time, and—can you imagine spending what he does on a suit and still look tacky? Well, he can. And you know, I'm smart, I'll be fine. I just need a firm with people around who can see my ideas for what they're worth."

Sharon, aged thirty, a consultant in a design firm, has also recently had an appraisal. She says that she can see "the writing on the wall," though she confesses that she was completely unaware of issues beforehand: "It was a bolt out of the blue. I keep thinking, Shouldn't I have seen this before? Because it would have been much nicer to go, or at least to plan to go, before this—well, what was really a dressing down. But there's nothing I can think of, even with the benefit of hindsight, that flagged this—no ball dropped, no criticism. It's just a matter of not being what they want, or think they want, or think I'll be, in the longer term. This kind of firm sheds a lot of people from time to time. A business like this has ups and downs, and when that happens, this happens, you know: the guys with clout lay the blame on the guys who can't defend themselves because they're not part of those key discussions. The big guys decide who gets credit and who gets the boot. So, apart from finding it hard not to feel stupid for not seeing what was clear as day to the partners—that I don't fit in—I'm ok with it. I clocked up some experience; I was paid—not as much as I deserve and not for all the hours I worked, but my debts didn't increase, at least. I just have to do some hard thinking about what I am good at, and where I might fit in."

Both Duncan and Sharon put a lot of energy into dissonance reduction: they try to square the negative judgment they receive in their workplace with their belief that they deserve praise and not blame. When an experience is painful, as any form of blame is, we try to reshape it, softening its edges, removing its sting, so we can absorb it and move on. This often involves replaying the event over and over in our thoughts. We may discuss it with a partner or friend, someone who is likely to confirm our point of view, and endorse our self-serving bias. Duncan's response to the message, "They think I'm no good," is remolded so that it is no longer a judgment of him, but a sign of the appraiser's worthlessness. This is the classic defense of impugning the character, judgment, motive, and even appearance, of the person who delivers a blow to one's esteem.[30]

Duncan's condemnation of Leslie may provide comfort, but this defense limits his ability to learn from the experience. Duncan cannot remember the points on which he was found wanting. When I press him on this, he says, only, "They say I didn't get the best deals, that other buyers had much higher profit margins, but that's rubbish. Really, he doesn't know what he's talking about."

Sharon also engages in dissonance reduction, but in a very

different way. She avoids turning her appraiser into a carica-
ture villain. She accepts that this is the kind of thing managers do in this kind of firm. She does not blame her manager
for finding fault with her. She does not claim that there is
something wrong with him (as Duncan does by calling his
manager "insecure"). Instead she looks at the firm's pattern of
hiring and firing, and challenges herself (Why didn't I see this
coming?). She notes what's positive about the outcome (she
was paid enough to avoid increasing her debts). She then looks
ahead to new possibilities.

These are two individuals responding, as individuals do,
in different ways; but Duncan and Sharon illustrate a common difference in men and women's responses. It is often said
that women take appraisals more personally than men, that
women are more praise dependent and particularly sensitive
to criticism.[31] Among the workers I interviewed,[32] though,
women handled negative appraisals with greater equanimity
than men.

Some argue that this difference arises from women's pro-
pensity to underestimate themselves, while men are more likely
to overestimate their abilities.[33] The difference in responses
may also be because women are more accustomed to neutral
or negative appraisals than men.[34] When Sharon prods her line
manager to explain why he assesses her input as "minimal," he
explains that he cannot credit her with recruiting additional
clients. Sharon is surprised because two big clients did come
to the firm after she and a coworker presented their ideas to
them. Her manager credits a coworker, who was male, with

these clients and describes Sharon's input as supportive. But Sharon sees no justification for this and concludes, "It really makes me feel distant from the whole thing. Maybe a little bit angry, but mostly just superior."

Where I found women more sensitive than men was in their responses to the implicitly patronizing messages of praise. When the chief operating officer of a think tank commends Felicity's foresight in backing up her presentation with data that the client peremptorily demanded, she fumes, "Has she only just noticed that I can do this? That I do it routinely? That I am always prepared with back up data?" When the president of her college tells Katy, "The way you handled that student was wonderful. It made me realize, 'There is a counselor worth her salt!'" Katy is dumbstruck: "He is impressed with that? That was the most straightforward case ever! It's a sliver of what I do. Is that the acme of my input, in his view?"

Praise in the workplace, as Lucy Kellaway observes, is "hellishly difficult to get right."[35] A friend of Kellaway's complained that her boss praised her for an easy task and then praised her diligence. Praise like this was a "love bomb [that] had gone off in her face and left her scarred." The underlying message that left her feeling "grim and demotivated" was that her good work on easy tasks could not be taken for granted and that she was good at working hard, but not driven or able or generally outstanding. In the workplace, as in our more intimate relationships, praise is complicated. When praise is out of sync with our goals and values and our own esteem, it can be as insulting as blame.[36]

Gender Bias and Judgment

Neither the manager who is surprised by Felicity's belt-and-braces competence nor the manager who overlooks Sharon's contribution to the workplace is likely to see him- or herself as biased. The manager would never say, "I believe a woman's work is worth less than a man's," but automatic bias slips beneath our radar.

One way to catch sight of embedded bias is through a series of exercises called the Implicit Association Test (generally referred to as IAT). This test measures the speed with which we associate certain qualities, positive or negative, with types of people.[37] The test reveals, repeatedly and often to the participant's dismay, a bias toward one group and against another— men over women, for example, or Caucasians over Africans, or Asians over Caucasians, or attractive people over plain people.

One of the most common exercises in the IAT teases out gender biases in the workplace. The exercise tests the speed with which people associate women and men with certain roles and abilities. The results show that most people, women and men alike, still associate women more strongly with supportive and nurturing roles, and men more strongly with careers, leadership, and power.[38] Even when, with sincere goodwill, we try to overcome bias, it often remains embedded, unconscious but active.

The tougher time women have in the workplace does not arise from a greater sensitivity to criticism. It does not arise because managers—men or women—make a conscious judgment that women are less able than men. It is not because women lack ambition or courage. More commonly it is because both women and men are slower to pick up on the strengths and impacts of women's performance. It is because both women's and men's judgments of others' abilities and potential are all too commonly shaped by implicit biases. Employers are more likely to overlook a woman's contribution to a team effort, more likely to see her in a supporting role, and less likely to focus on an idea she expresses.[39] This of course influences the employer's allocation of praise and blame.

Why Do Biased Judgments Persist?

One reason bias gains such a foothold in our judgments is that it hijacks a basic and normally useful learning mechanism. Our mind absorbs information through schema—patterns that organize and process experience efficiently. Mental schema prepackage information about what to expect. Without these, we would be far less efficient in recognizing ordinary things, such as a table or a chair or a pencil. Schema help us in interactions with people, too, as we draw on a mental store of responses and expectations about what they are likely to say and do. Still, while schemas help us navigate our social world, the associations packed within them can skew our judgment.

The psychologist Cordelia Fine compares mental schema to a litter of puppies sleeping in a warm, entwined heap;[40] when one puppy wakes up, others get restless and start to move around. In a similar way, associations gathered over time, from our own experiences, from exposure to others' views, from cultural representations in articles, films, and books, all wake up together. References to a certain group of people—whether it is women, Asians, homosexuals, Christians, Jews, or Muslims—stir up other information collected about that group. Even when we think we take a fresh and fair look at each individual, some stereotypical associations—either positive or negative—are likely to spring up as the brain goes about the difficult job of interpreting and judging humans.

We often think of prejudice as fixed and fused (usually in someone else's mind). But bias can be triggered by little cues, generating momentary prejudice in a mind that is ordinarily fair. Being shown pictures of glamorous models, for example, tends to make us more aware of a woman's physical appearance. Being shown a commercial in which women are behaving like airheads adjusts our expectations of women's intelligence downward. Likewise, exposure to images of women leaders makes it easier for us to associate a woman with leadership qualities.[41] Catching hold of and exposing bias can be particularly difficult because bias keeps changing its shape. Yet whatever its shape, it influences our judgments, positive and negative.

Implicit Bias and Judgment in the Workplace

Michelle, aged forty-nine, is applying for a partnership in an engineering consultancy firm. She has experience of how biases and biased judgments fluctuate, quiescent one moment while the next moment they snarl loudly. She explains, "Most of the partners and clients are welcoming and supportive. And *sometimes* I benefit from being what's still an oddity in engineering—a woman. There's a buzz when I do my stuff, and I may come out looking better because people are surprised I do it at all.[42] But other stuff goes on that really wears me down. Some older style men feel they have to be gallant. When I walked into the first interview, this old stick-in-the-mud smiled and pulled out a chair for me, and told me that I was the most attractive candidate they'd seen all week. Something like that—even a simple compliment on my shoes, usually from a woman—can poison the atmosphere."

Many women find covert bias in their workplace stressful and exhausting.[43] Praising a coworker or applicant for something that is irrelevant to her work (as Michelle was praised for her looks at the start of a professional interview) activates biased associations in all who hear it. However, as a culture shifts toward greater awareness of our own biases, our brains work harder to resist set patterns. When someone calls us to account, we may be more willing to reflect critically on our own responses.[44] As Michelle reflects, "A big, big change is that when someone patronizes you or sidelines you as a woman, you know there will be someone who picks up on this. You catch that beat, when one of those stupid comments bombs. It's a great comfort, let me tell you, because instead of me being patronized, he becomes the butt of a shared joke. That's a big change from twenty years ago."

This big change, however, is not sufficient to remove

all bias.[45] Most of us continue to see some people as more deserving of praise, depending on the group to which they belong. The persistence of embedded gender bias was recently exposed in an investigation of how even academic scientists judged applications.

In any science faculty in any distinguished university in most parts of the world, most people on an appointments committee want to select the best person for the job.[46] The best person is the one whose publications are strong enough to reflect well on the institution, who shows promise of further development, and who will work well with the teams of researchers already in place. The people on the appointments committee, women and men, are scientists themselves, rational thinkers, committed to the removal of bias, committed to allocating praise where praise is due. Most faculty members on such committees agree that any inherent differences between men and women's abilities in math and science are either very, very small, or nonexistent.[47] Nevertheless, a candidate named "John" is more likely to be appointed than the candidate named "Jennifer." [48]

In one study, 127 faculty members of highly respected universities, with research intensive science departments, rated applications for a science post: How competent were the candidates? What was the value of their research history? What was their potential? What would be an appropriate starting salary for the various candidates? [49] When the applicant was thought to be male, the candidate was rated as more competent than an identical applicant with a female name. A higher starting salary was proposed for the applicant identified as male than for an applicant with identical credentials but identified as a woman. The male applicant was also seen as a more desirable mentee than the identical female applicant. Both women and men made different judgments of the same applicant depending on whether the applicant was identified as male or female.

These judgments did not arise from a conscious prejudice against women's abilities, nor did they stem from a deliberate aim to exclude women. Here the efficient processing of information that so often aids our judgments left it vulnerable to unintended, unacknowledged, and grossly unfair biases.

Stereotypes and the Over-Eye

Other people's stereotypes impinge on us when they make unfounded assumptions about what we are like and what we are likely to do. When we clearly defy others' stereotypes, we may be condemned as an aberration. A prime minister who is a woman might be judged as "shrill," while a male prime minister acting as the woman does would be judged as "strong."[50] Looking through the distortions of bias, a normal woman does not show strength but a normal man does.

Stereotypes impinge on our self-judgments, too. Stereotypes infuse the over-eye, that inner voice drawing on social and cultural norms to remind us what others expect us to be. All too often, these judgments obscure our more personal, complex, and nuanced self-judgments. One of the most disturbing things about these biased judgments is that they can be activated by even very small cues in our environment.

Women, according to a common stereotype, are not naturally good at mathematics. Many women confidently dismiss such a stereotype, yet it may nonetheless have a measurable effect on them. In one alarming study, women were asked to record their sex at the beginning of a quantitative test, and this alone was enough to trigger the stereotype and impact their performance: they underperformed, compared to how they did when they were not asked to record "female" or "male" at the start of the test.[51] When women are in a minority when they take the test, they also do less well, for being in a minority is a reminder of the stereotype that women "don't do" math. When they have just watched a commercial in which women were behaving like airheads, or when they have just tried on a swimsuit as opposed to a sweater, then they perform less well than comparable women perform on the same test in more neutral conditions. A shift from swimsuit to sweater does not affect men's performance on the math test, because highlighting their gender does not trigger negative associations about mathematical ability.[52]

The boundaries between our own and others' judgments are highly permeable. We may feel we are resisting negative stereotypes but nonetheless internalize them. So, a bright teenage girl decides that science is not for her and a career woman believes she is not good enough to apply for promotion. Even those who defy stereotypes over and over again can suddenly fall under their spell. Perhaps Margaret Thatcher did, when she sought a voice coach to modify her "shrill" voice and when she joined the judgmental bigots by insisting,

"I didn't get here by being a strident female. I don't like strident females." [53] In speaking as a woman is expected to do, she was likely to be seen as underpowered and underconfident; in speaking assertively and with confidence, she was likely to be decried for being an unseemly woman. The bias embedded in stereotypes skews the judgment meter; regardless of how someone who is under the spell of a stereotype behaves, he or she is trapped within a negative assessment.

Can We Ever Avoid Bias in Our Judgments?

Our initial responses to people are informed by approach and avoidance tendencies linked to primitive survival assessments: Is it safe to approach this person, or should I avoid him? To be useful, to aid survival in the face of immediate danger, these appraisals have to be made quickly. So, within seven seconds of seeing someone we have never met, we infer from facial appearance, voice, and posture whether we like that person, whether we trust him or her, and whether we think that person is competent, aggressive, or kind.[54]

Over the past three decades an entire field of research has opened up to explore these fast judgments[55] based on rules of thumb that may have been useful at some points in our evolutionary or individual histories, but which now often lead us astray, preventing us from allocating praise and blame fairly. When I am interviewed for a job, my competence, likeability, and fitness for the job are likely to be assessed within the first seconds I enter the room. Whatever I do and say during the course of that interview may have little impact on that rapidly formed judgment.[56] It also seems that associations can be triggered, bizarrely, through the metaphors that infuse our language: we are more likely to judge a person as warm when we have been carrying a hot cup of coffee;[57] we seem more likely to judge a person as cold after we have carried a cold drink.[58]

For most of the previous century the unconscious was modeled as a cauldron of desires and emotions that we banned from consciousness. These unacknowledged forces led us to engage in strangely compulsive behavior, or slips of the tongue, or vivid or disturbing dreams. Over the past three decades, however, the mind's unconscious is more likely to be modeled as a fast response engine that shapes our judgments. The brain uses its powerful store of memories and associations to navigate our complex social environment, but the very mechanisms that underpin our genius for survival also leave our judgments vulnerable to bias.

How Much Do Praise and Blame in the Workplace Really Matter?

At the end of the day, many of us find release from the stress of workplace judgments as we chat to friends, eat with a partner, watch television, read or browse through magazines, shops, or the web. We seek reprieve from the daily grind of monitoring and adjusting judgments—others' as well as our own. It can be exhausting tracking these, questioning them, and refining them. In our private and comfortable social spaces, the judgment meter grows quiet, like a cat edging toward sleep. In this state, we may be hard pressed to list even a fraction of microjudgments that packed our day. We may shrug them off. After all, they are not part of who we really are, are they?

As powerful as the need for sex is the need to be positively engaged in one's community[59] and positively judged by others. Whether we get the praise we deserve in the workplace affects how healthy we are and how long we live. In fact, our sensitivity to others' judgments in the workplace became clear from studies done in the 1980s on the causes of heart disease among people in hierarchical organizations. At that time, it was thought that the pressure of being at the top of an organization was a special risk to health. The evidence, however, showed something very different.

Sir Michael Marmot, professor of epidemiology and public health at University College, London, led a study that looked at heart disease among British civil servants, as well as their overall health and longevity.[60] Marmot found that it was not the people at the pinnacle of an organization who suffered stress and subsequent ill health. These highfliers indeed carried the greatest burden of responsibility and had the greatest demands on their time; nevertheless, something seemed to protect them from stress-related illness. The workers sandwiched in the middle of an organization and those stuck at the bottom were most at risk.

The middle- and low-ranking civil servants felt more stress, Marmot discovered, because they had less power. The absence of power rather than the burden of power put their health at risk. Less power meant less status and less recognition and less credit for their hard work. The people at the top who had been thought at risk from excessive responsibilities actually benefitted from the power structure of praise and blame. Having more praise—in the form of respect and admiration relative to others—was a protection from illness.

Marmot was so struck by this surprising result that he set out to check these findings against a wide range of institutions and societies in different countries. He looked at data in the United States, Australia, Russia, Japan, and southern India. Again and again he found that once we are provided with the very basic needs of life, it is our place in the social hierarchy that most determines well-being. The higher our status, the more protected we are against illness; the lower our status, the greater our risk of illness and a shorter life.

Winning prizes, particularly those that attract wide public recognition, such as the Nobel Prize, has been found to add about four years to one's lifespan.[61] Low status, on the other hand, is, Marmot concluded, a "noxious element." It fills one's social environment with frustration, disappointment, and disregard and, possibly, generates the horns effect[62] whereby your low status overshadows any positive traits you may have and leads others to see everything about you in a negative light. These noxious elements are bad for one's health.

Other health hazards, such as smoking, drinking, or being sedentary or overweight arise within the unhealthy conditions of low status. Smoking, eating, and drinking offer comfort and may compensate us for the comfort we don't get from esteem or status. We may have little motivation to exercise, and little energy, when our mood is depressed by low status. Our daily experiences of praise and blame influence our behavior, for better or for worse. As Marmot discovered, "You are more likely to choose to smoke if you are low status than if you are high." [63]

The initial studies Marmot conducted were on men, where status was closely linked to the nature of their job. Subsequent research found that women were equally affected by status, though they interpreted status differently. Women were likely to focus on their general social standing; [64] their position at work and in the public world had less impact.

I believe that status for most people, men as well as women, is generally not about big things, nor is it granted once and forever like a medal. Status, or esteem, is the accumulated impact of small markers of praise and blame in our everyday lives: how we are greeted as we walk into work; how people talk to us; whether our ideas are heard at a meeting; whether, when we scan our social environment, we pick up cues that we are admired; whether, when we put in effort, our results are acknowledged and approved; whether, when we set our goals, we have a network of supporters who have high expectations of our success; and whether our judgments matter to others.

Status is often thought to come from wealth or title but it is really about relative praise[65] and whether we are given the benefit of doubt in others' judgments of us. People with high status are far more likely to have their efforts and achievements recognized. They have more opportunities to participate in their society and to gain further recognition. If they fail to shine, or even if they mess up, they may benefit from the halo effect, whereby what they do seems admirable, because people unconsciously alter their judgments according to the unacknowledged hypothesis that if you admire someone for one quality then his or her other qualities also seem admirable.[66] Perhaps we all need this crucial benefit of doubt, when our admirable qualities lift the shadow of our deficits.

Status, or relative esteem, is about money only when money becomes a symbol for praise.[67] The writer and philosopher Alain de Botton concludes that status is a proxy for the love that is steeped in praise. It provides assurance that we are valued members of a group and that the people on whom we depend delight in our existence. Our distress in low status, or disesteem, arises from the consequent vulnerability to being ignored or cast out, alone and in the wrong.[68]

Appropriate Praise and Blame Is Good for You, and the Organization

The Harvard psychologist George Valliant has spent five decades studying our long-term coping and thriving strategies. He believes that as important as it is for us to enjoy praise, it is also important for us to accept appropriate blame. Without the ability to tolerate blame, our judgment meter fails to function well. "No one," he observes, "is harder to reason with than the person who projects blame." [69]

Yet accepting blame is becoming increasingly rare in organizations.[70] Rosabeth Moss Kanter describes the damage to organizations that ensues as each employee blames the other rather than consider organizational change.[71] When the publicist is blamed for falling sales or when the accountant is blamed for deficits, then the entire organization is prevented from stepping back to take a fresh look at where problems might lie. Confronted with criticism and evidence of failure, partners, owners, and employees at all levels often use their ingenuity to deny or explain away evidence for decline and the necessity of change.[72]

Such dynamics occur even when the best minds are involved, even when the people concerned are those who would be predicted to be most respectful of actual evidence. The academic Edgar Schien said that acceptance of change occurs only when "survival anxiety" becomes greater than "learning anxiety."[73] How we—either as individuals or as part of an organization—respond to the threat of blame is key to survival, but no one should underestimate the potential for resistance to such learning, even when it seems in our best interests to do so.[74]

Surviving Praise and Blame in the Workplace

Learning how to survive in the workplace is only partly about excelling in the duties of the job itself. Survival depends on making sense of others' judgments, and finding ways to influence these or to avoid being demoralized by them. A common exercise run by executive coaches—those who train managers to get the most out of their team—focuses on accepting different personality types[75] with their accompanying different approaches to problems, to processing information, and to priorities. When Greg focuses on negative results and Ajit focuses on the positive ones, Greg says Ajit is in denial or deluded and Ajit feels that Greg refuses to acknowledge the firm's successes. When Michelle focuses on a statistical analysis of results over a ten-year period and Gavin goes with his gut, each thinks the other is blind or deluded. Instead, a leader is advised to make the best use of differences, to think about skill sets and complementary perspectives. This is intended to flex our responses and praise qualities that we might be inclined to blame. But this is just one of many tasks we need to address, for our judgment of coworkers goes far beyond our opinion of their actual work.[76]

Workplaces are as varied as individual families, but there are broad themes recognizable to anyone who works with other people, such as favoritism and scapegoating, spotlight grabbing and marginalization, inclusion and rejection. The judgments we experience in the workplace are informed by a range of unacknowledged biases: Who happens to find us attractive or appealing? Who happens to see similarities between the symmetry of our face and that of a despised cousin? Who finds our smile reassuring or commanding, because it is so like the one he remembers in his kind kindergarten teacher? Who finds our voice grating, and whose eyes dilate in admiration when we speak? Who admires our opinions of TV shows or books or politics, and who discounts our judgments? None of these characteristics has anything to do with how we do our job, but all are likely to have a great deal to do with whether we are praised or blamed for what we do.

WORKING well alongside others depends in large measure on how we read and respond to others. Our success also depends on our ability to monitor our own ordinary judgments, to know when to follow them and when to suspect them. Generally, we are much better at spotting the flaws and foibles of others' judgments than our own.[77] Asking ourselves whether we are being fair to others, what bias or blind spots distort our vision, and whether we are being as pig-headed as we think the people around us are involves humility and discipline. If we understand the workings of the judgmental human brain, ours will function better—both in the workplace and, as we see in the next chapter, in the particularly challenging realm of social media.

Social Media and the New Challenges to Our Judgment Meter

Low Information and Expert Judgments

IN MANY PROFESSIONS, it is necessary to evaluate people on the basis of very limited information. Police officers, customs officials, and lawyers are among those who frequently interact with people who lie, and their professional success depends on assessing character. Even so, the reliability of their judgments varies widely.[1]

Carolyn is a family lawyer who has to assess whether what someone is telling her—about assets, about children's needs, or about relationships—is true. She has to be alert to inconsistencies in self-praise and blame deflection: "I am not the kind of person to hit my wife," followed by "I only hit her once;" or "I don't have any funds my wife doesn't know about," and "There's only one private fund but that's for special expenses." She notes that game-changing information often slips out casually: "I've been totally in control of things lately, and only once in the past year did some coke." She knows that sincerity does not wipe out evidence: "I'm not the kind of person who leaves her child on its own!" a parent insists with heated self-righteousness to the neighbor who found the infant crying in an empty house.

After thirty years' experience, Carolyn prides herself on high-speed judgments. She acknowledges, though, that from time to time she believes someone who is lying or she distrusts someone who is being honest. These bad calls lead her to refine her observational skills even further. First she listens carefully to the voice: its steadiness, its timbre, and where in the body it sits. Does it come from deep within the chest, reverberating with personal feeling, or does it sit in the front of the mouth, which is more common when we are spinning a yarn? She also considers posture: does it express a willingness to connect; is it defensive, nervous, hostile, or overcontrolled? Then she notes eye movement. Carolyn challenges the common assumption that a steady and direct gaze is proof of truth telling. She believes that someone who looks directly into her eyes may be putting on a deliberate and false show of honesty. Instead, she looks for varied eye movement, and expects downward or sideways glances as a person reflects on the question and shapes genuine answers. Most important of all, she explains, is that she treats her judgments as probable rather than certain; she is always prepared to look at further evidence and revise her judgment.

Most of us assess people, initially, with only low-level information available to us. Our carefully evolved unconscious judgment meter rapidly processes a wealth of information from faces, voices, and body movements,[2] some of which is reliable, and some of which is not. Though we have seen how bias and defensiveness (such as threat-rigidity, or fear that we are being blamed) can impede reliable judgment, we generally accept that first impressions should be treated with caution and that we should be prepared to reassess when we know more. People, on the whole, are extraordinarily skilled at refining and flexing judgments in light of new evidence.

There is a new force in our environment, however, that is skewing our judgment meter. It increases the speed of our judgments but at the same time reduces reliability. It thrives on low-level information, makes good and complex information particularly difficult to process,[3] and diminishes the likelihood that we will gather new evidence. This new force is social media.

Social Media, Defective Judgments, and the New Adolescence

Facebook offers a sense of belonging and the opportunity to attract attention. It began in 2004 as a social networking site for one university, but now is open to anyone thirteen years or older.[4] Each month, 1.65 billion users are active on the site.[5] Users broadcast personal information, such as an engagement, a new job, a new partner. It allows us to keep abreast of friends' news without lengthy phone calls or letters. With social media, users can even show their friends what they are doing on holidays, at parties, on outings, by posting photos and videos on the site.

As compulsive communicators, we want to tell others what we are doing. We seek their attention and their approval.[6] Sensitive to this need, Facebook allows users to Like our posts and to post comments. As always, when judgments are solicited, there is the possibility of negative attention. There is no Dislike button on Facebook,[7] but users can signal disapproval with emojis and they can leave negative comments. For some users, failing to attract a high number of Likes is as disappointing as being shunned.[8]

Networking sites—Facebook, Instagram, Snapchat, and Twitter still lead in popularity though new sites gain hold month by month—have become part of many people's world, but they wield particular force in the lives of teens. These sites provide the blood supply of teens' social knowledge. Through these sites, teens can assure themselves that they are in the know or on point. Through these sites teens connect to their friends and enjoy the warmth of inclusion. Through these sites they also agitate other users' judgment meters, and from these today's teens feel they can never hide.

The Changing Judgment Meter

Nearly thirty years ago I conducted a study of teenage girls and their mothers.[9] Many of those teenage girls are now themselves mothers of teenagers, and I was able to contact fourteen of the thirty-six in my original study to explore how their perspective of adolescence had changed.

This was an exciting opportunity to return to the voices of those young girls who were struggling to wrest their own judgments from the powerful influences of parents and friends. I reread, along with these now midlife mothers, the full interview transcripts of the conversations we had had in the late 1980s,[10] when they were teens. As we then reflected on their past experiences, and their more recent experiences of mothering teens, each of the fourteen women emphasized the huge social and psychological shift brought about by social media. This, the mothers believed, presented new dangers of intrusive, distorting judgments.

Amy is now forty-three, and has a fourteen-year-old daughter, one year younger than Amy was at the time she participated in my original study. At the age of fifteen years, Amy had made a long list of what she saw as her physical defects: she thought her nose was "too thick," that her skin was "blotchy" and "doughy," and she suffered self-consciousness whenever she stood up or walked into a room: "I'm sort of standing in the thick of this thick body, and . . . the people watching me really make me sweat . . . I can't break through that awful cloud that just smothers me when I feel someone looking at me."[11] Amy gasps as I read these words, and comments, "That brings it back. Wow! What a thin skin I had. Is that normal? I guess that's just what Masha feels, for sure. But for me—well, I could then close the door to my room, and no one would be looking at me. I could escape. Masha can't, because, as she sees it, there's always social media. If she isn't on it, people she cares about are, and they are always judging her—her comments, her photos, her news. She's been having a rough time. Hearing you read out my own words, well, that's a real eye-opener, and my heart rushes out to my poor daughter."

When I speak to Masha, she explains what her mother meant by her having a rough time. Her friends are constant users of Instagram, which in many ways accentuates the most unsettling effects of Facebook. Users post images of themselves looking happy, looking interesting, and, Masha thinks, looking "really, really pretty and cool and everything a girl should be." She posted a photo of herself, one she had taken and chosen carefully after significant preparation and consultation with her friends. "I stared at it for so long it began to look weird. So I thought, Just do it. And right away I got a couple of really nice messages from my best friends, so I was in a good, happy place. But then these real nasties came out of nowhere." Masha's voice falters. She glances at her phone, then shudders, and hands her phone to me. "You read them," she says.

As I scroll through the comments, I find them dismissive rather than devastating: "How old is this chick? I can't tell if she's 10 or 35," and "Is that a wall on her head or *bangs*?" The worst was, "Even her shadow is ugly." These were mild compared to the cyberbullying that some teens experience, but reading negative comments about ourselves is never easy. In fact, the more negative the personal comments, the more likely we are to be obsessed by them[12]—even when we have no reason to value those judgments. As Masha says, these are from "people you don't know but who think they can trash you. And sometimes it's someone you do know, who thinks it's fun to be harsh."

When I first spoke to Ewan and Diana's mother, Linda,[13] she was thirteen years old. The teenage Linda had described a raw envy for the girl everyone would like, whom everyone would find pretty. Linda read out the words she spoke to me all those years ago and then read them again to Ewan and Diana. "I would love to make myself beautiful," she had said, "it would be like a base . . . something to feel sure about . . . I could go anywhere, do anything, and sort of feel safe." [14] The safety that Linda, at age thirteen years, imagined was that of approval and inclusion. Safety from negative judgment, from disapproval and exclusion, depended on her ability to attain an ideal beauty. But no one is safe from negative judgment and exposure to it is far greater online. Eighty-nine percent of teens between the ages of thirteen and seventeen years have been affected by messages that mock, demean, or intimidate them.[15] Of those teens, 54 percent feel angry, humiliated, and demotivated.[16]

For Linda's son Ewan, now thirteen, Facebook has become "a kind of nightmare." In response to his mother's, "Why don't you just ignore it? Just put it away," he explains "Ignoring what's going on is worse even than reading those messages calling me a 'sook' or 'lame dick' or any of the other things associated with the chess club. Or whatever else it is that people hate about me." His sister Diana, fifteen, insists that it cannot be as painful for her brother as it is for her: "I feel on such a high if I post a photo and get comments like 'Gorgeous' and 'Wow!' and 'Can I see more?' But it's like someone spitting straight at you, when you post something where you think you look really gorgeous and instead of Likes, you get smeared."

Diana continues to stare at her phone, scrolling through one of the sites. "You see all these perfect people on Facebook and Instagram," she says. "You see people who are famous— you know, with all these followers and stuff, and whatever they do is big news. Everything about them is kind of blessed. I have friends who are nearly Facebook famous. And you just want to put in your bid, you know, for success, and know that people think you're great." Ewan adds, "And you want to wash away the bad stuff. Or maybe just hang in there and answer back to all the bad stuff." Diana agrees that ignoring the sites is not an option. After all, "If you're not on social media, you don't exist." [17]

As I prepare to leave their family home, Linda hands me her phone, with an Instagram photo of her receiving a teaching award. As I offer my congratulations, she looks at her phone again and the pleasure drains from her face. "I'm a recent user of Instagram," she explains. "In fact, this is my first post." Linda pauses again, clearly reflecting on conversations with her teenage children. "I realize what they're up against. I started looking through Instagram, at all these happy photos, where everyone seemed to be gorgeous and interesting and thriving. Even people I know, like my cousins and their kids, seem enviable. I think, Here are all these people doing all these things. Am I doing enough? I get so . . . uneasy. Worse than that, to be honest. I felt small."

I am haunted by Linda's response. She has a distinguished career, with plenty of everyday praise, yet she feels diminished by the carefully composed praise-grabbing profiles of other social media users. Even the grown-ups, it seems, are daunted by the presentation of others' seemingly perfect lives.

Distorted Comparisons Distort Our Judgment Meter

As startled as I was by Linda's words, there is a lot of evidence showing that her response is common. Our internal judge is very sensitive to what psychologists call "social comparison." In the 1950s Leo Festinger realized that comparison was an important measure of self-appraisal.[18] We ask ourselves, How do I measure up to the people around me? and Looking at others, what should I expect of myself?

At a college reunion, I see some former classmates with the gloss of glamor and worldly success. Some work in the heart of government, some are forging ahead in the law courts, and in some an inner success shines through, though there may be no obvious acclaim behind it. As exciting as I find the high-fliers, as pleased as I am by the glowing signals of happiness and achievement, I feel something like Linda's unease at the polished medals, titles, and brand recognition. Such reunions are notoriously rife with the social comparison question, What happens to my esteem when I compare myself to others? At the end of the evening, we go our separate ways and pick up our ordinary lives, with those ups and downs that we often hide in social self-presentation. As our more concrete interests draw us in, the pressure of social comparison eases, and our sense of self stabilizes. But for those who spend time every day on social media, the aggravation of social comparison becomes a fixture in their daily life.

Every time we look on Facebook or Instagram or Snapchat—the three sites teens use most often[19]—we confront what seem like perfect faces, perfect lives. Intense users look at these sites several times each day.[20] They confront an apparent perfection linked not to reality but to highly selective user profiles. These would never stand up to face-to-face scrutiny. When we engage with people, when we exchange views and do things together—whether we are preparing a meal, deciding which film to see, or agreeing to edits of a team presentation—we learn far more about them than we possibly can learn from social media posts. Even casual interactions allow us to probe. We wonder, Are their ideas good? Do they listen? Are they fun? How deep are their passions? How original or fresh is their perspective? Our judgments are sometimes wrong, but when the information we have is corrupted by brevity, glamor, and pretense, then our judgments are not simply wrong, they are worthless.

Person to person, we catch the facial expressions as someone responds to us, the interest expressed with a dilated pupil, the disapproving or sympathetic intake of breath, the gentle or embarrassed laughter that expresses ease or discomfort with our presence. We get some sense of a person's subjective world, and we begin to assess that person within a living relationship, rather than through what Sherry Turkle calls the "bits and pieces" of some carefully presented, notional self[21] that would fragment under scrutiny. Social media users present themselves as they would like to be seen. It is as though their lives are airbrushed so that no rough edges, no imperfections, no self-doubt show through.

When we view others through that distorted, glamorizing lens, our own complex inner world feels deficient in comparison. This new judgment culture is succinctly described by the novelist Marian Keyes as the "relentless comparing of my insides with everyone else's outsides, and finding myself always coming up short."[22] Even when we can identify and articulate the underlying problem—the distortion in "comparing my insides with everyone else's outsides"—we may remain in its thrall. After all, the teens who as a group are most badly impacted by social media (though the impact is by no means restricted to teens) are able to articulate the problem. In Nancy Jo Sales's interviews with teenage girls, Sales heard Carrie reflect, "You assume so many things about people on social media without really knowing the truth, and it makes you think crazy things, based on the wrong information." Dara, also interviewed by Sales, says, "You compare yourself to them. It makes me more judgey, I guess."[23] Teens speak about having to "wake up and put on a mask and try to be someone else,"[24] but their awareness of the superficiality of social media based judgments does not diminish their power.

Judging other people—positively or negatively—is a basic

human activity but social media degrades it and turns it into an obsession. Positive feedback gives a momentary dopamine jolt, a rush of pleasure, as we bask in attention and praise.[25] This pleasure soon evaporates, though. Many users believe that having more followers, more Likes, more viewers is what they need. Eventually they find that more praise leaves them just as unsatisfied. Based on limited, contrived information about who we are, our dissatisfaction results not from insufficient praise but from its low quality.

Praise, Blame, and the Deficiencies of Social Media Judgments

One of the first studies establishing a link between internet use and self-dissatisfaction was published in 1998, before the rise of what became social media. Robert Kraut and his research team followed 169 people in 73 households during their first years online. Their resulting paper, entitled "Internet Paradox: A Social Technology that Reduces Social Involvement and Psychological Well-Being?"[26] showed that over that period, internet users' depression and loneliness increased. At that time, the internet was being used primarily for interpersonal communication, more like a telephone than a television. Nevertheless, instead of increasing social activity, internet use displaced it. People were becoming more isolated, but instead of remedying loneliness with face-to-face contact, they spent more time engaging in virtual contact. Subsequent research confirms a continuing link between high intensity Facebook use and unhappiness[27] and an unstable sense of self.[28] The problem, however, is only partly isolation; the greater problem is the distortion of judgment.

The judgment we crave—clear and focused approval and praise—is rarely available through social media. Praise has meaning within an active, responsive relationship. In face-to-face interactions, or even in phone conversations, we hear the microresponses in breath and voice; we get a full sense that someone is behind a judgment. When our photo or post gets lots of Likes, we feel a rush of pleasure only because we anticipate this interpersonal praise. In anticipation, the midbrain neurons release dopamine, a neurotransmitter of pleasure,[29] but expected satisfaction does not follow. If our focus remains on social media, we get into a cycle of anticipating pleasure, but getting no *satisfying* pleasure, and then seeking rewards through the same useless route.

Normally, when someone praises something I've done, I feel pleased that I have achieved something. I am also pleased and warmed by the approving relationship. I am pleased because I have made a positive impact on someone else's life. If I've merely posted a carefully posed photo, though, what significance does a fellow user's enthusiasm really have? Who is being admired? Why? Praise is powerful but it is also sensitive to what we value, what we think we deserve, and whose judgment we value.

When we see people constantly checking their social media sites, we often conclude they are addicted.[30] A more precise explanation is that they are driven by the hope of finding sat-

isfactory feedback. Social media can offer only a false promise: the more faceless the communication (such as texting and
instant messaging), the greater the dissatisfaction.[31] Regardless
of how many Likes we rack up on it, social media leaves our
thirst for praise unslaked.

Negativity Bias

Negative comments on social media have the same features
as positive ones. They are vague and diffuse and we rumi-
nate over unanswerable questions,[32] such as, Why are the
responses so negative? Why are people so disapproving of
me? or What has made them so angry? Ewan keeps checking his phone to make sense of the negative comments his
posts attract. He explains, "I want to understand what their
problem with me is." It might seem that bad experiences in
social media would deter someone from using it, but they
don't.[33] Instead we get hooked as we track what is said about
us, just as we do when gossip carries negative stories about
us or when someone insults us. It is very difficult, given our
obsession with judgment, to turn away, without argument,
redress, or retaliation, from negative judgments.

The power of nasty comments to hook our attention comes
from what is called the negativity bias.[34] Awareness of this
bias dates back to the 1930s and arose from a discovery by
Russian psychologist Bluma Zeigarnik. When Zeigarnik,
as a young student in Berlin, heard her professor comment
that waiters seemed to have a better memory for unpaid bills

than paid ones, she decided to explore this quirk of memory. By analyzing the content of dreams and of the unwelcome, distracting ruminations that can leave us so unsettled, she discovered that people are more likely to dream about, and brood upon, unfinished experiences.[35] A colleague of Zeigarnik, Maria Ovsiankina, further recognized that "unfinished business" generates persistent, intrusive thoughts. A very common theme in these unfinished experiences was negative judgments directed towards us.

Blame takes a long time for us to process—largely because it generates anxiety. When we cannot grasp what offense we have committed or what deficit we have revealed, we rehearse the insult over and over, trying to raze it. But often our brooding sharpens the negative thought and it becomes "a stone in one's shoe"—constantly irritating, constantly sore, impossible to ignore.

Throughout evolutionary history, any organism attuned to bad things would be more likely to survive. Evolutionary psychologists argue[36] that passing up positive outcomes may generate regret and lost opportunity, but these losses are not as terrible as ignoring danger. If one of my ancestors gave up the opportunity to engage with an interesting and intelligent group of early humans, then that would be sad. If early humans had ignored signs that a person was hostile, then they would not have passed on their genes to me. So, from an evolutionary perspective, the negativity bias is adaptive[37] but it wields a perverse power on social media, offering incentives to the perpetrators and stripping the victim of defense.

The Nasty Effect

"Can you kill yourself already?" an Ask.fr user demanded of sixteen-year-old Jessica Laney. Another user called her a "slut" and another a "fucking ass hoe."[38] As these negative comments escalated, they seemed to fill Jessica's entire world. She decided it was better to end her life than to endure the barrage of blame.

The tragic consequences of what is called cyberbullying are now widely recognized, and of great concern to parents, teachers, and legislators.[39] The perpetrators of these attacks, however, defy understanding. Do they begin the process with the intention of stirring trouble, or do they merely want to have their say? What relationship do their posted judgments have to their actual beliefs? Are they sick? Are they mean? Who are they?

People who attack others on social media often display empathy, self-control, and even tolerance in other contexts.[40] Their interpersonal behavior is sensitive and responsive, giving no sign that on social media they would become a bully.[41] They reveal a very different character on social media not because they normally hide a truly dark side, but because their judgment meter no longer registers their remarks as interpersonal behavior. Instead, they respond in a context in which both they and the people they address are no more than characters in a video game.[42]

Furthermore, the realm of social media thrives on quick, strong but shallow judgments—particularly negative ones.

Just as in our social lives reasoned and civil comments have far less impact than rude ones,[43] abusive comments attract more followers on social media. Outrage becomes a kind of entertainment wherein users compete for the stage. This competition—alongside the tendency for angry and negative views to be contagious—reinforces and escalates abuse. Furthermore, on social media, there is no immediate comeback of disapproval, so the bad behavior—and the dopamine jolt that accompanies it—get a free ride. The greater the personal insult, the more abusive the language, the more likely it is that others on the site will join the fray. This cycle of contagion is called "the nasty effect."[44]

The easy access users have to others' judgments can be thrilling—and as corrupting as power. The insults and abuse that are hurled are not seen as targeted at an actual person, who can be deeply hurt, whose relatives can be deeply hurt, and whose life can be overturned. After all, in this world, where users are reduced to profiles, where photos relay only bits and pieces of a person, indifference is more common than empathy. We do not see the unmistakable expressions of pain; there is no crack in the voice, no tearful eye or downturned mouth. There is no one to scoff at careless cruelty, no tensing around the eyes, no pull of muscle at the corner of a mouth to signal that this is unfair, that this is not going to end well. Then, when perverse approval for such abuse comes in the form of forwarded posts, additional followers, and like-minded comments, the nasty effect rather than good judgment is rewarded. Negative judgment spreads like an epidemic.

While it is often said that social media exposes us to a range of opinions, it is more likely to attract like-minded posts. This arises in part from our judgments about who is trustworthy and who is not: we tend to think that information and judgments from friends are more reliable than from people we do not know. When someone we like and admire expresses judgments different from our own, we are likely to engage with her perspective, if only to challenge it: "Why do you think that?" and "How can you be taken in by that politician?" But on social media, there is only a profile, only the comments, so no reason to engage with those whose views unsettle us.

In fact, users of social media sites are likely to unfollow or unfriend those whose judgments do not match theirs.[45] As we disregard comments that we disagree with, and read more posts that confirm our own, we may have the mistaken impression that what we are reading confirms of our own judgments. Moreover, the algorithms used by sites to catch a user's attention are derived from what he or she already looks at, thereby raising the probability that we will see judgments that are already aligned to ours.[46] The result is an echo chamber: one person voices an opinion and then others respond in agreement, just as, in an enclosed space, our own voice echoes back the very words we have spoken.[47] This echo effect reduces the impulse to question and reflect on judgments. It has been found to make us more rigid in our views and even more hostile to different views.[48] Hence we become not only more biased but also more indifferent to the damage wreaked by the nasty effect.

Careless Judgment

In 2012, Lindsey Stone's friend posted a photo on Facebook. In the photo Lindsey is crouched low, raucously shouting as she makes an obscene gesture. This would have seemed to be no more than a dumb photo[49] of a normally thoughtful woman, if it were not for the context. In this photo, Lindsey crouches next to the Tomb of the Unknown Solider in Arlington National Cemetery, where a sign reads "Silence and Respect."

At the time Lindsey posed for the photo, she and her friend saw themselves as having simple, silly fun, just as they did when they snapped themselves smoking in front of a No Smoking sign. The enticement to show off, the lure of positive feedback, and the lack of perspective are common on social media and are often referred to as the "online disinhibition effect."[50]

When we communicate through a digital device, we do not feel the complex presence of a human audience. Our mind seems to regress to a child's version of, "Look at me!" as we anticipate our follower's applause. Perhaps we feel a thrill of self-efficacy: "People are responding to my judgments!"[51] Perhaps we imagine the buzz of attracting new followers, who may be mistaken for admirers.[52] These incentives, along with the absence of real-person cues to remind us that there are other ways our behavior might be judged,[53] enclose us in a solipsistic bubble, far removed from critical reflection.

Lindsey Stone's post did not attract praise, after all. No one seemed to think she was cool to defy the sign. Initially, however, the blame was mild. A Facebook friend who had served in the military commented, "This is kind of offensive . . . it's tasteless."[54] For a few weeks, this photo remained just one of those silly, bad taste posts that social media attracts. Suddenly, however, the judgmental trend changed. Perhaps the outrage was fueled by the discrepancy between Stone's professional image—she held a job as a caregiver for vulnerable adults— for the comment "Fire Lindsey Stone" attracted 12,000 Likes. The negative judgments escalated with claims that she "hated the military" and was "a disgrace to America." It was those who flaunted their condemnation who attracted followers and admirers, while Lindsey's own life was transformed by the nasty effect.

There are many similar examples of particularly poor judgment from people whose judgment is ordinarily sound. Traveling to Africa on vacation, Justine Sacco posted tweets about "weird German dudes" and Africans with AIDS. At the time, Justine was a successful senior director of communications at a media and internet company. In her professional life she would have been quick to assess the associative power of a phrase, to avoid giving offense and to protect the esteem of both herself and her employer. However, in that enclosed infantile mindset so often generated by the eerie privacy of the digital device, her remarks seemed—to her, momentarily—cute, sassy, and even smart. Yet within hours, she was assaulted by tens of thousands of angry responses. "We are about to watch this . . . bitch get fired," an Instagram user gloated. Justine's career in public relations was over.[55]

These high-profile examples of poor judgment displayed on social media are not exceptions; they are symptoms of social media's power to corrupt judgment. In this impulsive, non-reflective process, judgment is prone to startling omissions. It fails to register context and perspective. The death of soldiers, their personal tragedies and professional sacrifices, are ignored. The simplicity and speed of messaging awakens stereotypes that would normally be avoided,[56] such as the careless association of Africans and AIDS, or being white with privileged protection. Just as a sightless bat finds its way around through subtle feedback effects, the resonance we feel in others' company refines and regulates our judgment meter. When there is only the digital device and unchallenged thoughts, when there is the power to proclaim judgment and no trigger for reflection, when the more extreme we are the more attention we get, the judgment meter becomes both hyperactive and dysfunctional.

Social Media Drains Empathy from Judgment

The overall effect of social media, originally promoted as a way of connecting to others, results in what Sherry Turkle calls "a crisis of empathy."[57] The remarkable human skill of mindsight, the ability to understand others and unite in tolerant communities, rests on our capacity for empathy. Yet recent studies[58] have found that nearly three-quarters of college students today appear, by the self-reported measures used in the study, to be less empathic than the average student was thirty years ago. The steepest drop occurred within the past ten years—the years in which social media grew. Empathy, as we see in the development of infants and young children, comes naturally to humans,[59] but can be suppressed when mindsight is compromised. Social media thins human dimensions. Other people become users or followers or virtual friends and leave empathy for an actual person out in the cold.

Another assault on judgment comes from the simplicity and consequent polarization of judgments on social media. This effect has been highlighted in interviews with people who promote extreme and offensive views. Jamie Bartlett, the director of the Center for the Analysis of Social Media, noted that trolling—generating vast waves of judgmental responses—adheres to a pattern. The brutal process begins when a message with highly negative content is posted and then attacked. In response to the attack, the negative judgment is repeated and also magnified. The terms of engagement are set: everyone who participates must judge whether he or she is for it or against it. Each iteration of judgment amplifies the extremes. The judgment becomes entrenched and simplified; compromise, conciliation, and reflection become increasingly irrelevant.

Bartlett describes the actions of Paul, who became an administrator of a Facebook group, as a typical case: "He started attacking Muslims on other Facebook pages, and they attacked him back, each side polarizing and radicalizing the other. Paul was living in an exciting Manichean world of friends and enemies, right and wrong—in which he was the chief protagonist."[60] The result is a fixed mindset in which people are either "them" or "us," and those in the "them" camp can be seen to suffer pain without triggering empathy.[61]

Distorted judgments based on "them" and "us," with bias toward the group we belong to and bias against other groups, extend far beyond social media, but no understanding of what social media does to our judgment is complete without understanding how quickly this mindset takes effect. The rapidly growing field of neuroscience provides crucial background to this process.

Brain activity is highly specialized across brain regions. Different regions are activated when we think about proto-emotions, such as pain and fear, on the one hand, and secondary emotions involving beliefs, needs, and context on the other. The pain matrix registers protoemotions such as anger, fear, joy, and sadness, and the mentalizing matrix registers the more complex secondary emotions[62] such as pride, longing, curiosity, doubt, and nervousness. Both brain networks are activated when we think about and make judgments of other people.

The first network registers others' pain and pleasure, using the same neural equipment with which we register our own pain.[63] When we see someone burn a hand, get hit by a car, or get stabbed, we really do "feel their pain:" the neural pain matrix of empathy looks very much like the neural activity registering our own pain. The intensity of the pain we witness also affects the neural activity: there is a high response when we witness someone being burned; there is more muted activity if we see someone stub her toe. The neural links between our own pain and the pain of others lay the groundwork of empathy. When empathy is switched on, we rush to offer aid, we make donations, we volunteer our services.

Empathy can trigger what Jonathan Haidt calls "the hive switch" that turns on group cooperation.[64] With the hive switch opened, other people are "like us," others' difficulties present us with a moral urgency, and we work to a common purpose, like bees belonging to the same hive. But the hive switch that generates group cooperation between *us* also generates intergroup competition and conflict, switching off empathy for *them*. When empathy is switched off because we see someone as belonging to an outside hive or group, it is possible to minimize or even enjoy their suffering.[65]

Empathy has two dimensions—that of pain and that of perspective. When we empathize we not only feel someone's pain, we also understand their thoughts, desires, and feelings. We understand the context in which they make choices and decisions. This is where a second neural network, the mentalizing matrix, comes in. The mentalizing matrix is activated when we wonder what someone else is thinking, when we consider how to explain someone's behavior, or when we predict what he or she might do.[66] But sometimes the mentalizing matrix breaks free of the pain matrix,[67] as a result of fear, or bias, or conflict, or extreme physical need. Sometimes this occurs because the "other" lacks the outline of a real person— as does a social media "user" or "follower." When this happens, we can imagine another's pain and shame, but feel either indifference or perhaps even *schadenfreude* —pleasure at the other user's pain. In this way, social media instigates a human crisis of judgment.

THE computer or tablet or phone screen is no substitute for a person's face with its multiple signals or for the voice with its varying emphasis and hesitation signaling that we are searching out the right word or phrase. Nor can those devices replace the activity of conversation in which ideas are collaborative, argument is welcomed and expected, and the sharing of different views is normal. These devices enforce rather than challenge stereotypes, drawing crude lines between fabricated divisions of "them" and "us," because they omit the rich contextual detail that fuels the far more subtle judgment meter that can be activated in our truly interpersonal lives.

9

Lifelong Judgments

THERE IS STRONG evidence that, overall, the human judgment meter has gained in empathy, nuance, and depth over the past millennia. The Princeton philosopher Peter Singer highlights the progress of our judgment meter across prehistory and history: at one time, empathic judgments were directed only at our nearest kin. Later, empathy came to include a wider community group, then expanded to the nation, and subsequently, expanded to the species.[1] What Singer calls "the expanding circle of empathy" has been powered through language, the exchange of ideas, and contact with diverse people.

The progress is uneven and often feels uncertain; it is beset by the same dips and slumps we see in a stock market index, but, like long term trends in a stock market, the rise is real. The cognitive scientist Steven Pinker presents compelling evidence that across millennia, violence—including murder, military conflict, genocide, torture, and child abuse—has decreased.[2] Of course judgment continues to be challenged by fear and by partisan biases, but over time, in aggregate, our behavior, our tolerance and our use of reason have improved as a result of "the better angels of our nature"—empathy, self-control, moral sense, and reason. These "better angels" gain in strength through the very activities that are driven by, and serve, our judgment meter. Because we are social beings, we are eager to elicit others' judgments, against which we test our own. Because we have an innate drive towards adventure, we come into contact with diverse people, and their diverse judgments. Because we have the capacity to reason, we may eventually revise and refine those judgments.[3]

It is the deeply personal history of our judgment meter, however, rather than the broad history of human judgment, that has been the focus of this book. A child's need to please the people she loves underpins a lifelong engagement with others' judgments. Starting in infancy, these are not infantile concerns, but symptoms of the stake we have as social beings highly invested in others' praise and blame. We constantly monitor others' responses to us. Several times each day, we are likely to ponder: Is she offended by what I just said? Have I just disappointed my father? What have I done to make my partner so angry? Why does my friend think I have betrayed her? Does my colleague now think I'm incompetent? Is her disapproval momentary or has there been a real shift in her perspective? Have I lost or gained esteem in their eyes? Is my position within this relationship still comfortable and still secure?

However secure our attachments, praise or blame from those we love remains a matter of profound interest. We care not only about the strength of the bonds between us, we also care whether they offer comfort and warmth and whether the space between us is filled with approval or disapproval.

Balancing others' judgments with respect for our own poses one of the most important challenges throughout our lives. To a very young child, stepping outside the warm circle of a parent's praise or being indifferent to a parent's blame is unthinkable. One might as well seek expulsion and the terrors of a wilderness.

The upheavals of adolescence are driven by the work teens do to distinguish their own judgments from those of their parents. At the same time, they fight to gain parents' admiration for their newly emerging self, just as they did in infancy. Those typical teen-parent arguments are not only with the parent in the room but also with the parent in the teen's head, the accrued memories of childhood praise and blame, and the persistent engagement with a parent's judgment. Teens turn to friends, who help them disentangle their own judgments, bit by bit, from those of their parents; in the process, however, a teen's judgments can become newly entangled with peer judgments. This marks the lifelong work we do in distinguishing between the influences that expand and validate our own judgments and those that silence, limit, or distort them.

As fundamental to human development as the urge to walk and talk is the quest to form and justify judgments of one's own. To this end we push ourselves outside our comfort zone; we engage in critical self-appraisal; we observe others and probe their judgments.

Throughout each day, our minds actively monitor our judgment meter. "Am I being fair?" and "Does she have any basis for her gripe against me?" and "How would my friend/partner/parent see this?" When we feel the barb of another's blame, we spring to our own defense, but doubts linger, stirring reflection: "Is this my fault?" and "Was I careless or thoughtless?" Through conversations, through reading, through debate, and through private reflection, we demonstrate our compulsion to be better at forming judgments.

Day in and day out, most people continue to test their judgments as they talk to a partner, gossip with a friend, read a book, listen to the news, or review the day's interactions when they prepare for bed. The efforts to hone and check our judgments are as much a part of our psychology as are the biases that arise from self-protection.

The basic human eagerness to test and refine judgments can be seen all around us. It emerges in the popularity of public debate. Intellectual arguments that challenge our judgments can be thrilling. They provide the buzz of healthy exercise as we practice defending and justifying our judgments, or enjoy the satisfaction of correcting them. In politics and public policy and morality and religion, debates spur us to identify and articulate our judgments, to explore the intricacies of praise and blame, parsing which belongs to whom, and why. Sometimes we enjoy simply observing debates, safe from the cut and thrust of attack and defense.

The urge to broaden our views is also demonstrated in the love of storytelling. We are, as the novelist Ian McEwan notes, "literary animals," relishing tales that involve key questions of who should be trusted and praised, who should be condemned, how we should treat those of whom we disapprove, and how we would deal with others' blame and our own injured pride.[4] Stories present imagined experiences that provide exercise for our judgment meter.[5]

The great novels satisfy us with narratives about small weaknesses in judgment as well as large moral failures;[6] they draw us in to the comedy of self-serving bias and the pathos of narrow-mindedness. The enduring popularity of many novels rests on the prominence of judgment as a driving force in the story of relationships. Jane Austen's *Pride and Prejudice* shows strong and vibrant characters mistakenly believing that their intelligence protects them from poor judgment; they then gossip with people who share their biases and they discount evidence that challenges their opinions. As they confront their pride and their prejudice, they are humbled, even shamed by the vulnerability of their judgment; but these hard lessons are essential for any story about intimate relationships to end well. As readers, we can learn about vulnerabilities in the human judgment meter without ourselves suffering shame, and we can be reminded that we sometimes fail to hear the deeper echoes within our own judgment meter.

The enduring popularity of theater arises from our eagerness to observe human predicaments, choices, and crises, to condense time so that the consequences of good and bad judgments are played out in a few hours. Drama, as we know it, begins with the conundrum of blame and praise, beginning with Sophocles' plays about family feuds. The medieval mystery plays offer a template for moving from blame (and sin) to praise (and acceptance). The special and privileged perspective of the audience, where we enjoy a surrogate experience, expands our perspective.

The power of praise, blame, and shame, the life-changing impact of others' judgment of us and ours of them are staple themes in the films and TV dramas we consume on a daily basis. These are filled with crises of embarrassment, humiliation, blame (both fair and unfair), bias, conflict and self discovery. Sometimes the plots and characters are easy on a lazy mind and endorse simplistic judgments, but people return again and again to those stories that have a wider resonance. Storytelling can push us beyond the boundaries of our own experience, either by presenting us with new, exotic possibilities or by prompting, through delicate and detailed observation, a finer vision than we might achieve unaided. Whether the stories are based on biography and history, or whether they are fictional, they offer new frames of reference for our evaluative emotions, since any really satisfying story contains surprising and satisfying nuances.

Finely judged detail, context, characterization, and narrative then become part of our register of responses. Stereotypes, whether directed toward others or ourselves, can be painstakingly dismantled with additional, high-quality information. In a powerful and intelligent narrative, characters that start off as blameworthy may morph into a praiseworthy character— or vice versa. We explore the inner lives of people we initially view as different and discover they are just like us.[7] The universal appeal of these mind-expanding and time-consuming activities indicates that they serve a highly useful purpose.

Alongside our judgments of others and our engagement with others' judgment of us is profound concern about how we judge ourselves. The need to think well of oneself is a powerful motivator, both for everyday behavior and long-term goals. The hidden economy of esteem that guides us the way the Gulf Stream drives the weather[8] is only in part a need to have esteem in others' eyes. Without a positive self-appraisal, we cannot feel comfortable in our own skin. Often we turn to a higher judge and submit to the terror of being "weighed found wanting,"[9] along with the hope that what makes us blameworthy will be washed away, allowing us to return to a state of praise.

Each turning point in our lives presents opportunities to look anew at our judgments. When we become parents, we look back to our child and adolescent judgments of our own parents. Sometimes we think, How could I ever have blamed my parents for being overprotective? Now I understand how they felt, because I know what I feel toward my own child. When we make a mistake, we may think, Why was I so intolerant of others, and so eager to shame them? Did I not realize how a good person could sometimes behave badly? When we suffer misfortune, we may realize that we blamed people who needed help as we need it now, and wonder why we were so sure they deserved blame.

Midlife presents new opportunities to look back with a

broader perspective over one's own judgments.[10] What is sometimes described as midlife crisis is a new, forceful confrontation with the over-eye that embodies others' views but obscures our own deeper judgment. Changing habits, seeking adventure, acting out of character arise from eagerness to escape other people's judgments. We wonder: Did I pursue this career, remain in this job, or accept this partner because I was seeking approval and avoiding disapproval from others? Have I been fair as I measure the force of my own judgments against those of others?

Our judgments include moral judgments, but they extend well beyond these. Some philosophers relegate these wider judgments to mere preferences [11] because they are personal and not always underpinned with universal principles. But when we praise and blame, we engage with profound beliefs and deep-seated emotions. These root us and guide us. Our judgment meter—our compulsion to judge others and to defend and disseminate our own judgments—is part of a vast machinery of judgment[12] that shapes the landscape of our interpersonal lives.

Our judgments have a history reaching back to early love, need, and fear. As they become more our own, our judgments offer insight into what it means *to us* to live well, to achieve, and to find meaning. They are key to our identity.

In fact, our judgments are more integral to who we are than our memories. It is widely recognized that brain damage can change one's personality: those who suffer dementia, for example, are sometimes perceived as no longer being the same person. The perception of whether or not someone is the "same person," though, depends far more on those responses and preferences and interactions shaped by judgment than on retention of their memory.[13] This may well be the one trait that is most closely linked to a person's success as a parent, friend, partner or colleague, or citizen, and yet the importance of that element—the judgment meter—has generally been seen as something we should suppress.

What if we could suppress it? What if we did not praise or blame, criticize or collude, or form alliances on the basis of shared judgments? Would human life be better if lived within a state of nonjudgment?

There is something very appealing about release from our constantly running judgment meter. As with everything that tasks our brain or our body, we benefit from periods of reprieve. Exercise and relaxation, enjoyment of films, friends, food, and art provide some of those spaces in which our judgments can feel safe, unchallenged, and unproblematic. Some common evasion techniques, such as drinking or binge watching and game playing, have less of an upside. There are also more sophisticated, formal techniques such as meditation and mindfulness.

Mindfulness is drawn from ancient practices of Buddhist meditation, which, since the 1970s, have been developed as secular techniques where we note our thoughts and feelings but strip away our judgments. In practicing mindfulness, many people find reprieve from the push and pull of everyday judgments. They become less reactive and defensive, and better managers of the strong emotions associated with their own feelings, both positive and negative. As a result, they feel more relaxed, more at peace; self-doubt, self-questioning, the whip of angry condemnation, and the wear and tear of self-righteousness subside. Many are capable of improved concentration.[14] In some cases it even seems to reduce chronic pain.[15]

These experiences are supported by brain imaging studies that show meditation can change brain activity; meditation appears to reduce, for a time, activity in the fear and pain centers of the brain.[16] Even so, mindfulness also poses significant risks, and these risks are often ignored.

Mindfulness, because it encourages a nonjudgmental and accepting approach to all our thoughts, means that some of our positive responses fall by the wayside along with the negative ones.[17] In shedding all judgment we deprive ourselves of much delight, joy, and motivation.

Mindfulness suspends our critical appraisal of thoughts, beliefs, and memories, and without this, psychologists have found, we are more susceptible to others' suggestions, even to the extent of adopting false memories.[18] One function of our judgment meter is to register a positive or negative opinion. But our judgment meter also assesses these initial responses. When we switch off judgment, we also switch off higher levels of assessment and discrimination.

Meditation techniques—including mindfulness—offer a place of mental rest and refreshment, but as a way of life they involve a profound disengagement from personal passions.[19] Further, because our emotions and their judgments, both of ourselves and others, are so essential to who we are, some people who practice mindfulness feel their identity fragment-ing, and consequently suffer greater anxiety and confusion as they try to navigate their lives.[20]

Judgments, I believe, are crucial to our dynamic and pas-sionate relationships. Hence, I emphasize the importance of understanding them and reflecting on them, rather than sup-pressing them, even though they will never be problem-free.

In observing how much energy and time and emotion goes into our judgments, in realizing that most people, generally, want to achieve fairness and balance in their judgments, we also see how vulnerable our judgments are to bias and simpli-fication. So how can we support our ongoing efforts to avoid the pitfalls of poor judgment while trusting the depth of our highly personal judgments?

First, we need to be motivated to explore and challenge our judgments. Motivation is often built on self-acceptance: when we accept that we are judgmental beings, that our judg-ment meter is essential to our lives as social humans, there will be less anxiety around noting and acknowledging our judg-ments. Common phrases such as "I'm not judging you," will be exposed as confused or disingenuous. Instead, the questions will arise, "What are my judgments?" and "Are they fair?"

This step will lead to the next one: identifying our judg-ments puts pressure on us to be open to fact checks: do my judgments about this person or about myself actually fit the facts as I know them, or am I making assumptions and fol-lowing response patterns that are outdated or inappropriate? Naming our judgments—or just catching sight of the role they play in our relationships—can help us separate the wheat from the chaff.

From the very beginning of psychology as a therapeutic "talking cure,"[21] naming our thoughts and feelings has been shown to relieve counterproductive responses. Now called "affect labeling," this naming of the emotional content of our thoughts can be seen to reduce activity in the amygdala (where anxiety and fear, and hence defensiveness, are triggered) and to strengthen frontal lobe response (involving reflection and impulse control).[22] In identifying the emotional force of common defenses and biases, both those that protect our esteem and those that diminish the esteem of others, we gain the tools to assess them.

Finally, we can focus on the impact our judgments have on our own lives through a series of reflective questions:

DO MY JUDGMENTS WORK FOR ME OR AGAINST ME? That is, Do I admire people who satisfy my needs, desires, values, and interests? Or do I approach and attach myself to people who lead me down dark alleyways and dead ends, where I invest a great deal of emotional energy without yielding satisfaction, pleasure, or meaning?

ARE MY JUDGMENTS FLEXIBLE AND RESPONSIVE? Do I absorb new information about people? As I reevaluate my views about others, do my emotions vacillate wildly or can I respond negatively to some aspects of a person without derailing the attachments and positions in which I am emotionally invested? Is there an adaptive balance between emotional stability and emotional rigidity, so that I can be loyal without being in denial? When my judgments are negative, are they nonetheless receptive to critical revision?

ARE MY JUDGMENTS SIMPLISTIC REFLECTIONS OF MY OWN INTERESTS? Do I distinguish between the magnitude of a fault and its impact on me? For example, am I able to see that a mistake that causes me great inconvenience or offense may arise from an inconsequential error on another's part?

AM I WILLING TO ENGAGE WITH OTHER PEOPLE'S JUDGMENTS? If I do so, am I willing to flex my own views?[23] Can I catch the working of an inner resistance when I look at evidence for a position I do not hold, or evidence presented by someone I dislike? Can I challenge this resistance, keep it in check, and follow the evidence in front of me? Can I hold in mind that a very different perspective might be justified?

AM I ABLE TO CATCH MYSELF MAKING UNWARRANTED ASSUMPTIONS ABOUT SOMEONE BASED ON HIS OR HER APPEARANCE, RELIGION, ETHNICITY, GENDER, OR POLITICAL AFFILIATION? Nothing flags vulnerability to this bias as clearly as a comfortable assurance that you are free of bias. Many of our responses contain unconscious associations. Some of these guide us to our deep values and we can use them as a compass, directing us to fulfillment. Other unconscious associations, however, result in responses that are unfair to others, and to ourselves. Acknowledging them and testing them must be a daily effort. This work should feel positive—because the judgment meter's vulnerabilities should not make us distrustful of all our responses.

CAN I TRUST MY JUDGMENTS EVEN WHEN THEY ARE STEEPED IN EMOTION? This is a crucial question that cannot be answered once and for all; it is a question we need to hold in our thoughts as we exercise our judgment meter, every day. It involves drawing on our abilities to distinguish emotions that illuminate from emotions that warp our environment.

FROM birth we are primed to scan and judge everything we encounter. From birth we experience others' judgments of us, as well as of the world we share. How we navigate the praise and blame that we receive every day, and that we ourselves constantly apportion to others, will shape our identity, behavior and relationships. These judgments stem from our profoundly individual interests and desires. A primary and lifelong task for each of us is to listen and learn from our judgment meter, while also challenging and being willing to revise it. Constant testing and refinement of our judgments can be exhausting and humbling, but it is also rewarding and exciting, and the best way of living well among the people we love, the people we need, and the people with whom we share our world.

ACKNOWLEDGMENTS

MUCH OF THE research here has been gathered over decades. Research support from Clare Hall, Cambridge, was essential to my work on teenagers and parents, and on midlife transition patterns. Newnham College, Cambridge, offered research support for additional work on teens and parents, on siblings, and on family systems more generally. The Leverhulme Trust supported my research on couples with the generous award of a Leverhulme Emeritus Fellowship. This funded visits to the Gottman Institute with its wealth of research data and analytical tools. Research like this is possible only with astounding cooperation from participants, and I remain forever in their debt. Their loyalty, patience, and persistent focus have been immensely rewarding and constantly serve as a reminder of the importance of doing justice to their input.

Many colleagues have contributed in various ways: Ruthellen Josselson not only participated but also guided our explorations of the pleasures and perils of friendships; Carol Gilligan's influence has come in many ways—through the illuminating power of her work as well as through her lightning-quick engagement with my own efforts to nudge psychology into a shape we can all recognize. James Gilligan's work on shame, and the need for daily reinforcements of praise, has provided a crucial foundation for this book. Janet Reibstein provided key contributions to my thinking about couples in general, and her research articles were enormously helpful in my understanding of the impact of marital disruption. Rae Langton provided a sounding board for some of the philosophical concepts I draw on; and philosopher Robin Zhang directed me to material that illuminates philosophy's burgeoning interest in judgments that extend beyond a strictly moral sphere. The proactive interest from W. W. Norton, both the London and New York teams, provided a tentative idea with the encouragement needed to grow into a book. Finally, this book would have neither life nor shape without the enthusiasm and guidance of my editor at Norton, Jill Bialosky. From conception to completion she has engaged with the ideas and supported their expression.

NOTES

Introduction

1. John Bargh, "First Second: The Preconscious in Social Interactions," *Unconscious Opinion*. Presented at the meeting of the American Psychological Society, Washington, DC, June 1994.
2. Richard J. Davidson and Sharon Begley, *The Emotional Life of Your Brain: How Its Unique Patterns Affect the Way You Think, Feel, and Live—and How You Can Change Them* (New York: Plume, 2012), 39.
3. Shelly L. Gable, Harry T. Reis, and Andrew J. Elliot, "Evidence for Bivariate Systems: An Empirical Test of Appetition and Aversion Across Domains," *Journal of Research in Personality* 37, no. 5 (2003): 349–72; Shelly L. Gable and Amy Strachman, "Approaching Social Rewards and Avoiding Social Punishments: Appetitive and Aversive Social Motivation," in *Handbook of Motivation Science*, ed. James Y. Shah and Wendi L. Gardner (New York: Guilford Press, 2008), 561–75; Charles S. Carver and Michael F. Scheier, "Feedback Processes in the Simultaneous Regulation of Action and Affect," in *Handbook of Motivation Science*, ed. James Y. Shah and Wendi L. Gardner (New York: Guildford Press, 2008), 308–24; Ronnie Janoff-Bulman, Sana Sheikh, and Sebastian Hepp, "Proscriptive Versus Prescriptive Morality: Two Faces of Moral Regulation," *Journal of Personality and Social Psychology* 98, no. 3 (2009): 521–37.
4. This particular study at the Elizabeth Garrett Anderson Hospital in London was never published, but it was among many studies on the timing and nature of what then was called "bonding."
5. Terri Apter, *The Confident Child* (New York: W. W. Norton, 2006).

6. Apter, *Confident Child*, 102–4.

7. Terri Apter, *Altered Loves: Mothers and Daughters During Adolescence* (New York: Ballantine, 1991); Terri Apter, *You Don't Really Know Me: Why Mothers and Teenage Daughters Fight, and How Both Can Win* (New York: W. W. Norton, 2004).

8. For example, Apter, *You Don't Really Know Me*, 66–73.

9. Apter, *Confident Child*; Apter, *You Don't Really Know Me*; Terri Apter, *Difficult Mothers: Understanding and Overcoming Their Power* (New York: W. W. Norton, 2012); Terri Apter and Ruthellen Josselson, *Best Friends: The Pleasure and Peril of Girls' and Women's Friendships* (New York: Crown, 1998).

10. Terri Apter, *Secret Paths: Women in the New Midlife* (New York: W. W. Norton, 1995).

11. These extensive sources will be cited in the endnotes throughout the chapters, but in particular I draw on the work of Peter Fonagy, James Gilligan, Robin Dunbar, Bruce Hood and Martha Nussbaum.

12. Robin Dunbar, "The Social Brain Hypothesis," *Evolutionary Anthropology* 6, no. 5 (1998), 178.

13. Bruce Hood, *The Self Illusion: Why There Is No "You" Inside Your Head* (London: Constable, 2012).

14. S.R. Ott and S.M. Rogers, "Gregarious Desert Locusts Have Substantially Larger Brains with Altered Proportions Compared with the Solitary Phase," *Proceedings of the Royal Society, B*, 277 (2010): 3087–96.

15. Every brain cell has dendrites, or branches, that reach out to other brain cells, forging connections between them. These connections, called synapses, carry electrical signals from brain cell to brain cell. When these synapses are stimulated over and over in the same way, pathways are formed that allow signals to be transmitted quickly and efficiently. These well-established patterns of neural connections are sometimes referred to as "hard-wiring" in the brain. The term "hard-wired" is often misused to suggest that some pathways are innate but even apparently permanent pathways are learned. For a concise account see Elaine Shiver, "Brain Development and Mastery of Language in the Early Childhood Years," Intercultural Development Research Association, http://www.idra.org/resource-center/brain-development-and-mastery-of-language-in-the-early-childhood-years/.

16. Robin Dunbar and Susanne Shultz, "Evolution in the Social Brain," *Science* 317, no. 5843 (2007): 1344–47.

17. Michael Marmot, *The Status Syndrome: How Social Standing Affects Our Health and Longevity* (New York: Holt Reinhart, 2005).

Chapter 1. The Beginnings of Human Judgment

1. Dan Siegel introduced the term *mindsight* to popular psychology. See Dan Siegal, *The New Science of Personal Transformation* (New York: Bantam, 2010). However, the substance of mindsight—the process of reflecting on our own internal world and understanding others in light of their internal worlds—is referred to as *mentalizing*, a concept developed in large part by Peter Fonagy. See Peter Fonagy et al., *Affect Regulation, Mentalization, and the Development of the Self* (London: Karnac Books, 2003).

2. We need to see other people as "intentional agents." See, for example, Michael Tomasello, "The Human Adaptation for Culture," *Annual Review of Anthropology* 28 (1999): 509–29; and Bruce Hood, *The Domesticated Brain* (Gretna, LA: Pelican, 2014).

3. William James, Chapter X ("The Consciousness of Self"), in *The Principles of Psychology* (New York: Holt, 1890), 291–401. James' actual quote reads, "I would not be *extant* today."

4. Carla Shatz, "MHC Class I: An Unexpected Role in Neuronal Plasticity," *Neuron* 64, no.1 (2009): 40–45. See also Anita Hendrickson, "Development of Retinal Layers in Prenatal Human Retina," *American Journal of Ophthalmology* 161 (2016): 29–35.

5. Teresa Ferroni et al., "Eye Contact Detection in Humans from Birth," *Proceedings of the National Academy of Sciences* 99 (2002): 9602–5.

6. Babies also show physical responsiveness to singing: memories of songs sung in early childhood remain with us throughout our lives and retain rich profound comfort of human connection. See Jayne M. Standley and Clifford K. Madsen, "Comparison of Infant Preferences and Responses to Auditory Stimuli: Music, Mother, and Other Female Voice," *Journal of Music Therapy* 27, no. 2 (1990): 54–97; and Eugenia Costa-Giomi, "Infants' Preferential Attention to Sung and Spoken Stimuli," *Journal of Research in Music Education* 63, no. 2 (2014): 188–94.

7. Dan Stern, *The Present Moment* (New York: W. W. Norton, 2004), 107.

8. Donald Winnicott introduced the term "good enough mother" to counter the notion of "perfect" mother while noting the importance

an ordinarily devoted mother has in the development of a child. Donald Winnicott, *The Child, the Family and the Outside World* (London: Penguin, 1964), 17, 44. Subsequent research by Ed Tronick shows that healthy development is likely when a parent is attuned to her infant's cues 30 percent of the time. Ed Tronick, *The Neurobehavioral and Social-Emotional Development of Infants and Children* (New York: W. W. Norton, 2007), 20.

9. Sylvia M. J. Hains and Darwin W. Muir, "Effects of Stimulus Contingency in Infant-Adult Interactions," *Infant Behavior and Development* 19 (1996): 49–61.

10. Alison Gopnik, Andrew Meltzoff, and Patricia Kuhl, *How Babies Think: the Science of Childhood* (London: Weidenfeld and Nicolson, 2001).

11. Susan T. Fiske, Amy J.C. Cuddy, and Peter Glick, "Universal Dimensions of Social Cognition: Warmth and Competence," *Trends in Cognitive Sciences* 11 (2007): 77–83.

12. Amanda L. Woodward, "Infants Selectively Encode the Goal Object of an Actor's Reach," *Cognition* 69 (1998): 1–34.

13. Christian Keysers, *The Empathic Brain* (Los Gatos, CA: Smashwords, 2011).

14. Keysers, *The Empathic Brain.*

15. As with vision, some people have better mindsight than others. Some people are mindblind, and do not naturally or easily grasp meanings and intentions through the face, voice, or body movements. This condition is known as Asperger's syndrome.

16. Charles Darwin, Chapter 13 ("Self-Attention-Shame-Shyness-Modesty: Blushing"), in *The Expression of the Emotions in Man and Animals* (London: John Murray, 1872), 325. However, the psychologist Dacher Keltner sees roots of the kind of embarrassment revealed by human blushing in other primates. After a fight, they may show embarrassment by looking away, lowering their head, and hunching or curling inward to appear smaller; this, Keltner argues, shows deference to the other's approval. See Dacher Keltner, *Born to be Good* (New York: W. W. Norton, 2009), 76–97.

17. Darwin, *The Expression of the Emotions.*

18. Keltner, *Born to Be Good.*

19. This marks the "Duchenne" smile identified by Paul Ekman. See Paul Ekman, *What the Face Reveals* (New York: Oxford University Press, 1998).

20. Hood, *The Domesticated Brain*, 272.

21. An exception would be a child who has given up hope that others will take notice of her. See John Bowlby, *Attachment and Loss,* vol. 1, *Attachment,* 2nd ed. (New York: Basic Books, 1983).

22. György Gergely, Katalin Egyed, and Ildikó Király, "On Pedagogy," *Developmental Science* 10 (2007): 139–46.

23. Bruce Hood, Doug Willen, and Jon Driver, "An Eye's Direction Detector Triggers Shifts of Visual Attention in Human Infants," *Psychological Science* 9 (1998): 53–56.

24. John H. Flavell, Susan G. Shipstead, and Karen Croft, "What Young Children Think You See When Their Eyes Are Closed," *Cognition* 8 (1980): 369–87.

25. James Russell, Brioney Gee, and Christina Bullard, "Why Do Young Children Hide by Closing Their Eyes? Self-Visibility and the Developing Concept of the Self," *Journal of Cognition and Development.*13, no. 4 (2012): 550–76. Other research shows, more broadly, children until the age of (at least) four years believe that seeing someone, or knowing someone is there, depends on being able to see the communication "flows" both ways. See Henrike Moll and Allie Khalulyan, " 'Not See, Not Hear, Not Speak': Preschoolers Think They Cannot Perceive or Address Others Without Reciprocity," *Journal of Cognition and Development* 18, no. 1 (2017): 152–62.

26. Michael von Grünau and Christina Anston, "The Detection of Gaze Direction: A Stare-in-the-Crowd Effect," *Perception* 24 (1995): 1296–1313.

27. Reginald Adam et al., "Effects of Gaze on Amygdala Sensitivity to Anger and Fear Faces," *Science* 300 (2003): 1536.

28. Sight is not the only way to exchange attention, mutually. A child who is blind from birth develops her or his sense of self and others' minds through touch: skin to skin, even in the form of holding someone's hand, provides immediate access to mutual presence, recognition and responsiveness. But for most children, mutual seeing is primary to a person's presence or absence.

29. Anthony DeCasper and William Fifer, "Of Human Bonding: Newborns Prefer their Mothers' Voices," *Science* 208, no. 4448 (1980): 1174–76. See also John Gottman and Julie Schwartz Gottman, *And Baby Makes Three* (New York: Crown, 2007), 31.

30. It has been commonly assumed in the past that people deprived of one sensory input learn to pay more attention to cues from their functioning senses. For example, blind people are more alert to auditory cues, and

deaf people are more alert to vision and touch. However, the compensatory work is now seen to be even more remarkable: the brain changes according to available experience and actually reorganizes itself in ways that heighten other senses. This adaptation is known as cross-modal plasticity—a type of neuroplasticity that often occurs in the wake of brain damage. See Cristina Kairns, Mark Dow, and Helen Neville, "Altered Cross-Modal Processing in the Primary Auditory Cortex of Congenitally Deaf Adults: A Visual-Somatosensory fMRI Study with the Double-Flash Illusion," *Journal of Neuroscience* 32, no. 28 (2012): 9626–38.

31. Philip Lieberman, *Eve Spoke: Human Language and Human Evolution* (New York: W. W. Norton, 1998).

32. Great strides have been made over the past three decades in animal communication. Identifying the meaning of sounds of other species is extraordinarily difficult, but it is clear that dolphins, for example, understand some elements of human language and have an intricate language of their own, a language that involves both aural and visual cues. See John Stuart Reid and Jack Kassewitz, *Conversations with Dolphins* (Los Angeles, CA: Story Merchant Books, 2013). See also Hal Hodson, "Decoding Dolphins: Dolphin Whistle Translated Instantly by Computer," *New Scientist,* March 29, 2014, http://www.newscientist.com/article/mg22129624.300-dolphin-whistle-instantly-translated-by-computer.html#.VVR6MNjbKcM.

33. Alice Graham, Philip Fisher, and Jennifer Pfeifer, "What Sleeping Babies Hear: a Functional MRI Study of Interparental Conflict and Infants' Emotion Processing," *Psychological Science* 24 (2013): 782–89.

34. However, babies processed the emotional tones in different ways. The babies who had been exposed to more arguments in their home showed greater alarm to anger than did those babies who had little experience of angry voices. See Graham, Fisher, and Pfeifer, "What Sleeping Babies Hear," 782–79.

35. Lawrence Kohlberg, *Essays on Moral Development,* vol. 2, *The Psychology of Moral Development: The Nature and Validity of Moral Stages* (New York: Harper & Row, 1984).

36. Richard Appignanesi, ed., *Introducing Melanie Klein* (Cambridge: Cambridge University Press, 2006), 173.

37. Neha Mahajan and Karen Wynn, "Origins of 'Us' versus 'Them': Prelinguistic Infants Prefer Similar Others," *Cognition* 124 (2012): 227–33.

38. Hood, *The Domesticated Brain,* 54–55.

39. Maciej Chudek et al., "Culture-Gene Coevolutionary Theory and

Children's Selective Social Learning," in *Navigating the Social World: What Infants, Children and Other Species Can Teach Us*, ed. Mahzarin R. Banaji and Susan A. Gelman (New York: Oxford University Press, 2012), 181–85.

40. Kiley Hamlin, Paul Bloom, and Karen Wynn, "Social Evaluation by Preverbal Infants," *Nature* 450 (2007): 557–59.

41. Hood, *The Domesticated Brain*, 55.

42. Michael Tomasello, *A Natural History of Human Morality* (Cambridge, MA: Harvard University Press, 2016).

43. Jens Kjeldgaard-Christiansen, "Evil Origins: A Darwinian Genealogy of the Popcultural Villain," *Evolutionary Behavioral Sciences* 10, no. 2 (2016): 109–22.

44. Richard Davidson and Sharon Begley, *The Emotional Life of Your Brain: How Its Unique Patterns Affect the Way You Think, Feel, and Live—and How You Can Change Them* (New York: Plume, 2012), 35.

45. Davidson and Begley, *Emotional Life*, 40.

46. The literature on distinguishing moral beliefs from personal preferences is vast. It includes Alfred J. Ayer, *Language, Truth and Logic* (London: Gollancz, 1936); Richard Mervyn Hare, *Moral Thinking: Its Levels, Method, and Point* (Oxford: Clarendon Press, 1981); David Hume, *Dialogues Concerning Natural Religion* (New York: Bobbs-Merrill, 1947); Immanuel Kant, *Critique of Practical Reason*, ed. Mary Gregor (Cambridge: Cambridge University Press, 1997); Immanuel Kant, *Critique of Pure Reason*, ed. Paul Guyer and Allen W. Wood (Cambridge: Cambridge University Press, 1998); Immanuel Kant, *Groundwork of the Metaphysics of Morals*, ed. Mary Gregor (Cambridge: Cambridge University Press, 1998); G.E. Moore, *Principia Ethica* (Cambridge: Cambridge University Press, 1903); and John Rawls, *A Theory of Justice* (Cambridge, MA: Harvard University Press, 1971).

47. See, for example, "World Thinkers 2013," *Prospect Magazine*, April 24, 2013, https://www.prospectmagazine.co.uk/magazine/world-thinkers -2013.

48. Jonathan Haidt presents a social intuitionist model of moral judgments in which moral judgments are based on automatically processed intuitions rather than conscious reasoning. Moral judgments, however, can be improved and tested by reason. A key text is Jonathan Haidt, *The Righteous Mind: Why Good People Are Divided by Politics and Religion* (New York: Vintage, 2013).

49. Jonathan Haidt, "The Emotional Dog and Its Rational Tail: A Social Intuitionist Approach to Moral Judgment," *Psychological Review* 108, no. 4 (2001): 814–34.

50. Charles Lord, Lee Ross, and Mark Lepper, "Biased Assimilation and Attitude Polarization: The Effects of Prior Theories on Subsequently Considered Evidence," *Journal of Personality and Social Psychology* 37, no. 11 (1979): 2098–109.

51. It is important to note that Jonathan Haidt nonetheless believes it is well worth scrutinizing judgments. He also believes that understanding the shape of others' judgments can make us more tolerant. See, for example, Haidt, *The Righteous Mind*.

52. Jonathan Haidt in fact has become an activist for reflection and revision of judgments through diversity and perspective taking. See his website HeterodoxAcademy.org.

53. Paul Slovic, Melissa Finucane, Ellen Peters, and Donald MacGregor, "The Affect Heuristic," *European Journal of Operational Research* 177 (2007): 1333–52.

54. The neuroscientist Antonio Damasio successfully challenged the persistent myth that emotion and reason were separate functions. He showed that emotional evaluations, and the approach and avoidance tendencies associated with these evaluations, play a crucial role in thought processes that were previously thought to be based on reason and logic only. See Antonio Damasio, *Descartes' Error: Emotion, Reason and the Human Brain* (New York: HarperCollins, 1995; reprint, New York: Penguin, 2005). Damasio presents evidence that a person can be excellent at reasoning, but without emotions that lend meaningful, evaluative engagement with his world, he cannot function. Without these evaluative emotions, you cannot interact meaningfully with others; you cannot make decisions about what to do and how to act, because you have no values and no priorities.

55. For a sustained and powerful argument about the intelligence of the emotions, see Martha Nussbaum, *Upheavals of Thought: The Intelligence of Emotions* (Cambridge: Cambridge University Press, 2004).

56. The social intuitionist model that puts emotion in charge of judgments does not rule out improving judgments through reason. In fact, Jonathan Haidt argues strongly in favor of using reason to understand our own and others' judgments, and to adjust them with reason. See, for example, Haidt, *The Righteous Mind*.

Chapter 2. The Chemistry, Economics, and Psychology of Praise

1. Christine P. Ellsworth, Darwin W. Muir, and Sylvia M. Hains, "Social Competence and Person-Object Differentiation," *Developmental Psychology* 29 (1993): 63–73.

2. Adam J. Guastella et al., "Does Oxytocin Influence the Early Detection of Angry and Happy Faces?," *Psychoneuroendocrinology* 34 (2009): 220–25.

3. Markus Heinrichs et al., "Selective Amnesic Effects of Oxytocin on Human Memory," *Physiology and Behavior* 83 (2004): 31–38.

4. Tania Singer et al., "Effects of Oxytocin and Prosocial Behavior on Brain Responses to Direct and Vicariously Experienced Pain," *Emotion* 8 (2008): 781–91.

5. Markus Heinrichs, Bernadette von Dawans, and Gregor Domes, "Oxytocin, Vasopressin and Human Social Behaviour," *Frontiers in Endocrinology* 30, no. 4 (2009): 548–77.

6. Michael Kosfeld et al., "Oxytocin Increases Trust in Humans," *Nature* 435, no. 7042 (2005): 673–76.

7. Betty Hart and Todd R. Risley, *Meaningful Differences in the Everyday Experience of Young American Children* (London: Brookes Publishing, 1995). See also Jennifer Henderlong and Mark R. Lepper, "The Effects of Praise on Children's Intrinsic Motivation: A Review and Synthesis," *Psychological Bulletin* 128, no. 5 (2002): 774–95.

8. Suzanne N. Haber, "The Primate Basal Ganglia: Parallel and Integrative Networks," *Journal of Chemical Neuroanatomy* 26, no. 4 (2003): 317–30.

9. Johan N. Lundström et al., "Maternal Status Regulates Cortical Responses to the Body Odor of Newborns," *Frontiers in Psychology* 5 (2003), http://dx.doi.org/10.3389/fpsyg.2013.00597.

10. Giacomo Rizzolatti and Laila Craighero, "The Mirror-Neuron System," *Annual Review of Neuroscience* 27 (2004): 169–92.

11. Andrew Meltzoff, "Born to Learn: What Infants Learn From Watching Us," in *The Role of Early Experience in Development*, eds. Nathan A. Fox, Lewis A. Leavitt, and John G. Worhol (Skillman, NJ: Pediatric Institute Publications, 1999), 1–10. Meltzoff's work, originally published in the 1970s, transformed understanding of how quickly babies engaged with others. Previously Jean Piaget believed that babies could not begin to imitate others until the age of nine months. There is, however, a new challenge to Meltzoff's classic findings: Janine Oostenbroek

et al., "Comprehensive Longitudinal Study Challenges the Existence of Neonatal Imitation in Humans," *Current Biology* 26, no. 10 (2016): 1334–38.

12. Andrew N. Meltzoff and M. Keith Moore, "Explaining Facial Imitation: A Theoretical Model," *Early Development and Parenting* 6, no. 34 (1997): 179–92.

13. Tanya L. Chartrand and John A. Bargh, "The Chameleon Effect: The Perception-Behavior Link and Social Interaction," *Journal of Personality and Social Psychology* 76 (1999): 893–910.

14. Jessica L. Lakin and Tanya L. Chartrand, "Using Nonconscious Behavioral Mimicry to Create Affiliation and Rapport," Psychological Science 14 (2003): 334–39.

15. Haim Ginott, *Between Parent and Child* (New York: Macmillan, 1965), 39.

16. John Vasconcellos, preface to *The Social Importance of Self Esteem*, eds. Andrew Mecca, Neil Smelser and John Vasconcellos (Berkeley: University of California Press, 1989), xi–xxi.

17. Robert Rosenthal and Lenore Jacobson, *Pygmalion in the Classroom: Teachers' Expectations and Pupils' Intellectual Development* (New York: Rineholt and Winston, 1968).

18. Another source for this assumption is known as the Hawthorne effect: workers at the Hawthorne works of Chicago's Western Electric Company improved productivity when they were told that they were being observed to see if different lighting made them more efficient. In one case, the old lightbulbs were replaced with exactly the same bulbs, yet the work rate improved. The study was meant to confirm that performance is related to what workers believe rather than to actual changes in the environment. However, the material was never written up, and it has now been lost. See Edwin Gale, "The Hawthorne Studies—A Fable For Our Times?," *QJM: An International Journal of Medicine* 97, no. 7 (2004): 4393–449, http://dx.doi.org/10.1093/qjmed/hch070.

19. For an excellent account of this process, see Ruthellen Josselson, *Playing Pygmalion: How People Create One Another* (Lanham, MD: Jason Aronson, Inc., 2007).

20. Roy F. Baumeister, Debra G. Hutton, and Kenneth J. Cairns, "Negative Effects of Praise on Skilled Performance," *Basic and Applied Social Psychology* 11 (2010): 131–48.

21. Ibid.

22. Ibid.

23. Terri Apter, *The Confident Child: Raising Children to Believe in Themselves* (New York: W. W. Norton, 1998).

24. Mary Budd Rowe, "Relation of Wait-Time and Rewards to the Development of Language, Logic, and Fate Control: Part II Rewards," *Journal of Research in Science Teaching* 11 (1974): 291–308.

25. Alfie Kohn, *Punished by Rewards: The Trouble with Gold Stars, Incentive Plans, A's, Praise, and Other Bribes* (New York: Houghton Mifflin, 1993).

26. Carol S. Dweck, "Motivational Processes Affecting Learning," *American Psychologist* 41, no. 10 (1986): 1040–48.

27. Carol S. Dweck, Chi-yue Chiu, and Ying-yi Hong, "Implicit Theories and Their Role in Judgments and Reactions: A World from Two Perspectives," *Psychological Inquiry* 6, no. 4 (1995): 267–85.

28. See Apter, *The Confident Child*; and William Damon, *Greater Expectations: Overcoming the Culture of Indulgence in America's Home and Schools* (New York: Free Press, 1995).

29. J. Patterson et al., "Improving Mental Health Through Parent Training Programmes," *Archives of Disease in Childhood* 87 (2002): 472–77.

30. Apter, *The Confident Child*.

31. Subsequent research has confirmed the ineffectiveness of inflated praise. See Eddie Brummelman, Jennifer Crocker, and Brad Bushman, "The Praise Paradox: When and Why Praise Backfires in Children with Low Self-Esteem," *Child Developmental Perspectives* 10, no. 2 (2016): 111–15.

32. Children prefer specific praise ("Great! I like the way you are sorting by shape!") to general praise ("Great!"). General praise has far less impact on a child's performance than descriptive praise; in some studies, general praise had the same effect as no praise. See Robert Ryan Scheer, "The Relative Effects of General Versus Descriptive Praise On a Card sorting Task" (PhD diss, University of Maryland, 1976).

33. This conversation was part of a new (not yet published) research project on the midlife women who, as teens, participated in the 1990 research of mothers and teenage daughters. The new project looks at their experiences of mothering teens. See Terri Apter, *You Don't Really Know Me: Why Teens and Mothers Fight* (New York: W. W. Norton, 2004); and Terri Apter, *Altered Loves: Mothers and Daughters During Adolescence* (New York: Ballantine, 1990).

34. Apter, *You Don't Really Know Me*.

35. This conversation was part of a new (not yet published) research project

on the midlife women who, as teens, participated in the 1990 research of mothers and teenage daughters. The new project looks at their experiences of mothering teens. See Apter, *You Don't Really Know Me* and Apter, *Altered Loves.*

36. This research was supported by the Leverhulme Trust.

37. This is an analogy I heard Arlie Russell Hochschild make in a seminar in Berkeley in 1988 when she was talking about her research on couples' division of labor in the home. Her observational research was written up in her book *The Second Shift: Working Parents and the Revolution at Home* (New York: Viking Penguin, 1989).

38. Geoffrey Brennan and Philip Pettit, "The Hidden Economy of Esteem," *Economics and Philosophy* 16 (2000): 33–98. Brennan and Pettit also consider cases where someone acts in ways that are more likely to accrue blame rather than praise. They argue that if someone's behavior *seems* irrational—which in this context means acting in ways that are likely to result in disesteem—then we are missing something. A teenager who drives recklessly seems to be risking disesteem; he or she is likely to be stopped, given a ticket, and may be deprived of a driver's license. Does this mean that his or her behavior is irrational in the economist's sense, which means acting in a way that is unlikely to achieve what the person wants to achieve? If the teen's motives were explored, it would become apparent that the esteem he is interested in is the esteem of his friends in the car; he wants to impress them with his bravado; he wants to be the one who can offer them the thrills he thinks they crave. His behavior may be stupid but it is not, in the economist's sense, irrational.

39. Brennan and Pettit, "The Hidden Economy of Esteem," 33–98.

40. "Judgment meter" is my term; Brennan and Pettit describe a "mutual invigilation" wherein we keep an eye on others in order to appraise them.

41. Brennan and Pettit, "The Hidden Economy of Esteem," 79.

42. Ibid., 33–98.

43. Recent studies show that we actually process the pleasure of monetary gain and the pleasure of esteem, or social status, in the same part of the brain (that is, the striatum). Caroline F. Zink et al., "Know Your Place: Neural Processing of Social Hierarchy in Humans," *Neuron* 58, no. 2 (2008): 273–83. As one neuroscientist in this study said, "the different types of reward are coded by the same currency system." Quoted in Nikhil Swaminathan, "For the Brain, Cash is Good, Status Is Better,"

Scientific American, April 24, 2008, https://www.scientificamerican.com/article/for-the-brain-status-is-better/.

44. "We may reward and punish each other just by being there and registering the character of one another's behavior. And the expectation of such rewards and punishments may lead us each to adjust our behavior accordingly" Brennan and Pettit, "The Hidden Economy of Esteem," 79.

45. Ola Svenson, "Are We All Less Risky and More Skilled Than Our Fellow Drivers?" *Acta Psychologica* 47, no. 2 (1981): 143–48.

46. Cordelia Fine, *A Mind of Its Own: How Your Brain Distorts and Deceives* (New York: W. W. Norton, 2008), 7 (notes on p. 171ff).

47. K. Patricia Cross, "Not Can, but *Will* College Teachers Be Improved?," *New Directions for Higher Education* 17 (1977): 1–15.

48. Ezra W. Zuckerman and John T. Jost, "What Makes You Think You're So Popular? Self Evaluation Maintenance and the Subjective Side of the 'Friendship Paradox'," *Social Psychology Quarterly* 64 no. 3 (2001): 207–23. See also, "It's Academic," *Stanford GSB Reporter*, April 24, 2000, 14–15.

49. Mark Alicke and Olesya Govorun, "The Better-Than-Average-Effect," In *The Self in Social Judgment*, eds. Mark Alicke, David Dunning, and Joachim Krueger, Studies in Self and Identity (Hove, UK: Psychology Press, 2005), 85–106.

50. Garrison Keillor, *Lake Wobegon Days* (New York: The Viking Press, 1985).

51. Vera Hoorens, "Self Enhancement and Superiority Biases in Social Comparisons," *European Review of Social Psychology* 4, no. 1 (1993): 113–39.

52. People who perform the worst in a task, whether it is driving a car or doing an exam or remembering names, are likely to overestimate their ability, whereas people who perform very well on these tasks are likely to underestimate their abilities. The underlying reason seems to be that those who are very able spot the mistakes they make and overestimate others' performance, whereas those who do not do well do not see where they have not succeeded. This is sometimes called "the double-curse of incompetence." See Joyce Ehrlinger et al.,,, "Why the Unskilled Are Unaware: Further Explorations of (Absent) Self-Insight Among the Incompetent," *Organizational Behavior and Human Decision Process* 105, no. 1 (2008): 98–121. See also Justin Kruger and David Dunning, "Unskilled and Unaware of It: How Difficulties in Recognizing

One's Own Incompetence Lead to Inflated Self-Assessments," *Journal of Personality and Social Psychology* 77 (1999): 1121–34. Here it is argued that poor performers provide inaccurate percentile estimates primarily because they are wrong about their own performance; top performers provide inaccurate estimates because they are wrong about other people.

53. W. Keith Campbell and Constantine Sedikides, "Self-Threat Magnifies the Self-Serving Bias: A Meta-Analytic Integration." *Review of General Psychology* 3, no. 1 (1999): 23–43.

54. James R. Larson, "Evidence For a Self-Serving Bias in the Attribution of Causality," *Journal of Personality* 45 (1977): 430–41.

55. Emily Pronin, Daniel Y. Lin, and Lee Ross, "The Bias Blind Spot: Perceptions of Bias in Self Versus Others," *Personality and Social Psychology Bulletin* 28, no. 3 (2002): 369–81.

56. This is drawn from a case described in Terri Apter, *Secret Paths: Women in the New Midlife* (New York: W. W. Norton, 1995), 287–90.

57. Fine, *A Mind of Its Own*, 9.

58. Adam Smith is more widely known for his view that rational self-interest and competition would lead to a flourishing and stable economy. Smith was also a serious moral philosopher and spent the last years of his life writing and rewriting a book called *The Theory of Moral Sentiments*, in which he tried to square moral beliefs, conscience, empathy, and altruism with the rational self-interest he had previously described as the most powerful social and economic force.

59. Adam Smith, "The Theory of Moral Sentiments," in *Glasgow Edition of the Works and Correspondence of Adam Smith*, Vol. 1, eds. D.D. Raphael and A.L. McFie (Oxford: Oxford University Press, 1982).

60. Ginott, *Between Parent and Child*, 39.

61. Ruthellen Josselson, *The Space Between Us: Exploring the Dimensions of Human Relationships* (San Francisco: Jossey-Bass, 1992).

Chapter 3. Blame: The Necessity and Devastation of Guilt and Shame

1. June P. Tangney, D. Mashek, and Jeffrey Stuewig, "Shame, Guilt, and Embarrassment: Will the Real Emotion Please Stand Up?," *Psychological Inquiry* 16, no. 1 (2005): 44–48.

2. E. R. Dodds, *The Greeks and the Irrational*, Sather Classical Lectures (Berkeley: University of California Press, 1951) distinguishes between

guilt that derives from a private sense of wrongdoing and shame that derives from public exposure of one's unacceptable behavior, but more recent research shows that both shame and guilt provide "immediate and salient feedback on our social and moral acceptability," and there is no empirical support for this public/private distinction. Solitary shame is as common as solitary guilt. June Tangney, "Recent Empirical Advances in the Study of Shame and Guilt," *American Behavioral Science* 38 (1995): 1132–45.

3. In the much-debated issue in the field called "blame and blameworthiness," moral and legal philosophers debate questions as to when blame is appropriate, but generally agree that it makes sense to blame someone who was a free agent, who understood what he or she was doing, and who could have acted differently. See, for example, Bernard Williams, *Morality: An Introduction to Ethics* (Cambridge: Cambridge University Press, 1972); and Bernard Williams, *Shame and Necessity* (Berkeley: University of California Press, 1993).

4. Examples of this discussion can be found in Jonathan Haidt, "Morality," *Perspectives on Social Science* 3 (2008): 65–72; and Dennis L. Krebs, "Morality: an Evolutionary Account," *Perspectives on Psychological Science* 3 (2008): 149–72.

5. Lawrence Kohlberg, "The Psychology of Moral Development: Moral Stages and the Idea of Justice," in *Essays on Moral Development,* vol. 1 (New York: Harper & Row, 1981); and Lawrence Kohlberg, "The Psychology of Moral Development: The Nature and Validity of Moral Stages," in *Essays on Moral Development,* vol. 2 (New York: Harper & Row, 1984). But see also Carol Gilligan, *In a Different Voice* (Cambridge, MA: Harvard University Press, 1983).

6. Daniel Goleman refers to this response as an "amygdala hijack." See Daniel Goleman, *Emotional Intelligence* (London: Bloomsbury, 1996), 79.

7. Raymond J. Dolan, "Emotion, Cognition and Behavior," *Science* 298 (2002): 1191–94; and Joseph LeDoux, "Emotion Circuits in the Brain," *Annual Review of Neuroscience* 23, no. 1 (2000): 155–84.

8. In both cases the insula and the corpus collosum (the largest white matter structure in the brain that connects the right and left hemispheres) are activated. See Naomi Eisenbreger and Matthew Leiberman, "Why Rejection Hurts: A Common Neural Alarm System for Physical and Social Pain," *Trends on Cognitive Sciences* 8, no. 7 (2004): 294–300,

quoted in Patricia Churchland, *Braintrust: What Neuroscience Tells Us About Morality* (Princeton, NJ: Princeton University Press, 2012), 39.

9. For a discussion of solitude as a "restorative niche," see Susan Cain, *Quiet: The Power of Introverts in a World that Can't Stop Talking* (New York: Broadway Books, 2012).

10. Quoted in Bruce Hood, *The Domesticated Brain* (Gretna, LA: Pelican, 2008), 229.

11. Hood, *The Domesticated Brain*, 230. Also Frans de Waal, "Second to the death penalty, solitary confinement is the most extreme punishment we can think of. It works this way, only, of course, because we are not born as loners;" see Frans de Waal, *Primates and Philosophers: How Morality Evolved*, eds. Stephen Macedo and Josiah Ober (Princeton, NJ: Princeton University Press: 2009), 5.

12. Sheldon Cohen et al., "Types of Stressors that Increase Susceptibility to the Common Cold in Healthy Adults," *Health Psychology* 17, no. 3 (1998): 214–23.

13. Steve W. Cole et al., "Social Regulation of Gene Expression in Human Leukocytes," *Genome Biology* 8 (2007): R189, doi:10.1186/gb-2007-8-9-r189.

14. Julianne Holt-Lunstad et al., "Loneliness and Social Isolation as Risk Factors for Mortality: A Meta-Analytic Review," *Perspectives on Psychological Science* 10, no. 2 (2015): 227–37.

15. Kipling D. Williams and Steve A. Nida, "Ostracism: Consequences and Coping," *Current Directions in Psychology* 20, no. 2 (2011): 71–75.

16. De Waal, *Primates and Philosophers*.

17. Rosnit Roth-Hanania, Maayan Davidov, and Carolyn Zahn-Waxler, "Empathy Development From 8 to 16 Months: Early Signs of Concern for Others," *Infant Behavior and Development* 34, no. 3 (2011): 447–58.

18. Martin Hoffman, "Empathy, Social Cognition, and Moral Action," in *Moral Behavior and Development: Advances in Theory, Research and Applications*, vol. 1, eds. William M. Kurtines and Jacob L. Gerwitz (New York: John Wiley and Sons, 1984).

19. Leslie Brothers, "A Biological Perspective on Empathy," *American Journal of Psychiatry* 146, no. 1 (1989): 10–19. For a helpful discussion see also Goleman, *Emotional Intelligence*, 102.

20. PTSD (post traumatic stress disorder) does not arise solely from one's own suffering; it can also be a consequence of what one has witnessed.

21. There is a physiological connection between observing pain and inflict-

ing pain. The signals we receive from our own responses to seeing pain present us with an "as if we were doing this to them" response. This suggests that we feel not only as if it were us but also as if we were causing someone pain. See Joshua Greene, *Moral Tribes* (New York: Penguin, 2014), 37. Greene cites a study showing that the vasoconstriction effect in watching pain being inflicted on someone else is specific to performing the pseudo-violent action oneself.

22. Greene, *Moral Tribes.*

23. Michael Tomasello, *A Natural History of Human Morality* (Cambridge, MA: Harvard University Press, 2016).

24. Tomasello imagines a human ancestor, the last of the great apes, living in groups in which cooperation and competition were beginning to emerge, would have had a sense of group identity (Us and Them) and a strong inclination to help others in need; without this basic and genuine empathy, Tomasello believes, we would not have become modern humans. See Tomasello, *A Natural History of Human Morality.*

25. Children are quicker to comply with "don't do this" than "do this". See Graznya Kochanska, "Committed Compliance, Moral Self and Internalization: A Mediational Model," *Developmental Psychology* 38, no. 3 (2002): 339–51.

26. Carsten K.W. De Dreu and Bernard A. Nijstad, "Mental Set and Creative Thought in Social Conflict: Threat Rigidity Versus Motivated Focus," *Journal of Personality and Social Psychology* 95, no. 3 (2008): 648–61.

27. Aaron Beck, *Cognitive Therapies and Emotional Disorders* (New York: Meridian, 1979).

28. W. Keith Campbell and Constantine Sedikides, "Self-Threat Magnifies the Self-Serving Bias: a Meta-Analytic Integration," *Review of General Psychology* 3, no. 1 (1999): 23–43.

29. Carol Tavris and Elliot Aronson, *Mistakes Were Made (But Not by Me): Why We Justify Foolish Beliefs, Bad Decisions, and Hurtful Acts*, new ed. (Boston: Mariner Books, 2008), 10.

30. Refers to the title of Tavris and Aronson's book, *Mistakes Were Made, But Not by Me.*

31. There is a related response known as the backfire effect whereby people not only reject evidence against their strongly held beliefs but, confronted with evidence that contradicts their beliefs, become more confident that their beliefs are justified. See Brendan Nyhan and Jason Reifler, "When Corrections Fail: the Persistence of Political Miscon-

ceptions," *Political Behavior* 32, no. 2 (2010): 303–10, doi:10.1007/s11109-010-9112-2.

32. Tavris and Aronson, *Mistakes Were Made*, 27.

33. Francine Patterson and Eugene Linden, *The Education of Koko* (New York: Holt, Rinehart and Winston, 1981).

34. Cordelia Fine, *A Mind of Its Own* (New York: W. W. Norton, 2006), 14. Fine here draws on a number of studies including Constantine Sedikides and Jeffrey David Green, "On the Self-Protective Nature of Inconsistency-Negativity Management: Using the Person Memory Paradigm to Examine Self-Referent Memory," *Journal of Personality and Social Psychology* 79, no. 6 (2000): 906–22; and Rasyid Bo Sanitioso, Ziva Kunda, and Geoffrey Fong, "Motivated Recruitment of Autobiographical Memories," *Journal of Personality and Social Psychology* 59, no. 2 (1990): 229–41.

35. Frederic Bartlett, *Remembering: A Study in Experimental and Social Psychology* (Cambridge: Cambridge University Press, 1932).

36. Childhood memories are particularly susceptible to revision because we fit in those memory fragments into the world we understand today. See Elizabeth F. Loftus and John C. Palmer, "Reconstruction of Automobile Destruction: An Example of the Interaction Between Language and Memory," *Journal of Verbal Learning and Verbal Behavior* 13 (1974): 585–89. See also Elizabeth Loftus, "Leading Questions and the Eyewitness Report," *Cognitive Psychology* 7 (1975): 560–72.

37. The second common pathway is rumination, or worry. See Peter Kinderman, Matthias Schwannauer, Eleanor Pontin, and Sara Tai, "Psychological Processes Mediate the Impact of Familial Risk, Social Circumstances and Life Events on Mental Health," *PloS ONE* 8, no. 10 (2013): 1–8, PMID: 24146890.

38. Alice Miller, *The Drama of Being a Child* (New York: Basic Books, 1995), 99–100.

39. James Gilligan, "Shame, Guilt, and Violence," *Social Research* 70, no. 4 (2003): 1149–80.

40. Ibid. See also James Gilligan, *Violence: Reflections on a National Epidemic* (New York: Vintage, 1997).

41. Sally S. Dickerson et al., "Immunological Effects of Induced Shame and Guilt," *Psychosomatic Medicine* 66, no. 1 (2004): 124–31.

42. In the 1980s a group of related women noticed that all the males in their family were prone to violence; among them they had committed rape, arson, and murder. They asked the world-famous geneticist Hans

Brunner to investigate whether there was some biological explanation. Brunner found what looked like a genetic explanation. Located in the X chromosome was a special variant of a gene (the MAOA gene). See H.G. Brunner et al., "Abnormal Behaviour Associated with a Point Mutation in the Structural Gene for Monoamine Oxidase A," *Science* 262 (1993): 578–80.

With this gene variant, neurotransmitters such as dopamine and serotonin are not broken down. Without these, those crucial conversations between the primitive areas of the brain and the executive part of the brain are impossible. The "conversations" soothe and control; they tell the easily reactive amygdala to hold on and calm down. Without this signaling, there is no curb on impulsivity and no reflection on the consequences of acting out. The "warrior gene" *prevents* certain brain processes or conversations from developing; hence Bruce Hood suggests it is more a lazy gene, failing to do an important job, than a gene programmed for violence (Hood, *The Domesticated Brain,* 141). So, once the brain's alarm is raised, negative emotions run wild.

Brunner's research was first published in the 1990s, before the complex field of epigenetics transformed our understanding of how genes work. At the time of Brunner's discovery, it was supposed that carrying this gene would be a reliable predictor of violent behavior. Courts even accepted genetic marking into evidence in criminal trials; someone charged with a violent offense might show he carried the particular MAOA variant and then argue, "My actions were caused by this gene; I cannot be held responsible."

It has since been discovered that one in every three people of European descent carries this gene variation. But eight out of ten males who carry this particular version of the gene show *no* evidence of *any* antisocial traits. It is only when a male with this gene variant grows up in certain conditions that this variation of the gene is switched on. The conditions that trigger the expression of violence include long-term physical, verbal, or sexual abuse—experiences that lead to "disesteem" or shame.

43. Antonio Damasio, *Descartes' Error: Emotion, Reason, and the Human Brain* (New York: HarperCollins, 1995), quoted in Jonathan Haidt, "The Emotional Dog and Its Rational Tail: A Social Intuitionist Approach to Moral Judgment," *Psychological Review* 108, no. 4 (2001), 825.

44. June P. Tangney, "Moral Affect: The Good, the Bad, and the Ugly,"

Journal of Personality and Social Psychology 61, no. 4 (1991): 598–607; June P. Tangney, Patricia E. Wagner, Deborah Hill-Barlow, Donna E. Marschall, and Richard Gramzow, "The Relation of Shame and Guilt to Constructive Versus Destructive Responses to Anger Across the Lifespan," *Journal of Personality and Social Psychology* 70 (1996): 797–809; Michael Ross et al., "Cross-Cultural Discrepancies in Self Appraisals," *Personality and Social Psychology Bulletin* 31, no. 9 (2005): 1175–88; and Paul Rozin, Jonathan Haidt, and Clark R. McCauley, "Disgust: The Body and Soul Emotion," in *Handbook of Cognition and Emotion*, eds. Tim Dalgleish and Mick J. Power (New York: John Wiley and Sons, 1999), 429–45.

45. Ralph Ellison's outstanding 1952 novel *Invisible Man* presents a compelling narrative of violence as a means of resisting social invisibility.

46. Anat Brunstein Klomek et al., "Bullying, Depression, and Suicidality in Adolescents," *Journal of the American Academy of Child Adolescent Psychiatry* 46 (2007): 40–49.

47. Matt Hamilton, "Father Fights Back Against Bullying After Son's Suicide," *Los Angeles Times*, October 19, 2013.

48. Ashley Davis, "Teen Gregory Spring Kills Self After Bullying, Bullying Continues on Condolence Page," June 26, 2013, http://www.opposingviews.com/i/society/family-says-9-year-old-boy-was-bullied-death.

49. Jenny Diski, "The Secret Shopper: The History of Shoplifting," *The New Yorker*, September 26, 2011, http://www.newyorker.com/magazine/2011/09/26/the-secret-shopper.

50. Philip Shenon, "His Medals Questioned, Top Admiral Kills Himself," *The New York Times*, May 17, 1996, http://www.nytimes.com/1996/05/17/us/his-medals-questioned-top-admiral-kills-himself.html.

51. Gilligan, "Shame, Guilt, and Violence," 1149–80.

52. Hood, *The Domesticated Brain*, 225–26.

53. Robert James R. Blair, "The Amygdala and Ventromedial Prefrontal Cortex: Functional Contributions and Dysfunction in Psychopathy," *Philosophical Transactions of the Royal Society B: Biological Sciences* 363, no. 1503 (2008): 2557–65. doi:10.1098/rstb.2008.0027.

54. Hervey Cleckly, *The Mask of Sanity: An Attempt to Clarify Some Issues About the So-Called Psychopathic Personality* (Eastford, CT: Martino Fine Books, 1988); and Paul Babiak and Robert Hare, *Snakes in Suits: When Psychopaths go to work* (New York: HarperBusiness, 1988), 38.

55. Colin J. Palmer et al., "'Subtypes' in the Presentation of Autistic Traits

in the General Adult Population," *Journal of Autism and Developmental Disorders* 45 (2015): 1291–1301.

56. There is no approved clinical diagnosis of psychopathy, though psychopathic characteristics are used in some criminal justice symptoms and are widely used in fiction and journalism. See the discussion of R. Hare, "Hare Psychopathy Checklist," in *Encyclopedia of Mental Disorders*, http://www.minddisorders.com/Flu-Inv/Hare-Psychopathy-Checklist.html. An earlier influential account of psychopathy can be found in Cleckly, *The Mask of Sanity*.

57. About 1 percent of the population has psychopathy characteristics and 25 percent of people in prison have psychopathic characteristics, so they are clearly at high risk for criminal behavior. See Adrian Raine and José Sanmartin, eds., *Violence and Psychopathy* (Dordrecht, Netherlands: Kluwer, 2001); and Jon Ronson, *The Psychopath Test: A Journey Through the Madness Industry* (New York: Riverhead, 2011).

58. It is estimated that 4 percent of corporate CEOs have psychopathic characteristics, which means they are overrepresented, by a factor of 400 percent. See Ronson, *The Psychopath Test*. See also Oliver James, *Office Politics: How to Survive in a World of Lying, Backstabbing and Dirty Tricks* (London: Vermillion, 2013).

59. Antonio R. Damasio, Daniel Tranel, and Hanna Damasio, "Individuals with Sociopathic Behavior Caused by Frontal Damage Fail to Respond Autonomically to Social Stimuli," *Behavioral Brain Research* 41 (1990): 81–94.

60. Christopher Patrick et al., "Emotion in the Criminal Psychopath: Fear Image Processing," *Journal of Abnormal Psychology* (1994): 103.

61. Jennifer Jacquet, *Is Shame Necessary? New Uses For an Old Tool* (New York: Pantheon, 2015).

62. See Ronnie Janoff-Bulman, Sana Sheik, and Sebastian Hepp, "Proscriptive Versus Prescriptive Morality: Two Faces of Moral Regulation," *Journal of Personality and Social Psychology* 96, no. 3 (2009): 521–37.

63. George Vaillant, *Triumph of Experience: Men of the Harvard Grant Study* (Cambridge, MA: Belknap Press, 2015).

64. Howard Tennen and Glenn Affleck, "Blaming Others for Threatening Events," *Psychological Bulletin* 108, no. 2 (1990): 209–32.

65. Kathleen A. Lawler et al., "The Unique Effects of Forgiveness on

Health: An Exploration of Pathways," *Journal of Behavioral Medicine* 28, no. 2 (2005): 157–67.

66. See Hood, *The Domesticated Brain.* 223.

Chapter 4. Family Judgments, Family Systems

1. For a highly complex mathematical model of some family interactions, see John Gottman, *The Mathematics of Marriage: Dynamic Nonlinear Models* (Cambridge, MA: MIT Press, 2005).

2. Jerry Lewis, Robert Beavers, John Gossett, and Virginia Phillips, *No Single Thread: Psychological Health in Family Systems* (Oxford, UK: Brunner/Mazel, 1976); Martha J. Cox and Blair Paley, "Families as Systems," *Annual Review of Psychology* 48 (1997): 243–67; and Linda Garris Christian, "Understanding Families: Applying Family Systems Theory to Early Childhood Practice," *Young Children* 61, no.1 (2006): 12–20.

3. These differences are roughly parallel to Diana Baumrind's description of authoritative versus authoritarian discipline. See Diana Baumrind, "Effects of Authoritative Parental Control on Child Behavior," *Child Development* 37, no. 4 (1966): 887–907.

4. 127 quarrels were recorded for Terri Apter, *You Don't Really Know Me: Why Mothers and Daughters Fight and How Both Can Win* (New York: W. W. Norton, 2004).

5. For a more detailed analysis of this and similar quarrels, see Apter, *You Don't Really Know Me.*

6. MRI (magnetic resonance imaging) scans show the physical structure of the brain. fMRI (functional magnetic resonance imaging) scans reveal blood flow within the brain, indicating which areas are active.

7. Sarah-Jayne Blakemore et al., "Adolescent Development of the Neural Circuitry for Thinking about Intentions," *Social Cognitive and Affective Neuroscience* 2 (2007): 130–39.

8. Ibid.

9. Richard Davidson and Sharon Begley, *The Emotional Life of the Brain: How Its Unique Patterns Shape the Way You Think, Feel and Live—And How You Can Change Them* (New York: Plume, 2012), 74.

10. For a general discussion, see "The Teen Brain: Still Under Construction," *National Institute of Mental Health,* 2011, https://infocenter.nimh.nih.gov/pubstatic/NIH%2011-4929/NIH%2011-4929.pdf; for a more detailed account see Francis Jensen, *The Teenage Brain: A*

Neuroscientist's Survival Guide to Raising Adolescents and Young Adults (New York: Harper Thorsen, 2015).

11. Davidson, *The Emotional Life of the Brain*, 74.
12. Apter, *You Don't Really Know Me*.
13. Ibid., 152–54.
14. Terri Apter, *Difficult Mothers: Understanding and Overcoming their Power* (New York: W. W. Norton, 2012), 46–47.
15. W. Keith Campbell and Constantine Sedikides, "Self-Threat Magnifies the Self-Serving Bias: a Meta-Analytic Integration," *Review of General Psychology* 3, no. 1 (1999): 23–43.
16. Eun Young Nahm, "A Cross-Cultural Comparison of Korean American and European American Parental Meta-Emotion Philosophy and Its Relationship to Parent-Child Interaction" (PhD Diss, University of Washington, 2006), 127.
17. Mathew Lieberman et al., "Putting Feelings into Words: Affect Labeling Disrupts Amygdala Activity," *Psychological Science* 18, no. 5 (2007): 421–28.
18. Sally Dickerson and Margaret Kemeny, "Acute Stressors and Cortisol Responses: A Theoretical Integration and Synthesis of Laboratory Research," *Psychological Bulletin* 1130 (2004): 355–91; and Sally Dickerson et al., "Immunological Effects of Induced Shame and Guilt," *Psychosomatic Medicine* 66, no. 1 (2004): 124–31.
19. For a review of relevant research see Daniel Funkenstein, "The Physiology of Fear and Anger," *Scientific American* 192, no. 5 (1955): 74–80.
20. Ibid. For a review of a number of studies, see *Anger, Aggression and Interventions for Interpersonal Violence*, eds. Timothy A. Cavell and Kenya T. Malcolm (Mahwah, NJ: Lawrence Erlbaum, 2007).
21. Neus Herrero et al., "What Happens When We Get Angry? Hormonal, Cardiovascular and Asymmetrical Brain Responses," *Hormones and Behavior* 57, no. 3 (2010): 276–83.
22. Apter, *Difficult Mothers*, 57–58.
23. Ibid., 43–47.
24. From 2000 to 2015 I worked at Newnham College, Cambridge, with duties comparable to those of a dean in a US college.
25. Karl Pillemer et al., "Mothers' Differentiation and Depressive Symptoms among Adult Children," *Journal of Marriage and Family* 72 (2010): 333–45.
26. Stephen Bank and Michael Khan, *The Sibling Bond* (New York: Basic Books, 2008).

27. Pillemer, Suitor, Pardo, and Henderson, "Mothers' Differentiation and Depressive Symptoms," 333–45.

28. Peg Streep, *Mean Mothers: Unloved Daughters and the Legacy of Hurt* (New York: Harper Collins, 2009).

29. Terri Apter, *The Myth of Maturity: What Teenagers Need from Parents to Become Adults* (New York: W. W. Norton, 2001), 56–60.

30. Robyn Skynner and John Cleese, *Families and How to Survive Them* (London: Methuen, 1983), 121.

31. Martha Nussbaum, *Upheavals of Thought: the Intelligence of the Emotions* (New York: Cambridge University Press, 2001).

32. Carol Gilligan, *The Birth of Pleasure: A New Map of Love* (New York: Knopf, 2002).

33. D. W. Winnicott, "Ego Distortion in Terms of True and False Self," in *The Maturational Process and the Facilitating Environment: Studies in the Theory of Emotional Development* (New York: International UP Inc., 1965), 140–52.

34. The internal spectator is explained in Chapter 2.

35. Smith's impartial spectator judges our behavior, motives, and manners according to our own highest standards, but infused with a genial and sympathetic perspective. See Adam Smith, "The Theory of Moral Sentiments," in *Glasgow Edition of the Works and Correspondence of Adam Smith*, Vol. 1, eds. D. D. Raphael and A. L. McFie (Oxford: Oxford University Press, 1982).

36. Philip Pullman, *His Dark Materials* (New York: Random House, 2007).

37. Matt Treeby et al., "Shame, Guilt, and Facial Emotion Processing: Initial Evidence for a Positive Relationship Between Guilt-Proneness and Facial Emotion Recognition Ability," *Cognition and Emotion* 30, no. 8 (2016): 1504–11.

38. Dana Crowley Jack, *Silencing the Self: Women and Depression* (Cambridge, MA: Harvard University Press, 1991).

39. Terri Apter, *Secret Paths: Women in the New Midlife* (New York: W. W. Norton, 1995).

40. Richard J. Davidson and Sharon Begley, *The Emotional Life of Your Brain: How Its Unique Patterns Affect the Way You Think, Feel, and Live—And How You Can Change Them* (New York: Plume, 2012), 41.

41. Ibid., 79.

42. This process is often referred to as "rupture and repair." See Allan Schore, *Affect Dysregulation and Disorders of the Self* (New York: W. W. Norton, 2003).

43. Davidson and Begley, *The Emotional Life of Your Brain*, 74.
44. There is evidence that many people balance these needs more successfully as they age. See, for example, Apter, *Secret Paths: Women in the New Midlife.*
45. Peter Fonagy et al., *Affect Regulation, Mentalization, and the Development of the Self* (New York: Other Press, 2002).
46. Peter Fonagy et al., "The Capacity for Understanding Mental States: The Reflective Self in Parent and Child and its Significance for Security of Attachment," *Infant Mental Health Journal* 12, no. 3 (1991): 201–18.

Chapter 5. Just Friends: Praise and Blame Between Peers

1. Brett Laursen et al., "Friendship Moderates Prospective Associations Between Social Isolation and Adjustment Problems in Young Children," *Child Development* 78, no. 4 (2007): 1395–1404.
2. Janice Kiecolt-Glaser, Jean-Philippe Gouin, and Lisa Hantsoo, "Close Relationships, Inflammation and Health," *Neuroscience and Biobehavioral Reviews* 35, no. 1 (2010): 33–38. See also John Cacoppo, James Fowler, and Nicholas Christakis, "Alone in a Crowd: The Structure and Spread of Loneliness in a Large Social Network," *Journal of Personality and Social Psychology* 97, no. 6 (2009): 977–91.
3. Terri Apter and Ruthellen Josselson, *Best Friends: The Pleasures and Perils of Girls' and Women's Friendships* (New York: Crown, 1998), 22–23. See also Robin Dunbar, *Grooming, Gossip, and the Evolution of Language* (Cambridge, MA: Harvard University Press, 1996).
4. Apter and Josselson, *Best Friends*, 20–25.
5. Apter and Josselson, *Best Friends*.
6. Eleanor Maccoby and Carol Nagy Jacklin, "Gender Segregation in Childhood," in *Advances in Child Development and Behavior*, vol. 20, ed. Hayne Reese (San Diego, CA: Academic Press, 1987), 239–87.
7. Bruce Hood, *The Domesticated Brain* (Gretna, LA: Pelican, 2014), 54–55.
8. G.M. Alexander and Melissa Hines, "Sex Differences in Response to Children's Toys in Nonhuman Primates (Cercopithecus Aethiops Sabaeus)," *Evolution and Human Behavior* 23 (2002): 467–79.
9. Amy Sheldon, "Pickle Fights: Gendered Talk in Preschool Disputes," *Discourse Processes* 13, no. 1 (1990): 5–31.

10. For example see Deborah Tannen, *You Just Don't Understand: Women and Men in Conversation* (New York: Morrow, 1991).

11. Sheldon, "Pickle Fights," 5–31.

12. Alexander and Hines, "Sex Differences in Response to Children's Toys," 467–79.

13. Gender differences are not "hard-wired." The rapidly developing field of epigenetics shows how experiences and environment switch genes on and off, presenting different possible pathways at each junction. A useful metaphor is that of a ball rolling along a terrain with many gullies and channels, some deep, some shallow. At critical points along the route, the ball may be directed into one of these channels. When a ball rolls into a deep channel, it tends to follow it; if it rolls into a shallow channel, the smallest jolt can eject it and it can easily find another route. [See Conrad Hal Waddington, *Organizers and Genes* (Ann Arbor, MI: The University Press, 1940).] The trajectory of the balls and the different routes they follow, and the chance events that direct them into or eject them from different channels, models the chances over a lifetime of individuals developing certain characteristics linked to genes. So, complying with norms of girls' friendship and playing with dolls rather than building train sets, or joining a chess club versus the debating society, will produce environments in which some skills are learned and other skills are not. Learning leads to new interests and routes of development, and closes others.

14. C.L. Martin and D. Ruble, "Children's Search for Gender Cues: Cognitive Perspectives in Gender Development," *Current Directions in Psychological Science* 13, no. 2 (2004): 67–70.

15. Apter and Josselson, *Best Friends*, 92–96.

16. Interview by Terri Apter, Washington, DC, 1997.

17. Apter and Josselson, *Best Friends*, 54–55.

18. Erika Nurmsoo, Shiri Einar, and Bruce M. Hood, "Best Friends: Children Use Mutual Gaze to Identify Friendship in Others," *Developmental Science* 15 (2012): 417–25.

19. Erving Goffman, *Interaction Ritual: Essays on Face-to-Face Behavior* (New York: Anchor Books, 1967); and Erving Goffman, *The Presentation of Self in Everyday Life* (Edinburgh: University of Edinburgh Social Sciences Research Centre, 1959).

20. Apter and Josselson, *Best Friends*.

21. See Niobe Way, *Deep Secrets: Boys' Friendships and the Crisis of Connection* (Cambridge, MA: Harvard University Press, 2011).

22. Sylvan Tomkins, *Affect, Imagery and Consciousness*, vol.1, *The Positive Affects* (New York: Springer, 1962).
23. Paul Ekman, *Emotions Revealed*, 2nd ed. (New York: Holt, 2007).
24. Christopher Boehm, *Hierarchy in the Forest: The Evolution of Egalitarian Behavior* (Cambridge, MA: Harvard University Press, 1999).
25. Robin Dunbar, "Gossip in Evolutionary Perspective," *Review of General Psychology* 8, no. 2 (2004): 100–110.
26. Ibid., 100.
27. Ibid.
28. Robin Dunbar, Niell Duncan, and Anna Marriott, "Human Conversational Behavior," *Human Nature* 8, no. 3 (1997): 231–46; and Dunbar, "Gossip in Evolutionary Perspective," 105.
29. Jeffrey G. Parker and Stephanie D. Teasley, "The Effects of Gender, Friendship and Popularity on the Targets and Topics of Adolescent Gossip" (paper presented at the biennial meeting of the Society for Research in Child Development, Indianapolis, IN, March, 1995).
30. Dunbar, "Gossip in Evolutionary Perspective," 100–110.
31. See Chapter 2 in this book.
32. Dunbar, "Gossip in Evolutionary Perspective," 100–110.
33. Apter and Josselson, *Best Friends*, Chapter 5 ("I'm Not Who You Think I Am") and Chapter 6 ("Promise You Won't Tell").
34. Apter and Josselson, *Best Friends*, 187.
35. Ibid., 132.
36. Ibid., 27.
37. Janet Lever, "Sex Differences in the Games Children Play," *Social Problems* 23 (1976): 478–87; and Barrie Thorne, *Gender Play: Girls and Boys at School* (Buckingham, UK: Open University Press, 1993).
38. Lever, "Sex Differences," 478–87; and Thorne, *Gender Play*.
39. B. I. Fagot, "Beyond the Reinforcement Principle: Another Step Toward Understanding Sex Role Development," *Developmental Psychology* 2, no. 6 (1985): 1102, table 3.
40. William Pollack, *Real Boys' Voices* (New York: Random House, 2001).
41. Matthias R. Mehl et al., "Are Women Really More Talkative Than Men?," *Science* 317 (2007): 82.
42. L. M. Janes and J. M. Olson, "Jeer Pressure: The Behavioral Effects of Observing Ridicule of Others," *Personality and Social Psychology Bulletin* 26 (2000): 474–85.
43. Way, *Deep Secrets*.
44. Fascinated by the discrepancy between the stereotypes of boys and

how boys actually spoke about themselves and their friends, Niobe Way interviewed a cross-section of boys in every year of high school. Growing up she had witnessed a sudden distance emerge between her brother and his closest childhood friend, his subsequent palpable sadness, and his reluctance to talk about it, ever. As a psychologist, she wanted to study boys' friendships and discover the inner workings and meanings of boys' friendship. She discovered they were articulate and impassioned as they spoke of friends, whom they looked upon as people they loved and admired, people on whom they depended and with whom they shared their deepest secrets. See Way, *Deep Secrets*.

45. Ibid., 12.
46. Ibid., 21.
47. Ibid., 1.
48. Ibid., 18.
49. Way, *Deep Secrets*.
50. For an account of the neuroscience of teens' risky behaviors, see B. J Casey, B. E. Kosofky and P. G. Bhide, eds., "Teenage Brains: Think Different," special issue, *Developmental Neuroscience* 36, no. 3–4 (2014): 143–358.
51. Jason Chein et al., "Peers Increase Adolescent Risk Taking by Enhancing Activity in the Brain's Reward Circuitry," *Developmental Science* 14, no. 2 (2011): F1–F10.
52. Way, *Deep Secrets*, 17.
53. Terri Apter, *The Myth of Maturity* (New York: W. W. Norton, 2001).
54. "Psychologist John Cacioppo Explains Why Loneliness is Bad for Your Health," *Institute for Genomics and Systems Biology*, January 25, 2011, http://www.igsb.org/news/psychologist-john-cacioppo-explains-why-loneliness-is-bad-for-your-health/.
55. Interview by Terri Apter. Cambridge, UK, May 24, 2011.
56. Yasuko Minoura, "A Sensitive Period for the Incorporation of a Cultural Meaning System: A Study of Japanese Children Growing Up in the United States," *Ethos* 20, no. 3 (1992), 304–39.
57. Janes and Olson, "Jeer Pressure," 474–85.
58. Apter and Josselson, *Best Friends*, 62–65.
59. Terri Apter, unpublished study on boys' friendships (Cambridge, UK, April–June 2011). I was working alongside a doctoral student on a study of boys' friendship. For various reasons the study was not completed.
60. Louisa Pavey, Tobias Greitemeyer, and Paul Sparks, "Highlighting

Relatedness Promoted Prosocial Motives and Behavior," *Personality and Social Psychology Bulletin* 37, no. 7 (2011): 905–17.

61. Jonathan Haidt, "The Emotional Dog and its Rational Tail: A Social Intuitionist Approach to Moral Judgment," *Psychological Review* 108, no. 4 (2001): 814–34, 822.

62. Tanya Chartrand and John Bargh, "The Chameleon Effect: The Perception-Behavior Link and Social Interaction," *Journal of Personality and Social Psychology* 76, no. 6 (1999): 893–910.

63. Elijah Anderson, *Streetwise: Race, Class, and Change in an Urban Community* (Chicago, IL: University of Chicago Press, 1990); and Anne Campbell, "Self-Definition by Rejection: The Case of Gang Girls," *Social Problems* 34 (1984): 451–66.

64. Roy Baumeister, Joseph Boden, and Laura Smart, "Relation of Threatened Egotism to Violence and Aggression: The Dark Side of High Self-Esteem," *Psychological Review* 103, no. 1 (1996): 5–33.

65. William F. Baccaglini, *Project Youth Gang-Drug Prevention: A Statewide Research Study* (Rensselaer: New York State Division for Youth, 1993).

66. Baumeister, Boden, and Smart, "Relation of Threatened Egotism to Violence and Aggression," 5–33.

67. Adam Watkins and Chris Melde, "Bad Medicine: The Relationship Between Gang Membership, Depression, Self-Esteem, and Suicidal Behavior," *Journal of Criminal Justice and Behavior* 43, no. 8 (2016): 1107–26, doi:0093854816631797.

68. Elijah Anderson, *The Code of the Street: Decency, Violence and the Moral Life of the Inner City* (New York: W. W. Norton, 1999).

69. Anderson, *The Code of the Street*, 33; and National Youth Gang Center, *1995 National Youth Gang Survey* (Washington, DC: U.S. Department of Justice, Office of Justice Programs, Office of Juvenile Justice and Delinquency Prevention, 1997), NCJ 164728.

70. David Brooks, "The Columbine Killers," *The New York Times*, April 24, 2004, http://www.nytimes.com/2004/04/24/opinion/the-columbine-killers.html.

71. Alexander Abad-Santos, "Who Is Dzhokhar Tsarnaev, the Man at the Center of the Boston Manhunt?," *The Atlantic*, April 19, 2013, https://www.theatlantic.com/national/archive/2013/04/who-is-dzhokhar-tsarnaev-boston/316095/.

72. Hood, *The Domesticated Brain*, 268.

73. This study was funded by Newnham College's Senior Members Support Fund 2015.

74. Anne Campbell, *The Girls in the Gang: A report from New York City* (New York: Basil Blackwood, 1984/1991).

Chapter 6. Intimate Judgments: Praise and Blame Within Couples

1. These words from The Book of Common Prayer are from one particular marriage ceremony, though high hopes for enduring praise and expectations that blame will be minimal and transient are shared by most modern couples.
2. From marriage ceremonies in Game of Thrones.
3. These twelve couples were heterosexual couples. I have begun a study on gay and lesbian couples and have yet to find any significant differences in the ways praise and blame are expressed, or how praise and blame impact the relationship.
4. Funded by the Leverhulme Trust via an award of a Leverhulme Emeritus Fellowship 2015/16.
5. Here is a standard outline of the first session in marital therapy: http://www.marriage-couples-counseling-new-york.com/what-to-expect-in-your-first-meeting/. See also Kim Therese Buehlman, John Mordechai Gottman, and Lynn Fainsilber Katz, "How a Couple Views Their Past Predicts Their Future: Predicting Divorce from an Oral History Interview," *Journal of Family Psychology* 5, no. 3–4 (1992): 295–318.
6. John Gottman, *Why Marriages Succeed or Fail* (New York: Simon and Schuster, 1995).
7. John Gottman, *The Mathematics of Marriage* (Cambridge, MA: MIT Press, 2005).
8. Gottman, *Why Marriages Succeed or Fail*, 26.
9. John Gottman developed the Specific Affect Coding System (SPAFF) integrating Paul Ekman's Facial Affect Coding System (FACS) with coded observations of couples. So complex and detailed is the coding that initially it took 25 hours to code 15 minutes of interactions, but this has now been reduced to 45 minutes per 15 minutes. Though even 6 minutes of interactions, carefully analyzed, is a strong predictor of marital survival versus divorce, the usual assessment involves observations over a three-hour period. See John Gottman and Julie Schwartz Gottman, *The Empirical Basis of Gottman Couples Therapy* (Gottman Institute, 2013), https://www.gottman.com/wp-content/uploads/EmpiricalBasis-Update3.pdf. The 6 minutes of time is discussed by Malcolm Gladwell in "The Theory of Thin Slices: How a

Little Bit of Knowledge Goes a Long Way," in *Blink: The Power of Thinking Without Thinking* (London: Allen Lane, 2005).

10. Gottman reports that he is able to predict with 95 percent accuracy which couples will divorce and which couples will remain in a committed marriage. There are, however, some questions surrounding this claim. First, much of the data does not involve a forecast but a formula in which the marital status of the couple at six years is already known; second, the base rate of divorce (16 percent of couples will divorce after six years of marriage) seems not to have been factored in; third, the way this prediction is presented often gives the impression that the predictive reliability applies to each couple, as opposed to statistical probability across a large group of couples.

11. Gottman, *The Mathematics of Marriage*, 5–6.

12. Ibid., 18.

13. The tendency to be more easily influenced by blame than by praise arises from what psychologists call the negativity bias. Roy Baumeister et al., "Bad is Stronger than Good," *Review of General Psychology* 5, no. 4 (2001): 323–70.

14. Different types of negative responses carry different weight. Overt blame, involving criticism (for example, "You are the problem. Your faults or deficits are what make me unhappy") and contempt ("You are less than you should be; you matter less than me") predict early divorce, within five years of marriage. Emotional disengagement is predictive of divorce at a later date, approximately 16.2 years after marriage. Data are from the Gottman Institute, Seattle, WA, 2014. See also John Gottman, *The Seven Principles for Making Marriage Work*, revised ed. (New York: Harmony, 2015).

15. The elevated cortisol levels that accompany initial neophobia, or wariness of getting very close to a stranger, are transformed to the thrill of a newly discovered person. See A. de Boer, E. M. van Buel, and G. J. Ter Horst, "Love Is More Than Just a Kiss: A Neurobiological Perspective on Love and Affection," *Neuroscience* 201 (2012): 114–24.

16. See Chapters 2 and 4 in this book.

17. A discussion of Dana Crowley Jack's "over-eye" is included in Chapter 3 of this book.

18. Idealization actually diminishes the power of praise in marriage. See Jennifer Tomlinson et al., "The Costs of Being Put on a Pedestal: Effects of Feeling Over-Idealized," *Journal of Social and Personal Relationships* 31, no. 3 (2014): 384–409.

19. Given the importance of close relationships to human survival, being accused of damaging a relationship is likely to arouse terrible guilt. See Bruce Hood, *The Domesticated Brain* (Gretna, LA: Pelican, 2008), 211.

20. Gottman, *The Mathematics of Marriage*, 29.

21. These defenses against blame are discussed in Chapter 3 of this book.

22. Harold L. Rauch et al., *Communication, Conflict, and Marriage* (San Francisco, CA: Jossey-Bass, 1974), 2.

23. Fritz Heider, *The Psychology of Interpersonal Relations* (New York: John Wiley and Sons, 1958).

24. June Tangney et al., "Relation of Shame and Guilt to Constructive Versus Destructive Responses to Anger Across the Lifespan," *Journal of Personality and Social Psychology* 70 (1996): 797–809.

25. Occasional blame between couples seems inevitable, but when it is persistent and predictable, rather than getting used to it, some people become sensitized so that even the hint of blame triggers a violent response. See Sara J. Shettleworth, *Cognition, Evolution, and Behavior*, 2nd ed. (New York: Oxford University Press, 2010).

26. This process is known as the confirmation bias: Raymond Nickerson, "Confirmation Bias: A Ubiquitous Phenomenon in Many Guises," *Review of General Psychology* 2, no. 2 (1998): 175–220.

27. Gottman, *The Mathematics of Marriage*, 11.

28. Ibid.

29. Tangney et al., "Relation of Shame and Guilt," 797–809.

30. Carol Tavris and Elliot Aronson, *Mistakes Were Made (But Not by Me): Why We Justify Foolish Beliefs, Bad Decisions, and Hurtful Acts*, new ed. (Boston: Mariner Books, 2008), 171.

31. *Flooding* is a term initially used by Paul Ekman. See Paul Ekman, "Expression and the Nature of Emotion," in *Approaches to Emotion*, eds. Klaus R. Scherer and Paul Ekman (Hillsdale, NJ: Lawrence Erlbaum Associates Press, 1984), 319–44.

32. Gottman, *Why Marriages Succeed or Fail*, 95. These data are based on heterosexual couples. Among lesbian couples stonewalling still occurs, so it is important to note that stonewalling is not an exclusively male defense. See also John Gottman, *The Seven Principles of Making Marriage Work* (New York: Harmony, 2015).

33. Gottman, *Why Marriages Succeed or Fail*, 94–95.

34. Ibid., 94.

35. An excellent description of the impact of infidelity can be found in

Shirley Glass and Jean Coppock Staeheli, *Not "Just Friends": Rebuilding Trust and Recovering Your Sanity After Infidelity* (New York: The Free Press, 2008).

36. These brain areas are the amygdala, nucleus accumbens, ventral tegmental area (VTA), cerebellum, and pituitary gland.

37. Oxytocin (and prolactin) are often referred to as "female hormones" because of their bonding function during birth and breast-feeding, but they are also involved in the bonding process between males and their newborn infants. See Ilanit Gordon et al., "Prolactin, Oxytocin, and the Development of Paternal Behavior Across the First Six Months of Fatherhood," *Hormones and Behavior* 58 (2010): 513–18.

38. De Boer, van Buel, and Ter Horst, "Love Is More Than Just a Kiss," 114–24.

39. The elevated cortisol levels that accompany initial "neophobia" or wariness of getting very close to a stranger are transformed to the thrill of a newly discovered person. See de Boer, van Buel, and Ter Horst, "Love Is More Than Just a Kiss," 114–24.

40. Maggie Scarf, *September Songs* (New York: Riverhead Books, 2008), 238.

41. Scott Edwards and David Self, "Monogamy: Dopamine Ties the Knot," *Nature Neuroscience* 9 (2006): 7–8.

42. Ever since very different patterns of social behavior and pair bonding were noted in two closely related species—the monogamous prairie vole and the polygamous meadow vole—the question of human fidelity has been revved up a notch. There is a particular vasopressin receptor (called V1A) that is expressed in higher levels in the faithful prairie vole than in the promiscuous meadow vole. In an experiment where the V1A gene of the prairie vole was transferred into the (ventral fore) brain of the meadow vole, the meadow voles then showed greater preference for a particular mate. So, while in both species, vasopressin (one of the attachment hormones) and dopamine (a reward hormone) regulate pair bond behavior, one particular receptor seems to make the difference between fidelity and promiscuity (Miranda M. Lim et al., "Enhanced Partner Preference in a Promiscuous Species by Manipulating the Expression of a Single Gene," *Nature* 429 [2004]: 754–57). Comparable variations in neural receptors have been found in human males, particularly in dopamine receptors. The hypothesis, based on the questionable assumption that in "casual" sex the risks are high but

the rewards are substantial, is that there is a special dopamine rush—a particularly delicious reward—for infidelity that men with a specific variant of the dopamine receptor (called D4) find irresistible (Justin Garcia et al., "Associations Between Dopamine D4 Receptor Gene Variation with Both Infidelity and Sexual Promiscuity," *PLoS One* 5 [2003]: 1–6). These observations are intriguing, but there is no scientific basis to assert a cause and effect link between a person's genes and his or her fidelity or promiscuity. Humans as a species are flexible in their social and sexual behavior.

43. Monogamy probably developed as a reproductive strategy between 20,000 and 40,000 years ago, arising from the child-rearing requirements of a more complex social world. See Sarah Blaffer Hrdy, *Mothers and Others: The Evolutionary Origins of Mutual Understanding* (Cambridge, MA: Harvard University Press, 2011).

44. Caryl E. Rusbult, John M. Martz, and Christopher R. Agnew, "The Investment Model Scale: Measuring Commitment Level, Satisfaction Level, Quality of Alternatives, and Investment Size," *Personal Relationships* 5 (1998): 357–91; and Caryl E. Rusbult, "Commitment and Satisfaction in Romantic Associations: A Test of the Investment Model," *Journal of Experimental and Social Psychology* 16 (1980): 172–86. Discussed by John Gottman, Julie Gottman, and Dan Siegel, *The Science and Creation of Fidelity and Infidelity* (handout distributed under license by the Gottman Institute, 2014).

45. Gottman, Gottman, and Siegel, *The Science and Creation of Fidelity and Infidelity*.

46. Ibid.

47. Janet Reibstein, "Commentary: A Different Lens for Working with Affairs," *Journal of Family Therapy* 35, no. 4 (2011): 368–80 (published online in 2013).

48. Ibid.

49. Ibid.

50. These consist of the twelve couples I followed over an eighteen-month period, meeting with them at three-month intervals and inviting them to keep diaries of the relationship, which we then discussed, all three of us, during the meetings. This work was funded by the Leverhulme Trust.

51. Robin Stern, *The Gaslight Effect: How to Spot and Survive the Hidden Manipulation that Others Use to Control Your Life* (New York: Harmony, 2007).

52. The film is based on the 1938 play *Angel Street* by Patrick Hamilton.

53. Roy F. Baumeister, Arlene M. Stillwell, and Todd F. Heatherton, "Guilt: An Interpersonal Approach," *Psychological Bulletin* 115, no. 2 (1994): 243–67.

54. Reibstein, "Commentary: A Different Lens for Working With Affairs," 368–80; Denis de Rougemont, *Love in the Western World*, trans. Montgomery Belgion (New York: Fawcett, 1956).

55. The betrayer's grief at seeing his fallen image in a partner's eyes is sensitively discussed in Glass, *Not "Just Friends,"* 116.

56. Tavris and Aronson, *Mistakes Were Made*, 177.

57. Gottman, *Why Marriages Succeed or Fail*; John Gottman and Julie Gottman, *The Marriage Clinic* (New York: W. W. Norton, 1999); and Julie Schwartz Gottman, *The Marriage Clinic Casebook* (New York: W. W. Norton, 2004).

58. R. L. Weiss and M. C. Cerreto, "The Marital Status Inventory: Development of a Measure of Dissolution Potential," *The American Journal of Family Therapy* 8 (1980): 80–86.

59. Christina Stoessel et al., "Differences and Similarities on Neuronal Activities of People Being Happily and Unhappily in Love: a Functional Magnetic Resonance Imaging Study," *Neuropsychobiology* 64, no. 1 (2011): 52–60.

60. Gottman, *The Mathematics of Marriage*, 19.

61. Some research indicates, however, that couples can be trained to focus on the positive traits of their partner. Elizabeth A. Robinson and M. Gail Price, "Pleasurable Behavior in Marital Interaction: An Observational Study," *Journal of Consulting and Clinical Psychology* 48 (1980): 177–88. Robinson and Price found that in couples described as "unhappy," the partners observed only 50 percent of the other's positive overtures but each could be trained to catch sight of more positive behavior.

62. Ibid.

63. Gottman and Gottman, *The Marriage Clinic.*

64. Gottman, *The Mathematics of Marriage*, 165. The process and challenges of healing after an affair can be seen in far greater detail in John Gottman, Julie Schwartz Gottman, and Dan Siegel, *Healing From After An Affair—Gottman Couples Therapy* (distributed under license by The Gottman Institute, 2014). See also John Gottman and Julie Schartz Gottman, *Aftermath of a Fight or Regrettable Incident* (distributed under license by The Gottman Institute, 2015).

Chapter 7. Professional Dues: Praise and Blame in the Workplace

1. Ben Dattner, *The Blame Game: How the Hidden Rules of Credit and Blame Determine Our Success or Failure* (New York: Free Press, 2011), 3.
2. Denise M. Breaux et al., "Politics as a Moderator of the Accountability Job Satisfaction Relationship: Evidence Across Three Studies," *Journal of Management* 35, no. 2 (2009): 307–26.
3. Peter Hom and Angelo Kinicki, "Towards a Greater Understanding of How Dissatisfaction Drives Employee Turnover, *The Academy of Management Journal* 44, no. 5 (2001): 975–87.
4. Wayne A. Hochwarter et al., "Strain Reactions to Perceived Entitlement Behavior by Others as a Contextual Stressor: Moderating Role of Political Skill in Three Samples," *Journal of Occupational Health Psychology* 15, no. 4 (2010): 388–98.
5. Will Felps et al., "Turnover Contagion: How Coworkers' Job Embeddedness and Coworkers' Job Search Behaviors Influence Quitting," *Academy of Management Journal* 52, no. 3 (2009): 545–61.
6. Song of Songs 7:4 (New King James Version).
7. My title at the UK university was senior tutor, but the duties are that of dean in a US college.
8. EU Grant, Fifth Framework, *Work/Life Balance* (Ralfa.org and Newnham College, 2003).
9. Oliver James, *Office Politics: How to Thrive in a World of Lying, Backstabbing and Dirty Tricks* (London: Vermillion, 2013).
10. Dattner, *The Blame Game*.
11. Sayre's law is cited in Charles Issawi, *Issawi's Laws of Social Motion* (New York: Hawthorn Books, 1973), 178.
12. The question as to whether observing behavior changes behavior is one that can neither be ignored nor overcome. The Hawthorne effect, sometimes called the observer effect, was identified in the 1930s when researchers were trying to assess the effect of lighting on work productivity; after a time they concluded that the lighting was incidental, and what affected workers' productivity was being observed. See Elton Mayo, "Hawthorne and the Western Electric Company," in *The Social Problems of an Industrial Civilisation* (London: Routledge, 1949), 60–76. This interpretation however has been subsequently questioned. See Steven Levitt and John List, "Was There Really a Hawthorne Effect at the Hawthorne Plant? An Analysis of the Original Illumination Experiments," *American Economic Journal: Applied Economics* 3, no. 1 (2011): 224–38.

13. Bruce Hood, *The Domesticated Brain* (Gretna, LA: Pelican, 2008), 14–15.

14. James, *Office Politics*, 219.

15. Junhui Wu, Daniel Balliet, and Paul A.M. Van Lange, "Gossip Versus Punishment: The Efficiency of Reputation to Promote and Maintain Cooperation," *Scientific Reports* 6 (2016), doi:10.1038/srep23919.

16. Richard Davidson and Sharon Begley, *The Emotional Life of Your Brain: How Its Unique Patterns Affect the Way You Think, Feel, and Live—And How You Can Change Them* (New York: Plume, 2012), 246.

17. "Perhaps 'blamed' is too strong a word, but it is directionally correct," write Jean-Francois Manzoni and Jean-Louise Barsoux. See "The Set-Up To Fail Syndrome," *Harvard Business Review*, March–April 1998.

18. EU Grant, Fifth Framework, *Family Friendly Policies in Workplaces* (Ralfa.org and Newnham College, Cambridge, 2003).

19. Manzoni and Barsoux, "The Set-Up To Fail Syndrome."

20. This compares to approximately 1 percent in the general population. See Paul Babiak and Robert D. Hare, *Snakes in Suits: When Psychopaths Go to Work* (New York: HarperBusiness, 2006).

21. Nathan Brooks and Katarina Fritzon, "The Emergence of Noncriminal Psychopathy," paper presented to the Australian Psychological Society Congress (Melbourne, September 2016).

22. This interview was conducted by Terri Apter on 4 April 2003 in Cambridge, UK, for a research project on Family Friendly Practices funded by an EU Grant. Fifth Framework, *Work/Life Balance* (Ralfa.org and Newnham College, Cambridge: 2003).

23. Jean Twenge and Keith Campbell, *The Narcissistic Epidemic: Living in the Age of Entitlement* (New York: Free Press, 2009).

24. See Nick Gowing and Chris Langdon, *Thinking the Unthinkable: A New Imperative for Leadership in the Digital Age* (London: Chartered Institute of Management Accountants, 2016).

25. James, *Office Politics*.

26. Ibid., 173.

27. Hannah Seligson, *New Girl on the Job* (New York: Citadel, 2008).

28. See Dick Grote, "The Myth of Performance Metrics," *Harvard Business Review*, September 12, 2011, https://hbr.org/2011/09/the-myth-of-performance-metric.

29. For one of the best discussions about how setting targets risks creating perverse incentives, see Onora O'Neill, "A Question of Trust" (BBC Reith Lectures, Cambridge, UK, 2002), http://downloads.bbc.co.uk/rmhttp/radio4/transcripts/20020403_reith.pdf.

30. Steven Rsin, Steven J. Spencer, and Steven Fein, "Prejudice as Self-Image Maintenance: Affirming the Self through Derogating Others," *Journal of Personality and Social Psychology* 73, no. 1 (1997): 31–44.

31. See, for example, James, *Office Politics*; but also Broverman et al., "Sex-Role Stereotypes and Clinical Judgments of Mental Health," *Journal of Consulting and Clinical Psychology* 34, no. 1 (1970): 1–7.

32. In a research project involving a consultancy firm, a university, a public hospital, and a supermarket, I interviewed 17 people at different levels. Funded by an EU Grant, Fifth Framework, *Family Friendly Practices in Workplaces* (Ralfa.org and Newnham College, Cambridge, 2003).

33. Sylvia Beyer, "Gender Differences in the Accuracy of Self-Evaluation of Performance," *Journal of Personality and Social Psychology* 59, no. 5 (1990): 960–70. See also Heather Sarsons and Guo Xu, "Confidence Men? Gender and Confidence: Evidence Among Top Economists," *Harvard Scholar*, July 14, 2015, https://scholar.harvard.edu/files/sarsons/files/confidence_final.pdf.

34. Bonita C. Long and Sharon E. Kahn, *Women, Work, and Coping: A Multidisciplinary Approach to Workplace Stress* (Toronto: McGill Queens University Press, 1993).

35. Lucy Kellaway, "Kudos to Bosses Who Use Praise Wisely," *Financial Times*, May 24, 2009, https://www.ft.com/content/093cc1c6-9154-438d-b5bb-386cc352ce1c?mhq5j=e1.

36. Wulfe-Uwe Meyer, "Paradoxical Effects of Praise and Criticism on Perceived Ability," *European Review of Social Psychology* 3 (1992): 259–83.

37. Makzarin Banaji and Anthony Greenwald, *Blindspot: Hidden Biases of Good People* (New York: Delacorte Press, 2013); and Ali Rezaei, "Validity and Reliability of the IAT: Measuring Gender and Ethnic Stereotypes," *Computers in Human Behavior* 27, no. 5 (2011): 1937–41.

38. This evidence is from the Gender-Career IAT. You can take it online yourself, and see how you score: https://implicit.harvard.edu/implicit/user/agg/blindspot/indexgc.htm.

39. Banaji and Greenwald, *Blindspot*; see also Dattner, *The Blame Game*, 61.

40. Cordelia Fine, *A Mind of Its Own: How Your Brain Distorts and Deceives* (New York: W. W. Norton, 2007), 155; and Mark Chen and John A. Bargh, "Nonconscious Behavioral Confirmation Processes: the Self-Fulfilling Consequences of Automatic Stereotype Activation," *Journal of Experimental and Social Psychology* 33, no. 5 (1997): 541–60.

41. Banaji and Greenwald, *Blindspot*; and Rezaei, "Validity and Reliability of the IAT," 1937–41.

42. The surprise when a person defies a stereotype often serves the purpose of maintaining the bias: concluding that an outstanding engineer is an exceptional woman leaves intact the assumption that most women lack the skills to be an engineer. See Ziva Kunda and Kathryn C. Oleson, "When Exceptions Prove the Rule: How Extremity of Deviance Determines the Impact of Deviant Examples on Stereotypes," *Journal of Personality and Social Psychology* 72, no. 5 (1997): 965–79.

43. Caryl Rivers and Rosalind Barnett, *The New Soft War on Women: How the Myth of Female Ascendance Is Hurting Women, Men—And Our Economy* (New York: Tarcher, 2015).

44. See Richard Crisp, *The Social Brain: How Diversity Made the Modern Mind* (London: Robinson, 2015).

45. Cordelia Fine uses the term "bigot goggles" to describe seeing the world through biased eyes: Fine, *A Mind of Its Own*, 145.

46. Many universities are eager to demonstrate their lack of bias and to improve the diversity of their staff. There is a shared understanding that appointing a woman would be good for the department. Despite all this, despite the good will toward women students in math and sciences, despite pressure from the 2012 report from the President's Council of Advisors to increase training and appointments of women in math and science, selection committees assess male candidates more highly than female candidates with comparable CVs: President's Council of Advisors on Science and Technology, "Engage to Excel: Producing One Million Additional College Graduates with Degrees in Science, Technology, Engineering, and Mathematics" (Washington, DC, Executive Office of the President: 2012), https://obamawhitehouse.archives.gov/sites/default/files/microsites/ostp/pcast-engage-to-excel-final_2-25-12.pdf.

47. Elizabeth S. Spelke, "Sex Differences in Intrinsic Aptitude for Mathematics and Science? A Critical Review," *American Psychologist* 60 (2005): 950–58.

48. Ernesto Reuben, Paola Sapienzo, and Luigi Zingalis, "How Stereotypes Impair Women's Careers in Science," *Proceedings of the National Academy of Sciences* 111, no. 12 (2014): 4403–8; and Lisa Williams, "The Problem with Merit-Based Appointments? They're Not Free from Gender Bias Either," *The Conversation*, July 29, 2015, http://theconversation.com/the-problem-with-merit-based-appointments-theyre-not-free-from-gender-bias-either-45364. See also European Commission for Research and Innovation, "Meta-Analysis of Gender and Science

292 NOTES

Research," (Brussels: European Commission, 2012), https://ec.europa.eu/research/swafs/pdf/pub_gender_equality/meta-analysis-of-gender-and-science-research-synthesis-report.pdf.

49. Corinne A. Moss-Racusin et al., "Science Faculty's Subtle Gender Biases Favor Male Students," *Proceedings of the National Academy of Sciences* 111, no. 2 (2012): 16474–79.

50. John Campbell, *Margaret Thatcher*, vol. 1, *The Grocer's Daughter* (London: Jonathan Cape, 2000).

51. Claude M. Steele, *Whistling Vivaldi: How Stereotypes Affect Us and What We Can Do* (New York: Norton, 2010), 119–20, 149; and David Sadker and Karen R. Zittleman, *Still Failing at Fairness: How Gender Bias Cheats Girls and Boys in School and What We Can Do About It* (New York: Scribner, 2009); and Irene V. Blair, "The Malleability of Automatic Stereotype and Prejudice," *Personality and Social Psychology Review* 6, no. 3 (2002): 242–61.

52. B.L. Frederickson et al., "That Swimsuit Becomes You: Sex Differences in Self-Objectification, Restrained Eating, and Math Performance," *Journal of Personality and Social Psychology* 75, no. 1 (1998): 269–84.

53. Referenced by Jenni Murray, "What Did Margaret Thatcher Do for Women?," *The Guardian*, April 9, 2013, https://www.theguardian.com/politics/2013/apr/09/margaret-thatcher-women.

54. Janine Willis and Alexander Todorov, "First Impressions: Making Up Your Mind After a 100-Ms Exposure to a Face," *Psychological Science* 17, no. 7 (2006): 592–98.

55. For an excellent account see Daniel Kahneman, *Thinking: Fast and Slow* (New York: Penguin, 2012).

56. Alexander Todorov et al., "Inferences of Competence from Faces Predict Election Outcomes," *Science* 308, no. 5728 (2005): 1623–26; and Jeremy Biesanz et al., "Do We Know When Our Impressions of Others Are Valid? Evidence for Realistic Accuracy Awareness in First Impressions of Personality," *Social Psychological and Personality Science* 2, no. 5 (2011): 452–59.

57. John A. Bargh and Idit Shalev, "The Substitutability of Physical and Social Warmth in Daily Life," *Emotion* 12, no. 1 (2012): 154–62, doi:10.1037/a0023527.

58. Bargh and Shalev, "The Substitutability of Physical and Social Warmth in Daily Life."

59. Edgar Schien, *Career Dynamics: Matching Individual and Organizational Needs* (New York: Addison-Wesley, 1978).

60. Michael G. Marmot et al., "Health Inequalities among British Civil Servants: The Whitehall II Study," *Lancet* 337, no. 8754 (1991): 1387–98.

61. Michael Marmot, *The Status Syndrome* (London: Bloomsbury, 2005).

62. *Collins English Dictionary*, 12th ed. s.v. "horns and halo effect."

63. Improved lifestyles would improve health, but only by about a third. See Marmot, *The Status Syndrome*, 46.

64. "A socioeconomic measure that reflects the nature of the job best predicts the social gradient in mortality in men. A measure that reflects the general social standing best predicts the social gradient in women" (Marmot, *The Status Syndrome*, 43).

65. This sensitivity to relative praise may seem distinctively human, but it is shared by other primates. Frans de Waal's work on monkeys and chimpanzees shows that other primates also experience envy, or concern over the relative value of a reward. De Waal showed animals protesting when another member of their species got a better treat for the same amount of "work." A monkey that has been satisfied with celery and cucumber will protest when another monkey is given a sweeter treat of a grape and will then, in a funk, refuse to accept the lesser treat of the celery or cucumber. They reject their own food when they see that a neighbor is getting better food. See Sarah F. Brosnan and Frans B.M. de Waal, "Monkeys Reject Unequal Pay," *Nature* 425 (2003): 297–99.

66. The phrase "halo effect" was first used in 1920 by the psychologist Edward Thorndike who found that officers usually judged "their men" as being either good right across the board or bad. There was little mixing of traits; few people were said to be good in one respect but bad in another. See Edward Thorndike, "A Constant Error in Psychological Ratings," *Journal of Applied Psychology* 4, no. 1 (1920): 25–29. See also Richard Nisbett and Timothy D. Wilson, "The Halo Effect: Evidence for Unconscious Alteration of Judgments," *Journal of Personality and Social Psychology* 35, no.4 (1977): 250–56.

67. Even if everyone had the same income, Marmot points out, there would still be differences in status with corresponding differences in health. See Marmot, *The Status Syndrome*, 63.

68. Alain de Botton, *Status Anxiety* (New York: Vintage, 2005).

69. George Vaillant, *Adaptation to Life* (Boston: Little, Brown), 162.

70. See Gowing and Langdon, *Thinking the Unthinkable: A New Imperative for Leadership in the Digital Age* (London: Chartered Institute of Management Accountants, 2016).

71. Rosabeth Moss Kanter, *When Giants Learn to Dance: the Definitive Guide to Corporate Success* (New York: Simon and Schuster, 1990).

72. Entire societies also are vulnerable when things go wrong and no one is willing to accept blame. Jared Diamond gives terrifying examples of entire societies that collapse rather than accept and adapt to change. Wars raged in Easter Island while one group blamed another for their plight, not noticing that a remedy they could easily take themselves was near to hand. See Jared Diamond, *Collapse: How Societies Choose to Fail or Survive* (London: Allen Lane, 2005).

73. Diane L. Coutu. "Edgar Schein: The Anxiety of Learning—The Darker Side of Organizational Learning," *Harvard Business School Working Knowledge*, quoted in Ben Dattner, *The Blame Game*, 145.

74. For an account of how change can be effective through self-awareness, see the discussion by a former chair and CEO of IBM: Lou Gerstner, *Who Says Elephants Can't Dance?* (New York: Collins, 2002).

75. The most common categorization of personality types for this purpose is based on Myers-Briggs Type Indicator (MBTI). Isabel Myers and Katherine Briggs drew on Carl Jung's categorization of the different ways people process and organize their thoughts, make decisions and set priorities. Executive coaches using MBTI are likely to emphasize how understanding one's own preferences and approaches, and those of others, helps get the most out of employees. See Carl Jung, *Modern Man in Search of a Soul* (Orlando, FL: Harcourt, 1933); and Isabel Briggs Myers et al., *MBTI Manual: A Guide to the Development and Use of the Myers-Briggs Type Indicator*, 3rd ed. (Mountain View, CA: Consulting Psychologists Press, 1998).

76. The Myers-Briggs Type Indicator has recently come under heavy criticism for its lack of scientific basis. With its allocation of a fixed personality type, there is a suggestion that assessments generate predictions about how people work in a team and how individuals will respond in a wide range of situations. As Professor John Rust says, "The test chops you. It leads people to believe they have a type, which is more like astrology." See Murad Ahmed, "Is Myers-Briggs up to its job?," *Financial Times*, February 11, 2016, https://www.ft.com/content/8790ef0a-d040-11e5-831d-09f7778e7377?mhq5j=e1. See also Annie Murphy Paul, *The Cult of Personality* (Washington, DC: Free Press, 2004).

77. Andrew Greenwald, "The Totalitarian Ego: Fabrication and Revision of Personal History," *American Psychologist* 35 (1980): 603–18.

Chapter 8. Social Media and the New
Challenges to Our Judgment Meter

1. Confidence in one's judgment is not related to accurate judgment of people, and many who believe they are expert at, for example, determining whether someone is lying or telling the truth, are right as often as they would be in random guessing. See Aldert Vrij, Par Anders Granhag, and Stephen Porter, "Pitfalls and Opportunities in Nonverbal and Verbal Lie Detection," *Psychological Science in the Public Interest* 1, no. 13 (2010): 89–121.

2. Leanne ten Brinke, Dayna Stimson, and Dana Carney, "Some Evidence for Unconscious Lie Detection," *Psychological Science* 25 (2014): 1098–1105.

3. Michela Vicario et al., "The Spreading of Misinformation Online," *Proceedings of the National Academy of Sciences* 113, no. 3 (2015): 554–59.

4. Thirteen years is the lower age limit set by Facebook, though some state laws impose additional restrictions.

5. This is as of March 2016. Facebook Newsroom.

6. Matthew Lieberman, *Social: Why Our Brains Are Wired to Connect* (New York: Broadway Books, 2014).

7. Facebook management considered but then decided against a Dislike button, presumably because it is out of keeping with the upbeat façade of the site. See Sam Colt, "Facebook May Be Adding a 'Dislike' Button," *Inc.*, December 12, 2014, https://www.inc.com/business-insider/facebook-may-be-adding-a-dislike-button.html, though this has not yet been rolled out. See also Christopher Zara, "Facebook Is Testing Out a Dislike Button, But There's a Catch," *Fast Company*, March 6, 2017, https://news.fastcompany.com/facebook-is-testing-out-a-dislike-button-but-theres-a-catch-4031826. They did however add emoji that signal "wow," "sad," and "angry." These, as well as the facility for leaving comments, are well-equipped to express decisive disapproval.

8. See Nancy Jo Sales, *American Girls: Social Media and the Secret Life of Teenagers* (New York: Knopf, 2016).

9. Terri Apter, *Altered Loves: Mothers and Teenage Daughters* (New York: Ballantine, 1991).

10. The study was first published in 1990, but the interviews were conducted between 1986 and 1989.

11. Apter, *Altered Loves*, 32.

12. Ashley A. Anderson et al., "The 'Nasty Effect': Online Incivility and Risk Perception in Emerging Technologies," *The Journal of Computer-Mediated Communication* 19, no. 3 (2013): 373–87.

13. Linda is quoted in Apter, *Altered Loves*, 29–30.

14. Ibid., 29.

15. "Online Bullying," *Bitdefender Resource Center*, October 6, 2011.

16. Pew Research Center, *Teens, Technology and Social Media Overview 2015: Smartphones Facilitate Shifts in Communication Landscape for Teens* (Washington, DC: Pew Research Center, 2015), http://www.pewinternet.org/files/2015/04/PI_TeensandTech_Update2015_0409151.pdf.

17. In 2012, Jessica Laney hanged herself after a barrage of comments declaring her a "slut" and demanding, "Can you kill yourself already." "Online Bullying," *Bitdefender Resource Center*, October 6, 2011. Jessica Cleland took her own life at the age of nineteen after a storm of Facebook messages, some from friends, telling her they hated her. See Sales, *American Girls*, 221.

18. Leo Festinger, "A Theory of Social Comparison Processes," *Human Relations* 7, no. 2 (1954): 117–40.

19. Pew Research Center, *Teens, Technology and Social Media*.

20. According to the 2015 Pew report "Teens, Technology and Social Media," teens say they are on social media "constantly." As far as was measured, more than half (56 percent) of teens—defined in this report as those ages thirteen to seventeen—go online several times a day, and 12 percent report once-a-day use. Just 6 percent of teens report going online weekly, and 2 percent go online less often.

21. Sherry Turkle, *Reclaiming Conversation: The Power of Talk in a Digital Age* (New York: Penguin, 2015).

22. Marian Keyes, "Mind Your Head," *Sunday Times*, March 8, 2015, https://www.thetimes.co.uk/article/mind-your-head-xnnz860vw3p.

23. Sales, *American Girls*, 138.

24. Diandra, quoted by Sales, *American Girls*, 218.

25. Luke Clark et al., "Gambling Near-Misses Enhance Motivation to Gamble and Recruit Win-Related Brain Circuitry," *Neuron* 61 (2009): 481–90. For the real power of anticipatory pleasure, see Wolfram Schultz, Peter Dayan, and P. Read Montague, "A Neural Substrate of Prediction and Reward," *Science* 275 (1997): 1593–99.

26. Robert Kraut et al., "Internet Paradox: A Social Technology That Reduces Social Involvement and Psychological Well-Being?," *American Psychologist* 53, no. 9 (1998): 1017–31.

27. Ethan Kross et al., "Facebook Use Predicts Declines in Subjective Well-Being in Young Adults," *PLoS One* 8, no. 8 (2013): doi:10.1371/journal.pone.0069841; Joy Goodman-Deane et al., "The Impact of Communication Technologies on Life and Relationship Satisfaction," *Computers in Human Behavior* 57 (2016): 219–29; and Morten Tromholt, "The Facebook Experiment: Quitting Facebook Leads to Higher Levels of Well-Being," *Cyberpsychology, Behavior, and Social Networking* 19, no. 11 (2016): 661–66.

28. Markus Appel et al., "Intensity of Facebook Use Is Associated With Lower Self-Concept Clarity: Cross-Sectional and Longitudinal Evidence," *Journal of Media Psychology: Theories, Methods, and Applications* (2016), doi:10.1027/1864-1105/a000192.

29. Clark et al., "Gambling Near-Misses Enhance Motivation to Gamble," 481–90.

30. I do not believe that "addiction" is an apt metaphor; the problem is that the "jolt" of pleasure is short-lived and we expect more from praise. So the problem resides in our expectations: we expect praise to offer reassurance and warmth; when we get only a hint of this, we feel we have not had enough, so we search for more. What is needed is to get this pleasure from a different source.

31. Joy Goodman-Deane et al., "The Impact of Communication Technologies on Life and Relationships Satisfaction," 219–29.

32. Dr. Patti M. Valkenburg, Jochen Peter, and Alexander P. Schouten, "Friend Networking Sites and Their Relationship to Adolescents' Well-Being and Social Self-Esteem," *CyberPsychology & Behavior* 9, no. 5 (2006): 584–90, doi:10.1089/cpb.2006.9.584.

33. The teenage girls Nancy Jo Sales interviewed would not be dissuaded by bad experiences from using social media. Some feared being left out of a common pool of communication, while some remained hopeful that, next time, they would attract praise. See Sales, *American Girls*.

34. David E. Kanouse and L. Reid Hanson, "Negativity in Evaluations," in *Attribution: Perceiving the Causes of Behavior*, ed. Edward Ellsworth Jones et al. (Morristown, NJ: General Learning Press, 1972); and Roy F. Baumeister, Ellen Bratslavsky, and Catrin Finkenauer, "Bad Is Stronger than Good," *Review of General Psychology* 5, no. 4 (2001): 323–70.

35. Bluma Zeigarnik described this effect, called the Zeigarnik effect, in 1938. See Bluma Zeigarnik, "On Finished and Unfinished Tasks," in

A Source Book for Gestalt Psychology, new edition, ed. Willis D. Ellis (Hyland, NY: The Gestalt Journal Press, 1938), 1–15.

36. Baumeister, Bratslavsky, and Finkenauer, "Bad is Stronger than Good," 323–70.

37. Of course individuals differ in degrees of negative focus. Stronger memory of negative things is associated with depression; see Jonathan Roiser and Barbara Sahakian, "Hot and Cold Cognition in Depression," *CNS Spectrums* 18, no. 3 (2013): 139–49. Stronger focus on negative things has also been shown to be associated with conservative versus liberal politics; see Drew Weston, *The Political Brain: The Role of Emotion in Deciding the Fate of the Nation* (New York: PublicAffairs, 2007).

38. See Sales, *American Girls,* 36.

39. See, for example, "Report Cyberbullying," U.S. Department of Health & Human Services, http://www.stopbullying.gov/cyberbullying/how-to-report/; Department for Education, "Cyberbullying: Advice for Headteachers and School Staff," November 2014, https://www.gov.uk/government/uploads/system/uploads/attachment_data/file/374850/Cyberbullying_Advice_for_Headteachers_and_School_Staff_121114.pdf; "Bullying and Cyberbullying: Facts and Statistics," National Society for the Prevention of Cruelty to Children, https://www.nspcc.org.uk/preventing-abuse/child-abuse-and-neglect/bullying-and-cyberbullying/bullying-cyberbullying-statistics/.

40. Some psychologists take a very different view, arguing that internet trolls have dark personality traits—narcissism, or grandiosity and lack of empathy; Machiavellianism, or self-centeredness; cynical and manipulative; and psychopathy, or selfishness, impulsiveness and lack of remorse. See Erin Buckels, Paul Trapnell, and Delroy Paulhus, "Trolls Just Want to Have Fun," *Personality and Individual Differences* 67 (2014): 97–102; and Jonathan Bishop, "The Effect of De-individuation of the Internet Troller on Criminal Procedure Implementation: An Interview with a Hater," *International Journal of Cyber Criminology* 7, no. 1 (2013): 28–48.

41. Charles Notar, Sharon Padgett, and Jessica Roden, "Cyberbullying: A Review of the Literature," *Universal Journal of Educational Research* 1, no. 1 (2013): 1–9.

42. Michael Walrave and Wannes Heirman, "Cyberbullying: Predicting Victimization and Perpetration," *Children and Society* 25, no. 1 (2009): 59–72.

43. This quote is from a New York Times piece written by two of the researchers, Dominique Brossard and Dietram Scheuffle; see Dominique Brossard and Dietram Scheuffle, "This Story Stinks," *New York Times Sunday Review*, March 2, 2013, http://www.nytimes.com/2013/03/03/opinion/sunday/this-story-stinks.html.

44. Anderson et al., " 'The 'Nasty Effect'," 373–87.

45. Filippo Menczer, "Fake Online News Spreads Through Social Media Echo Chambers," *Scientific American*, November 28, 2016, https://www.scientificamerican.com/article/fake-online-news-spreads-through-social-echo-chambers/.

46. Menczer, "Fake Online News."

47. Del Vicario et al., "The Spreading of Misinformation Online," 554–59.

48. This is also an example of the confirmation bias, where we see more clearly evidence that supports our beliefs and discount evidence that counters our beliefs; in this case the confirmation bias results in an echo chamber.

49. Lindsey Stone is quoted by Jon Ronson, " 'Overnight, Everything I Loved Was Gone': The Internet Shaming of Lindsey Stone," *Guardian*, February 21, 2015, https://www.theguardian.com/technology/2015/feb/21/internet-shaming-lindsey-stone-jon-ronson.

50. John Suler, "The Online Disinhibition Effect," *CyberPsychology & Behavior* 7, no. 3 (2004): 321–26.

51. Matthew S. Eastin and Robert LaRose, "Internet Self-Efficacy and the Psychology of the Digital Divide," *Journal of Computer-Mediated Communication* 6, no. 1 (2000), doi:10.1111/j.1083-6101.2000.tb00110.x.

52. Robert LaRose, "Cybercompulsions: Media Habits, Media Addictions and the Internet," in *Impact and Issues in New Media: Towards Intelligent Societies*, eds. Paul S.N. Lee, Louis Leung, and Clement Y. K. So, Hampton Press Communication Series (Cresskill, NJ: Hampton Press, 2004).

53. Indeok Song et al., "Internet Gratifications and Internet Addictions: On the Uses and Abuses of the New Media," *CyberPsychology and Behavior* 7, no. 4 (2004): 384–94.

54. Quoted in Ronson, " 'Overnight, Everything I Loved Was Gone'."

55. Both these cases are discussed by Jon Ronson, *So You've Been Publicly Shamed* (New York: Riverhead Books, 2015).

56. Consider the problems discussed by Daniel Kahneman; see Daniel Kahneman in *Thinking: Fast and Slow* (New York: Farrar, Straus and Giroux, 2013). There are times when nonreflective thought facilitates

observation, understanding, and expert performances, but there are also many times when it makes us stupid.

57. Sherry Turkle, *Reclaiming Conversation: The Power of Talk in a Digital Age* (New York: Penguin, 2015).

58. Sara H. Konrath, Edward H. O'Brien, and Courtney Hsing, "Changes in Dispositional Empathy in American College Students over Time: A Meta-Analysis," *Personality and Social Psychology Review* 15, no. 2 (2011): 180–89.

59. Empathy in infants and young children is discussed in Chapters 1–3 in this book. See also J.K. Hamlin, K. Wynn, and P. Bloom, "Social Evaluation by Preverbal Infants," *Nature* 450 (2007): 557–59.

60. Jamie Barlett, "Who Are the People in the Dark Corners?," *BBC Magazine*, April 28, 2015, http://www.bbc.com/news/magazine-32446711.

61. Anneke Buffone and Michael Poulin, "Empathy, Target Distress, and Neurohormone Genes Interact to Predict Aggression for Others— Even Without Provocation," *Personality and Social Psychology Bulletin* 40, no. 11 (2014): 1406–22.

62. Rebecca Saxe and Nancy Kanwisher, "People Thinking about Thinking People: The Role of the Temporo-Parietal Junction in 'Theory of Mind'," *Neuroimage* 19, no. 4 (2003): 1835–42; Liane Young et al., "The Neural Basis of the Interaction Between Theory of Mind and Moral Judgment," *Proceedings of the National Academy of Sciences* 104, no. 20 (2007): 8235–40; and Emile Bruneau, Nicholas Dufour, and Rebecca Saxe, "Social Cognition in Members of Conflict Groups: Behavioural and Neural Responses in Arabs, Israelis and South Americans to Each Other's Misfortunes," *Philosophical Transactions of the Royal Society B: Biological Sciences* 367, no. 1589 (2012): 717–30.

63. However, only the part of the neural pain network involved in affect or emotional feelings is activated when we see someone else in pain, not the neural sensory network. See Tania Singer et al., "Empathy for Pain Involves the Affective but Not Sensory Components of Pain," *Science* 303 (2004): 1157–62.

64. Jonathan Haidt, *The Righteous Mind: Why Good People are Divided by Politics and Religion* (New York: Vintage, 2013), 228.

65. One study found that white doctors often underestimate the pain suffered by non-white patients. See Matteo Forgiarini, Marcello Gallucci, and Angelo Maravita, "Racism and the Empathy for Pain on Our Skin," *Frontiers in Psychology* 2, no. 108 (2011): 1–8.

66. Mina Cikara et al., "Their Pain Gives Us Pleasure: How Inter-group Dynamics Shape Empathic Failures and Counter-Empathic Responses," *Journal of Experimental and Social Psychology* 55 (2014): 110–25.

67. For a neuro-imaging study of empathy being shut off in actual conflict, while the mentalizing matric continues to function, see Cikara et al., "Their Pain Gives Us Pleasure," 110–25.

Chapter 9. Lifelong Judgments

1. Peter Singer, *The Expanding Circle: Ethics, Evolution and Moral Progress* (Princeton, NJ: Princeton University Press, 2011).

2. Steven Pinker, *The Better Angels of Our Nature: Why Violence Has Declined* (New York: Penguin, 2012). Pinker takes the title of his book from Abraham Lincoln's first inaugural address. He uses it to encompass empathy, self-control, moral judgment, and reason.

3. Steven Pinker focuses on the decline of violence over millennia. This decline can be seen in the decreased magnitude of homicide, military conflict, genocide, torture, and child abuse. Other studies, looking at different measures, present evidence that young people (represented by a study of seventy-two college students) are 40 percent less empathic than were similar young people at the turn of the twenty-first century. The authors of this study hypothesize that this decline is linked to social media and excessive competition. See Sarah H. Konrath, Edward H. O'Brien, and Courtney Hsing, "Changes in Dispositional Empathy in American College Students Over Time: A Meta-Analysis," *Personality and Social Psychology Review* 15, no.2 (2010): 180–198. While the view of declining empathy may be more common, and may "feel" right, Singer's and Pinker's evidence is compelling.

4. Jonathan Gottschall and David Sloan Wilson, eds., *The Literary Animal: Evolution and the Nature of Narrative*, Rethinking Theory (Evanston, IL: Northwestern University Press, 2006).

5. fMRI studies showed heightened responses in the so-called empathy network and the area involved in social decision making (the dorsomedial prefrontal cortex) after reading complex fiction. See Chun-Ting Hsu, Markus Conrad, Arthur M. Jacobs, "Fiction Feelings in Harry Potter: Haemodynamic Response in the Mid-Cingulate Cortex Corresponds with Immersive Reading Experience," *Neuroreport* 25, no. 17 (2014): 1356–61; and Diana I.Tamir et al., "Reading Fiction and

Reading Minds: The Role of Stimulation in the Default Network," *Social Cognitive and Affective Neuroscience* 11, no. 2 (2016): 215–24.

6. There is evidence that literary fiction boosts emotional skills more than popular fiction. Fiction filled with stereotypical characters (as in many examples of popular fiction) may enforce a perspective in which people are seen in terms of their roles or race, while reading even a few pages of literary fiction boosts recognition of others' emotions. See David Comer Kidd and Emanuele Castano, "Reading Literary Fiction Improves Theory of Mind," *Science* 342, no. 6156 (2013): 377–80.

7. Singer, *Expanding Circle*; and Singer, *Better Angels of our Nature*.

8. Geoffrey Brennan and Philip Pettit, "The Hidden Economy of Esteem," *Philosophy and Economics* 16 (2000): 77–98.

9. Daniel 5:27 (New King James Version); see also Job 31:6 (New King James Version).

10. We cannot, however, be sanguine about the continued increase in wise judgment. Elderly people have been found to revert to adopting the stereotypes they learned when they were young. There is sometimes an age-related decline in the area of the brain that inhibits sloppy associations. In cases where the frontal lobes atrophy with age, a person is likely to exhibit greater stereotyping and bias. See Brandon Stewart, William von Hipel, and Gabriel Radvansky, "Age, Race, and Implicit Prejudice: Using Process Dissociation to Separate the Underlying Components," *Psychological Science* 20, no. 2 (2009): 164–68.

11. The literature on distinguishing moral beliefs from personal preferences is vast. It includes Alfred J. Ayer, *Language, Truth and Logic* (London: Gollancz, 1936); Richard Mervyn Hare, *Moral Thinking: Its Levels, Methods, and Point* (Oxford: Clarendon Press, 1981); David Hume, *Dialogues Concerning Natural Religion* (New York: Bobbs-Merrill, 1947); Immanuel Kant, *Critique of Practical Reason*, ed. and trans. Mary Gregor (Cambridge: Cambridge University Press, 1997); Immanuel Kant, *Critique of Pure Reason*, eds. and trans. Paul Guyer and Allen W. Wood (Cambridge: Cambridge University Press, 1998); Immanuel Kant, *Groundwork of the Metaphysics of Morals*, ed. and trans. Mary Gregor (Cambridge: Cambridge University Press, 1998); G. E. Moore, *Principia Ethica* (Cambridge: Cambridge University Press, 1903); and John Rawls, *A Theory of Justice* (Cambridge, MA: Harvard University Press, 1971).

12. Joshua Greene, *Moral Tribes: Emotion, Reason and the Gap Between Us and Them* (New York: Penguin, 2013).

13. Nina Strohminger and Shaun Nichols, "Neurodegeneration and Identity," *Psychological Science* 26, no. 9 (2015): 1469–79.

14. Jeffrey M. Greeson, "Mindfulness Research Update: 2008," *Complement Health Practice Review* 14, no. 1 (2009): 10–18.

15. Research at the Stanford Center for Back Pain is exploring how real-time fMRI neurofeedback, mindfulness based stress reduction, cognitive behavioral therapy, and acupuncture treatment impact chronic back pain. See Ying Jiang et al., "Perturbed Connectivity of the Amygdala and Its Subregions with the Central Executive and Default Mode Networks in Chronic Pain," *Pain* 157, no. 9 (2016): 1970–78.

16. Richard J. Davidson et al., "Alterations in Brain and Immune Function Produced by Mindfulness Meditation," *Psychosomatic Medicine* 65, no. 1 (2004): 564–70.

17. Pablo Briñol et al., "Treating Thoughts as Material Objects Can Increase or Decrease Their Impact on Evaluation," *Psychological Science* 24, no. 1 (2012): 41–47.

18. Psychologists at the University of California, San Diego, conducted memory tests on 153 undergraduates who were randomly put into three groups. The group exposed to mindfulness meditation was more likely to "remember" (incorrectly) seeing words than either of the other two groups. In a further study students were put in two groups, one of which was trained in mindfulness techniques. After training, this group was significantly more likely to "recall" words not seen, compared to responses before training. See Brent M. Wilson et al., "Increased False-Memory Susceptibility After Mindfulness Meditation," *Psychological Science* 26, no. 10 (2015): 1567–73.

19. There is, however, a practice called compassion meditation that, according to one study, heightens the brain's response to emotional cues. If further research bears this out, and longitudinal data shows improved compassion and responsiveness, then this form of meditation could be used to facilitate the activity of the judgment meter, rather than to escape it. See Antoine Lutz et al., "Regulation of the Neural Circuitry of Emotion by Compassion Meditation: Effects of Meditative Expertise," *PLoSOne* 3, no. 3 (2008): 1–10, doi: 10.1371/journal.pone.0001897.

20. Kathleen B. Lustyk et al., "Mindfulness Meditation Research: Issues

of Participant Screening, Safety and Procedures and Researcher Training," *Advances in Mind-Body Medicine* 24, no. 1 (2009): 21–30.

21. Sigmund Freud, *Five Lectures on Psycho-Analysis* (New York: Penguin, 1995), 8–9.

22. Mathew Lieberman et al., "Putting Feelings into Words: Affect Labeling Disrupts Amygdala Activity," *Psychological Science* 18, no. 5 (2009): 421–28.

23. According to Jonathan Haidt, the willingness to engage with other people's feelings and judgment is central to getting along. See Jonathan Haidt, *The Righteous Mind: Why Good People Are Divided by Politics and Religion* (New York: Vintage, 2013).

24. For a sustained argument on trusting our own emotions, see Carol Gilligan, *Meeting at the Crossroads* (Cambridge, MA: Harvard University Press, 1993). See also Miriam B. Raider-Roth, with a forward by Carol Gilligan, *Trusting What You Know: The High Stakes of Classroom Relationships* (San Francisco, CA: Jossey-Bass, 2005).

INDEX